BOOKS BY BILL HYBELS

Christians in the Marketplace
Laws that Liberate
Who You Are When No One's Looking
Too Busy Not to Pray
Seven Wonders of the Spiritual World

Who You Are When No One's Looking

Choosing Consistency, Resisting Compromise

Bill Hybels

edited by La Vonne Neff

IVP Books

An imprint of InterVarsity Press
Downers Grove, Illinois

InterVarsity Press
P.O. Box 1400, Downers Grove, IL 60515-1426
World Wide Web: www.ivpress.com
E-mail: email@ivpress.com

*InterVarsity Press® is the book-publishing division of InterVarsity Christian Fellowship/USA®, a student
movement active on campus at hundreds of universities, colleges and schools of nursing in the United States of
America, and a member movement of the International Fellowship of Evangelical Students. For information
about local and regional activities, write Public Relations Dept., InterVarsity Christian Fellowship/USA, 6400
Schroeder Rd., P.O. Box 7895, Madison, WI 53707-7895, or visit the IVCF website at <www.intervarsity.org>.*

Scripture quotations, unless otherwise noted, are from the Revised Standard Version of the Bible, *copyright
1946, 1952, 1971 by the Division of Christian Education of the National Council of the Churches of Christ in
the U.S.A., and are used by permission.*

Cover photograph: Jon Feingersh/The Stock Market

ISBN 978-0-87784-945-2

Printed in the United States of America ∞

Library of Congress Cataloging-in-Publication Data

Hybels, Bill.
  Who you are when no one's looking.
  1. Virtues.   2. Character.   3. Christian ethics.
4. Christian life—1960-.   I. Neff, LaVonne.
II. Title.
BV4630.H93   1987   241   87-16856
ISBN 0-87784-945-5

P	47	46	45	44	43	42	41	40	39	38	37	36	35	34	33	32
Y	22	21	20	19	18	17	16	15	14	13	12	11	10	09	08	07

1. CHARACTER: Preserving Endangered Qualities   7

2. COURAGE: Overcoming Crippling Fears   13

3. DISCIPLINE: Achieving Success through Delaying Gratification   23

4. VISION: Looking beyond the Obvious   35

5. ENDURANCE: Crashing through Quitting Points   47

6. TENDER LOVE: Walking in Someone Else's Moccasins   57

7. TOUGH LOVE: Insisting on Truth in Relationships   67

8. SACRIFICIAL LOVE: Giving without Giving Out   81

9. RADICAL LOVE: Breaking the Hostility Cycle   93

10. The **CHARACTER** of Christ   103

1
CHARACTER

Preserving Endangered Qualities

Character—the word is seldom used in the Bible, and we don't see it very often in newspapers or hear it on television. Yet we know what it means, and we immediately recognize its absence.

People who never use the word *character* look around them at junior-high promiscuity, busy abortion clinics and the current epidemic of sexually transmitted diseases, and they mourn the passing of morality. They see elected officials taking bribes, business leaders demanding kickbacks and investors parlaying inside information into untold wealth, and they lament the demise of integrity. Or they read about battered wives, jobless husbands and abused children, and they wonder what is happening to caring.

Character, a wise person once said, is what we do when no one is looking. It is not the same as reputation—what other people think of us. It is not the same as success or achievement. Character is not what we have done, but who we *are*. And although we often hear of tragic lapses of character, describing its absence does not tell the whole story.

Endangered Character Qualities

People give evidence of strong character in hundreds of ways every day:

☐ A woman confronts her terror of public speaking so she can tell her church congregation about her miraculous answer to prayer. That's *courage.*

☐ A man vows to get up twenty minutes early every morning to jog around the block, and he keeps his vow. That's *discipline.*

☐ A high-school teacher patiently draws out an inattentive student and discovers she is a gifted writer. That's *vision.*

☐ A college student, overwhelmed by tests and term papers, considers dropping out, but decides to stay and study instead. That's *endurance.*

These four traits are all on my "endangered character quality" list. They aren't glamorous, and they aren't easy. Therefore a lot of people try to get along without them. But strangely enough, the most endangered quality of all is the one that we all think we want—*love.*

Unfortunately, when we say we want the character quality of love, most of us mean only that we want to be loved. We hope people will admire us and treat us affectionately, and we will try to do the same for them. But people of character go beyond the warm fuzzies to the hard work of loving. They do this in many different ways, often without realizing that they are showing strength of character:

☐ A woman refuses to make any more excuses for her husband when he misses work because of a hangover. That's *tough love.*

☐ A man notices his daughter's tear-stained face, and so he sits down and encourages her to tell him what's on her heart. That *tenderhearted love.*

☐ A parent gives up an attractive job promotion so the family can stay in the town where they have made friends and put down roots. That's *sacrificial love.*

☐ A young widow offers forgiveness to the drunken driver who hit and killed her husband. That's *radical love.*

Love, says the apostle Paul, is the most important Christian character trait (1 Cor 13:13), and it is probably the least understood. That is why I have devoted the second half of this book to it. But it is extremely difficult to learn to love unless we also have other character traits: the courage to do what needs doing; the discipline to make decisions and carry them out; the vision to see far into the future and deep into people's hearts; and the endurance to keep going in spite of ridicule, discomfort or simple boredom. That is why I have given the first half of the book to these foundational character qualities.

Developing a Strong Character

Some people reading the table of contents might be tempted to draw up a chart. "Let's see," they would say, "I'm weak on courage, and so I'll give myself two months to work on that one. Six weeks will probably cover discipline, and I'm sure I can handle vision in two weeks at most. I'll just skip endurance, and that will give me two months on each kind of love. If I follow this plan, in one year I'll have a strong character."

Benjamin Franklin reports in his *Autobiography* that he tried that approach, and it didn't work. As soon as he mastered one good trait and went on to the next, the first one started slipping out of his grasp. Character cannot be developed through good resolutions and checklists. It usually requires a lot of hard work, a little pain and years of faithfulness before any of the virtues are consistently noticeable in us.

Developing character, however, does not have to be a grim task. There are secrets to developing each of the character qualities, and I have shared them in each chapter. More important, Jesus Christ—the only person who has ever consistently excelled in every virtue we could name—offers to develop his character in us as we follow him. This is an offer we can hardly refuse!

Salvation Is Free

Please keep one very important fact in mind as you read this book: *No matter how wonderful your character is, it will never be wonderful enough to earn God's approval.* This is not a book about how to get God to sit up and notice you or how to improve your heavenly credit rating. As important as character is, it is not a way to earn salvation. That is because salvation cannot be earned—not even by courage, discipline, vision, endurance and love.

Salvation is a gift from the heavenly Father to us. It cost him everything—the death of his beloved only Son. It costs us nothing. Hard work cannot earn it; neither can good behavior or sterling character. The only way we can enjoy a relationship with God is by coming to Jesus Christ, our hands outstretched and empty, and saying, "Lord, I want to follow you. Please take me into your family, scrub me, give me new clothes and make me like you." And Jesus will do exactly that. He will take us as we are and assure us that we are his forever. Then—slowly at first, but surely—he will mold us and shape us until we resemble him.

This book is for two kinds of people. First, it is for you who, whether Christian or not, admire character strength and see the urgent need for it in our society and in yourself. I hope to show you how to get where you want to go. Second, it is for you who, having given your life to Christ, yearn for spectacular transformations and dazzling displays of virtue. I hope to show you that you are already well on the way to character strength, even if the path is humbler than you expected.

Character is our world's most pressing need. If all five billion of us had strong characters, there would be no wars, no hunger, no family breakups, no crime, no poverty. We will not live in such a perfect world until Christ returns and the earth is made new, but, in the meantime, we should not despair. To the extent that our own characters grow stronger, the world will be a better place.

So take courage—a very good place to start.

2
COURAGE
Overcoming Crippling Fears

I have an embarrassing admission to make: I saw *Rocky I* three times. What's more, I saw *Rocky II* three times and *Rocky III* twice, and I even saw *Rocky IV*. I have to admit that each one sent a little tingle up my spine. Not because I think these are especially good movies. They just happen to be about a great subject—courage.

I've always been fascinated by courage. When I was a boy, my dad bought a sailboat in Ireland and sailed it back across the Atlantic Ocean through a hurricane. Before leaving home, he had collected a library of books so that he would know what he was in for, and I read them all. Many of these were books about disasters at sea, and they all included a scene where people were lined up on the deck as the ship went down, wondering what to do because there were not enough life jackets to go around. Some guy would always say, "Here, take mine." As I read that, my breath would get short and my pulse would start to race.

Whenever I hear of someone showing courage instead of cowardice, I find myself saying, "That's what I want to be like." I wish I had more courage. I do not want to be debilitated by fear or paralyzed by anxiety. I do not want to cave in under difficult circumstances and compromise my convictions or give up on difficult challenges. I do not want to be a coward; I want to be courageous. This is a biblical wish, for in 2 Timothy 1:7 Paul says, "God did not give us a spirit of timidity but a spirit of power."

Courage in the Ordinary

I regret the fact that we usually hear about courage only when someone does some extreme act of heroism that attracts media attention—carrying an old woman out of a burning building, diving into an icy pond to save a drowning child, risking gunfire while dragging a buddy to safety. I love these stories, but they seem bigger than life. Dramatic, once-in-a-lifetime opportunities never seem to happen to ordinary folk like you and me. But the older I get, the more I understand that it takes a great deal of courage to face life's ordinary, everyday challenges.

Every single day we make choices that show whether we are courageous or cowardly. We choose between the right thing and the convenient thing, sticking to a conviction or caving in for the sake of comfort, greed or approval. We choose either to take a carefully thought-out risk or to crawl into a shrinking shell of safety, security and inactivity. We choose either to believe in God and trust him, even though we do not always understand his ways, or to second-guess him and cower in corners of doubt and fear. These choices come our way every day, rapid fire. We face them so frequently that we forget that we are even making them, and we sometimes find ourselves going with the flow instead of carefully making courageous choices.

Courage to Be Vulnerable

People say that Christianity is for weak people, cowards and quiche eaters. I have always been fascinated by that accusation, because in my experience the exact opposite is true. It takes a great deal of old-fashioned courage to be a Christian. My faith demands the best I have. In fact, a lot of courage is required even to become a Christian. The Bible says that, to become a Christian, you have to own up to your sins before a holy God. That takes courage.

At the beginning of every semester, professors say, "On such-and-such a date, your term paper will be due." But it is easy to get sidetracked with different activities, and when the due date is tomorrow, you suddenly realize that your paper is not ready. You go to the teacher's office and say, "Prof, you wouldn't believe what happened to me. My Aunt Ethel took ill, the library lost the one reference book I most needed and the dog ate the final draft of my paper right after I pulled it out of the typewriter." You say anything but the truth, hoping the professor will be merciful and give you a break.

Probably very few of you ever walked into the professor's office and said, "You made an assignment several months ago. It was fair, and I understood it clearly. Unfortunately, I played too many hands of cards and too much racquetball. I neglected to do what I should have done. I was undisciplined, and I procrastinated. Now I don't have the assignment done. I make no excuses; it was my fault. Do whatever you think is right." Why don't people operate that way? Because it is painful to own up to the truth about our behavior. It takes courage.

When I talk with people about Christianity, I tell them, "You've got to repent before a holy God. You have to tell him the truth about yourself—that you've lied, you've hurt people, you've cheated; you've been greedy, dishonest, unfaithful to your spouse, self-centered." When I say that, I see terror in their eyes. They do not want to be that open and vulnerable. They shift in their seats. They look at their watches and wonder how to get out of such confrontation.

What is going on? Inside them, a voice is saying, "Confession would be painful and humiliating, and it would make you feel uncomfortable and exposed, but it's the right thing to do and you have to do it." At the same time, another voice is saying, "Don't look at yourself that closely. Take it easy. Go with the flow. Cover your tracks."

Too many people cave in to their fears and say, "I just can't do it. It would be too embarrassing, too humiliating." So they say ridiculous things like "Who, me, a sinner? No, not me. Harry's awful, and Mary's wicked, but I've lived a pretty good life. I may have made a few minor mistakes in judgment—nobody's perfect—but not many, mind you. Nothing serious."

When I hear that kind of response, I have a strong urge to say, "Pal, you're gutless. You know what you should do, but you're too chicken to do it. You don't have the guts to tell God the truth about who you really are. You're afraid of the pain, the embarrassment. You're too frightened to admit the obvious." I also want to add, "If you're too chicken to repent, then please don't ever say Christianity is for weak people. Apparently it's for people with more courage than you have." If it takes courage to *become* a Christian, it takes even more courage to *be* a Christian.

Courage to Follow

We used to play a game at summer camp in which we would blindfold one of the kids and have him or her run through a wooded area, relying on a friend for verbal directions to help navigate. "Turn to the left; there's a tree coming!" "There's a log in front of you—*jump!*" Some kids would not trust the verbal directions whatsoever. They would shuffle their feet and walk very slowly, even though their friends were shouting that the way was clear. Other kids would trot along, and a few would go like gangbusters. All the kids, though, had to fight the urge to tear off the blindfold so that they could see what was ahead. It takes a great deal of courage to follow another person's lead.

As Christians, we sometimes feel like those blindfolded children. Paul says in 2 Corinthians 5:7, "We walk by faith, not by sight." We are not alone in the woods, though—God "shall direct thy paths" (Prov 3:6 KJV). But following Jesus Christ demands an enormous amount of courage. Quite often his leadings sound illogical, irrational, countercultural. Sometimes he is so challenging that I say, "No, I think I'll just crawl back into my shell and play it safe." Then a voice inside me says, "Where's your courage, Hybels? Get up and walk. You can trust God."

Cowards do not last long on their spiritual pilgrimages. They shrivel up and disappear. It takes enormous courage to repent and become a Christian. It takes enormous courage to follow God's leadings in the Christian life. Some of his callings demand the best that you can summon. Some of his tests stretch you to the limit. Some of his adventures evoke great fears and doubts. Truly, spiritual courage is on the endangered character-quality list.

Relational Courage

Another kind of courage is also in danger of extinction today— *relational courage.* I try not to give two-cent answers to hundred-dollar questions, but when people ask me what it takes to build a meaningful marriage, I say, "courage."

For a marriage relationship to flourish, there must be intimacy. It takes an enormous amount of courage to say to your spouse, "This is me. I'm not proud of it—in fact, I'm a little embarrassed by it—but this is who I am." It also takes courage to look your spouse in the eye and say, "Our marriage is in serious trouble, and we've got to do something about it." What do most people do? They put their problems on the back burner and go their own directions. While they pursue their own careers and their own recreations, the marriage disintegrates from lack of courage. They did not have the courage to put on the gloves and say, "Let's fight for this marriage. Let's go to a marriage retreat. Let's see a marriage counselor. Let's get together with another couple we respect. Let's lay it out on the table and solve these problems instead of running from them." It takes courage to fight off the "greener grass" temptations, to work through layer after layer of masks, cover-ups and defense mechanisms, to keep working on that marriage year after year. Relational courage does not apply only to the husband-wife relationship. It also takes courage to raise kids. How often I see parents backing off from proper discipline because they don't want to endure their kids' disapproval! The kids throw a tantrum and say "I hate you," and the parents give in. If you want to raise your children the way God wants them raised, you will have to let the little tyrants get mad. Show some courage and say, "You don't intimidate me, little one. This is the right thing to do, and this is what you're going to do."

It also takes relational courage to build significant relationships with friends, to look another person in the eye and say, "Isn't it time we stopped talking about the weather and the stock market and started talking about what's going on in your life and mine? Isn't it time we became brothers?" Not many men have the courage to challenge each other, to fight for each other's spiritual and relational growth. But I have learned over the years that I will never be a success in my marriage, with my kids or with my friends, without courage.

Courage to Be Moral

We could discuss many other kinds of courage—vocational courage, courage to face difficult circumstances, moral courage. How much courage must you summon to operate ethically in the marketplace? What kind of guts does it take to be honest? We don't want to offend customers, and so we say, "The shipment will be there Monday," when we know it won't leave the warehouse until Wednesday. We want people to think we are honest, and so we say, "I report all my income" when in reality we have a drawerful of unreported check stubs at home. April 15 is a great day to separate courageous people from cowards, because that is when moral courage hits us in the wallet.

How much courage is required to stay sexually pure in a sex-crazed culture? How much is required to stick to a conviction when everyone at the office, at school or in the neighborhood says, "You're hopelessly idealistic, old-fashioned, and a little bit strange—in fact, you're a religious fanatic"?

How to Grow in Courage

But how do you become courageous? Do you make a wish? Say a prayer? Wave a wand?

You grow in courage when you *face your crippling fears.* Sometimes we think courageous people were born without fear. In actuality, courageous people are ordinary people like you and me who began at some point to face their fears rather than running from them.

When I was growing up, my dad saw that I was a timid guy, and so he always challenged me to do things I was afraid to do. When I was in grade school, for example, he'd take me down to our produce company and bark out, "Billy, go out and back in that semi." I'd been driving tractors for several years, but I'd drag myself into the cab of that forty-foot rig just shaking with fear. Sometimes it would take me forty-five minutes, and the truck would be half-jackknifed against the dock. But when I crawled out, my knees shaking, Dad would say, "Good job." The next time he would ask me to do it, it would be just a little bit easier.

Sometimes when Dad and I were in our sailboat on Lake Michigan, coming in between two cement piers with huge waves tossing the boat one way and then the other, he would say, "I've got to go down below—you take over the helm." I knew exactly what he was doing: waiting until I was terrified out of my mind, and then putting me in control. One minute the boat would be heading right toward one cement barrier, and the next minute a wave would pitch it over to the other side. About the time I eventually managed to get the boat where it belonged, Dad would come up and say, "Now that wasn't so bad, was it?" The next time it was a little bit easier.

Dad treated me the same way when I was learning to fly. Meigs Field is one of the most dangerous airports in the United States. Right off the lakefront in downtown Chicago, it is surrounded by water and has high crosswinds. So, of course, whenever we flew to Chicago on business from Kalamazoo, my dad would make me land at Meigs Field even though several other airports were available. But every time I did it, it got a little easier.

Every fear that is faced and overcome becomes a building block. Each success gives you a new sense of confidence. You grow in courage as you face your crippling fears. You also grow as you *surround yourself with good models.* The Bible says, "Bad company ruins good morals" (1 Cor 15:33). If you spend time with spineless people, you will probably become spineless yourself. Unfortunately, we are often surrounded by people who cave in, quit, compromise and play it safe as part of their daily routine. But if you want to grow in courage, make a calculated choice to increase your exposure to courageous people. Read autobiographies of courageous people; articles about courage; and Bible stories about people like Moses, Daniel, Esther and Paul who, though petrified, went ahead in faith and grew.

Finally, you grow in courage as you *allow your mind to be*

transformed. Sooner or later you begin to understand the centrality of courage in all walks of life. Courage is not an isolated, optional character quality. It is not merely a nice trait for people who want it but unnecessary for those who are not interested in it. Courage is foundational to being a Christian.

It takes courage to begin a walk with Christ, to reach out your hand and trust him. It takes courage to lead a life of obedience to Christ. It takes courage to be moral and to build significant relationships with your spouse, your children and with your friends. It takes courage to expand a business, change your major or start a new career. It takes courage to leave home or to go back home.

Courage—we all need it, and God wants us to have it. "God did not give us a spirit of timidity but a spirit of power." But you cannot sit still and expect courage to come and find you. You have to go after it.

3
DISCIPLINE

Achieving Success through Delaying Gratification

Some people seem to succeed at everything they try. They have successful careers; they relate well to their families; they may be involved in church and community activities; they are active, growing Christians—they are even physically fit. When you get close to people like this and try to determine just how they manage to fulfill so much of their potential, you find that in almost every case one quality plays a significant role—*discipline.*

By contrast, other people have an embarrassing string of setbacks, disasters and failures. If you get close to them, and if they are honest with themselves and with you, they will probably offer you a candid appraisal of why these calamities have befallen them. "Well, you know, I just started to let things slide," they may say. "I put off doing my homework." "I neglected to follow up leads." "I didn't keep my eye on the store." "I didn't push my chair back from the bar." "I stopped making my calls." "I didn't watch the till." "I didn't take care of myself." "I didn't spend time with my family." "I thought problems would solve themselves." The list of reasons for failure could go on and on, but most of them stem from one conspicuous lack—*discipline.*

Discipline is one of the most important character qualities a person can possess. It plays a key role in developing every area of life. But how many highly disciplined people do you know? Can you quickly think of five people that are truly disciplined in all areas of their lives? Are you disciplined yourself? God has given me hundreds of acquaintances, and only a small fraction of them demonstrate discipline to a significant degree. Not that people do not want to be disciplined—they do. But discipline, I fear, is an endangered character quality.

In various polls, I have asked people what character quality they would most like to have more of; usually one of the top responses is discipline. But there is a great deal of confusion as to what discipline really is and how to practice it. People do not know how to develop greater levels of discipline and put it to work for them in everyday life.

What, then, is this thing we don't understand but want more of? I can give you a two-word explanation of this confusing character quality that defines it, captures its essence and uncovers what is really at its core. These two words are easily remembered—you can think about them during the day and use them in your conversation. Discipline is *delayed gratification.*

First, the Bad News

According to Scott Peck in his book, *The Road Less Traveled,* "Delaying gratification is a process of scheduling the pain and pleasure of life in such a way as to enhance the pleasure by meeting and experiencing the pain first and getting it over with."

He adds, "It is the only decent way to live." I couldn't agree more.

Did you ever watch a normal, well-adjusted, blossoming, disciplined boy eat a piece of cake? He carefully carves around the frosting and eats the cake part first. When he gets done with that, his eyes get a little bit bigger and he attacks the frosting. It's the only decent way for a kid to eat cake. For that matter, did you ever watch an adult eat Neopolitan ice cream? Usually vanilla goes first, then strawberry, then chocolate. Well-developed cake- and ice-cream eaters know how to increase their satisfaction by using the principle of delayed gratification.

It takes continual parental prompting over a period of years before most children learn to use this principle, but those who mature properly eventually learn that they will not enjoy dinner and after-dinner activities if they have homework hanging over their heads or if they know the dog needs a bath. That is why well-disciplined students attack their responsibilities—their schoolwork and chores—as soon as possible after school. Once these tasks are finished, they can enjoy the rest of the evening.

As people move out of adolescence into adulthood and the job market, they usually knowingly and of necessity enter the work force near the bottom rung of the ladder. They willingly put up with long hours, short vacations, repetitive tasks and minimal pay because they know that, if they endure the entry-level discomfort for a while, the payoff will eventually come in the form of more flexible hours, higher pay, longer vacations, more responsibility, more interesting tasks. They are practicing delayed gratification: purposefully scheduling the pain early, trusting that a much more enjoyable phase will result. This principle, which works well in the job market, can be applied to many other situations as well.

For example, delayed gratification is important to spiritual life. As a pastor, I have often heard people say, "I've learned something over the years. If I discipline myself to spend ten or fifteen minutes early in the morning in a quiet place getting a proper perspective on my walk with the Lord—writing down some thoughts, reading my Bible, listening to a tape, praying—the whole rest of my day seems much more satisfying." Listen closely to what these people are saying. If I roll out of the sack while the house is still cold and invest my time and energy on something worthwhile, then the rest of the day will be better. This is delayed gratification as it pertains to the spiritual walk.

Delayed Gratification in the Family

Discipline also pertains to the relational life. Married couples who understand the value of discipline say to each other early in their relationship, "Let's work very hard on this marriage right now. Let's face all our conflicts as they arise. Let's not let things slide. Let's do whatever it takes right now to make our marriage mutually satisfying." This may require a lot of hard work, and it may be uncomfortable or even painful at times, but it brings wonderful results in the form of more fulfilling and satisfying days ahead.

Sometimes my wife, Lynne, and I get together with couples who are experiencing pain in their marriage. After talking with them we often realize that, even if they have been married twice as long as we have, they are just now dealing with things that we took care of during our first two or three years of marriage. As problems arose or conflicts surfaced between them, they would refuse to face them. It was too uncomfortable, and so they pretended nothing was wrong. Rather than endure present discomfort for the sake of future happiness, they let things slide. The result of their lack of discipline, of course, was escalating discomfort that eventually became intolerable. They would have been much better off saying, "Let's go through the pain right now so that we'll have a longer time of pleasure ahead."

Delayed gratification is also important in training children. A lot of parents are unwilling to make the sacrifices that are necessary in order to meet their children's deepest needs. A promotion at work, a TV show, or a nap on the sofa may all seem much more enticing than playing Candy Land with a three-year-old. There's no question about it: it is hard to devote yourself wholeheartedly and regularly to bringing up your children properly. But hard work during the children's early, impressionable years usually forms strong characters in them. Parents who discipline themselves to do this, trusting God for the strength to keep going, are likely to enjoy the payoff of a lifetime of solid relationships with their children.

No Pain, No Gain

Achieving good physical condition is impossible without discipline and delayed gratification. People make a calculated decision to forgo certain culinary ecstasies because they want good news at weigh-in time. The delay is worth it when they look at themselves in their new slacks in front of the full-length mirror. At the health club where I work out we say, "Why do we do these things? Because it feels so good when we stop." There's some truth to that. When you take the pain for forty-five minutes or an hour, you feel better about yourself. Your muscle tone is good. You feel alert. You enjoy satisfaction that lingers all day and into the night.

It's the same thing with handling finances. If there is any area where delayed gratification must be practiced, this is it. You experience pain or discomfort when you make a conscious choice not to spend money on something you would really like to have, but as your nest egg grows and your investments mature, you say, "I did it the right way."

Discipline is not hard to understand, then, if you can remember the words *delayed gratification.* But understanding discipline and practicing it are two different things. The key to practicing discipline can be described in three words—*advance decision making.* Here's what I mean.

Advance Decision Making

Once you make up your mind that the only decent way to live is to schedule the pain and the tough challenges first so that you can enjoy the pleasure, the rewards, and the payoff later, then you have to take an important practical step. You must make advance decisions as to *how* you are going to practice discipline in the various dimensions of your life.

For instance, physical health is a dimension that is very important to me. I come from a family with chronic heart problems on both sides. Two uncles on one side and two uncles on the other had heart attacks and died before they were fifty. My dad died at fifty-three. And trouble started showing up in my medical reports when I was fifteen. So, for me, there is no playing games with my health. I know I need to do something about it.

I understand intellectually that I must first endure the pain of running and weightlifting if I am going to experience the satisfaction of feeling well and being healthier. That is, I *understand* discipline. But understanding alone is not enough to improve my health; I must put my beliefs into practice. I *practice* discipline when I make the decision, in advance, that Monday through Friday at 3:30 I will leave the office and go to the health club to work out.

I made that decision several years ago, and I regularly write it on my calendar. Still, every day at about 3:15 my body starts sending signals: "You don't want to work out today. You're a little sore down here, a little tired up there. You're awfully busy in your work. You really don't want to leave now, do you?" A big part of me does not want to work out, you see, and so we start this little argument.

"Yeah, well, I should go."

"Oh, but you can skip a day now and then. After all, you don't want to turn into a fanatic."

So goes the debate. If every day at 3:30 I made the decision whether or not to go work out, I would not work out very often. When it came right down to the moment of packing up and leaving, with all those emotions and voices converging on me, I would probably cave in most of the time. But I practice advance decision making. Because I have already decided to go to the club, I ignore arguments against going, no matter how persuasive they may sound.

"Sorry," I say to my body, "I'd like to hear you out, but I can't do anything about it. It's already been decided. It's on my calendar. You're not going to reverse the decision. It's done." My body may groan, but it gets itself to the weight room. Advance decision making has become a powerful way to implement the practice of discipline in my daily life.

Money Mastery

Advance decision making works in financial planning just as well as in maintaining physical health. Lynne and I put our family budget together at the beginning of each year. We pray about it, we agree on it, and we put it down on paper. Then we covenant together—that is, we make an advance decision—to abide by our budget, come what may.

Payday comes, and what happens? "I saw the most wonderful lamp. It has our name written on it. And it's on sale." We start smiling at each other. "It would look perfect on that little table, and it would make the room so much brighter. We really *need* it." Without an advance decision about our budget, we would probably run out and buy that lamp right then. But because we have agreed to live by our budget, we look at the figures and ask, "Is it in there, or isn't it?" If it isn't, that's too bad; the decision has already been made. We don't fight about it or try to backtrack. We live by it.

Personal Relationships

Advance decision making is extremely important in one area where, sadly, it is rarely applied—relationships. If a husband and wife, for example, are going to continue to nurture their relationship and grow, they need at least one night a week of interaction time alone. Lynne and I call it our *date night.* For several years I have been encouraging the married couples of our church to take weekly private time together. Almost everybody agrees that the idea is good, even essential. Few couples actually do it on a regular basis, however. I am convinced that the people who stick to it every week, month in and month out, have made the advance decision to do so. They have a standing appointment with each other, and a regular babysitter comes in at a prearranged time so that they can keep it. It's all arranged in advance; so when the time comes, they do it.

Most important of all, advance decision making is an important factor in our relationship with God. We know we are saved by grace and not by hard work or planning or discipline. Our spiritual life is God's gift to us, just as our physical life was given to us with no effort on our part. But without practicing discipline, we will not grow spiritually any more than we would grow physically if we neglected the disciplines of eating, sleeping and exercising.

If you have any interest whatsoever in fulfilling your spiritual potential, it is essential that you begin to practice advance decision making in your spiritual life. I have discovered three things that I must do if my spiritual life is going to flourish. First, I need to participate regularly in worship services at my church. Second, I need a daily time of personal interaction with the Lord. Third, I need fellowship with other believers in some type of Christian service. If I do not actively participate in these three endeavors, I wilt. I feel spiritually frustrated, and it seems as if God is not using me. Sooner or later every true believer comes to an understanding of what it takes for him or her to flourish as a Christian—the minimum daily or weekly requirements of a healthy spiritual life. And this is where discipline enters in.

When you determine what has to happen on a regular basis for you to flourish in Christ, it is time to make some advance decisions. If in order to grow spiritually you need to be part of the body of Christ when it gathers to worship, make an advance decision to be there—and go. Say, "All right, I *will* be with the body of believers when it assembles. I *will* attend church every Sunday morning." Don't wait until Saturday night when you get in late and then ask, "Do I feel like setting the alarm?" Don't ask, "Who's speaking? What's the message about?" Don't look out the window to see what the weather is like. Go because you have already decided to do so.

In the same way, if you need personal time with the Lord each day, find the time, block it off on your calendar, and keep the appointment. Perhaps you have your devotional time when you get up in the morning, when you arrive at your office, during your lunch hour or before you go to bed at night. You might spend the time reading the Bible, praying, writing in your journal or listening to a tape—anything that strengthens you in your walk with the Lord. Structure your time and activities in whatever way best suits your needs, but do not leave your time with the Lord to chance. Make the advance decision to keep your daily appointment with him, and keep it without fail.

Sticking with Discipline
When you come to the point in your spiritual life of saying, "I'm going to harness the powers of discipline and commit myself to meeting my minimum requirements," you are really saying, "I'll do what it takes. I'm willing to go through the discomfort and pain of the investment stage first so that I can experience the blessedness of flourishing as a Christian the rest of my life." You

are making an advance decision to delay gratification as long as necessary to achieve the results you most desire. That's discipline.

The essence of discipline, then, is delayed gratification, and the key to practicing discipline is advance decision making. But some of you are saying, "I can't do this alone." You heartily believe in delayed gratification and you have frequently tried advance decision making, but your efforts fall short. Somehow your high resolves melt in the heat of temptation or the pleasant warmth of laziness.

Good news—God does not expect you to do it alone. He knows you need brothers and sisters running along with you (in fact, that's one reason Christians come to God as a church and not just as individuals). If you need help in sticking to your decisions, harness the power of *accountability*. Ask two or three friends to hold you accountable for your decisions. Tell them, "I've made these advance decisions because I really want the payoff. Please hold me to them." This is a tremendous boost to discipline. In addition, God says in his Word that the Holy Spirit helps you produce discipline in your life (Gal 5:23). You can depend on his aid.

What's in This for Me?

Discipline without rewards would eventually seem rather grim. Fortunately, the payoffs of a disciplined life are enormous. Chicago Bears linebacker Mike Singletary is a member of my church. I have been to his home and I have seen the impressive collection of training equipment he has set up in his basement. "Mike," I said, "the Bears have tens of thousands of dollars worth of workout equipment at Halas Hall. Why do you want more in your basement?"

"I want to go overboard," Mike told me. "I'm willing to pay any price, because, when game time comes, I want to be ready." That's why, after a full day of practice, Mike often goes home, walks down to his basement and continues to work out. What are the payoffs for him? Being able to play pro football; playing in the Super Bowl; being named all-pro for three seasons.

Discipline will bring payoffs in whatever area of life you apply it. The payoff for spiritual discipline is a stable Christian life—maturity, usefulness, satisfaction, contentedness. The payoff for relational discipline is a flourishing marriage and family life along with a network of significant relationships. The payoff for physical discipline is a fit body, increased energy, resistance to sickness, lower insurance rates, higher concentration levels and increased self-worth. The payoff for financial discipline is freedom from debt and the satisfaction of knowing your little nest egg is growing.

The rewards of discipline are great, but they are seldom immediate. When the world clamors for instant gratification and easy solutions, it is hard to choose the way of discipline instead. But you will never build a walk with God, a marriage, a body or a bank account by obeying the world's law of instant gratification. Payday will come in its own time, if you endure the pain and put your nose to the grindstone now.

Delayed gratification. Advance decision making. Accountability. These six words define discipline and tell how to achieve it. The rewards of a disciplined life are enormous, and they are within your reach if you are willing to make the effort. Which area of your life most needs discipline? When are you going to take the first step?

4
VISION

Looking beyond
the Obvious

The story is told of two prisoners in one small cell with no light except what came through a tiny window three feet above eye level. Both prisoners spent a great deal of time looking at that window, of course. One of them saw the bars—obvious, ugly, metallic reminders of reality. From day to day he grew increasingly discouraged, bitter, angry and hopeless. By contrast, the other prisoner looked through the window to the stars beyond. Hope welled up in that prisoner as he began to think of the possibility of starting a new life in freedom.

The prisoners were looking at the same window, but one saw bars while the other saw stars. And the difference in their *vision* made a huge difference in their lives.

A business leader told me that, in his opinion, there is a shortage of visionaries entering the marketplace. "There are lots of nuts-and-bolts people in business these days," he said, "people who will do exactly what they're told to do, exactly the way they're told to do it—no more, no less. There are plenty of robots, but precious few idea people. We need people with imagination, people who think overtime, who find ways to make improvements or increase efficiency."

A church leader called me long distance to see if I could suggest the name of a pastor who might be available to lead his congregation. He made it very clear that he did not want someone who would simply come to the church and preserve the status quo. "We are looking for a pastor with vision," he said.

A single woman told me not long ago that she was praying that God would lead her to a man who, in her words, "really knows where he is going, who is willing to take risks, who will keep me guessing." In other words, she wanted God to find her a visionary. "But," she sadly said, "I'm not sure there are many of those around anymore." I wanted to tell her she was being overly pessimistic, but I couldn't. There are a lot of nuts-and-bolts people who will do exactly as told, and there are a lot of people firmly committed to preserving the status quo, but there are not many visionaries around anymore.

Why Are Visionaries Hard to Find?

Vision is on my endangered character quality list along with courage and discipline. The reason is simple: it takes too much work to be a visionary. It's much easier just to go with the flow and do what's expected. It takes courage to break out of conventional thought patterns. It takes confidence and daring to risk failure with a new idea or a new approach. Visionaries tend to fail many times before they ever succeed, and most people feel too fragile to take risks. They would rather be safe and secure.

It also takes a lot of old-fashioned perspiration to be a visionary. It takes discipline to sit down with a pencil and paper and vow not to get up from your desk until you come up with five new ways to do something, three new ways to improve something or two new options for salvaging something that is in danger of disintegrating. It takes endurance to get on your knees and stay there until God supernaturally ignites a fresh thought in your mind. It takes hard work to plan for what could happen in six months, a year, three years or five years in your business, family, marriage or ministry. It probably won't ever happen anyway, so why dream? It's a lot easier to see bars than stars.

Many of us seem to think that dreams, grandiose plans, inventions and creative bursts are reserved for writers, physicists, composers and artists. They are not for ordinary people with ordinary vocations, ordinary families and ordinary relationships. But I think that God disagrees with that kind of thinking. I think he would say that vision, like courage and discipline, is a character trait that can be stimulated and developed in anyone who is willing to understand what it really is and then to work hard at making it part of everyday life. Everyone can choose to look at bars or at stars. In fact, everyone makes that choice several times every day.

Seeing Solutions   Def. 1

Vision can be defined in many ways; I offer three definitions covering three aspects of this important character quality. First, *vision is the God-given ability to see possible solutions to the everyday problems of life.* Visionary people are solution oriented, not problem oriented. There is a tremendous difference between those two approaches.

In Luke 16:1-9 Jesus tells a parable so unusual that many teachers would rather turn the page and go on than try to understand it. It is the parable of a crooked accountant (traditionally, an "unjust steward") who used creative bookkeeping techniques.

His boss eventually caught on and decided to give him his termination notice. But while the accountant still had a few days left to work, he said to himself, "I have a problem. I'm going to lose my steady paycheck. I'm too old to dig ditches and too proud to panhandle. I'm going to have to solve this somehow."

So the accountant did an unethical but ingenious thing: he called some of the people who owed his boss money. "How much do you owe us?" he asked.

One man answered, "A hundred measures of wheat."

"I'll tell you what," the accountant said. "Change your copy of the invoice, and I'll change mine. Put down that you owe us only fifty measures."

"Well, thanks," said the man. "That's a very nice thing for you to do. If you ever need a favor, call me up."

"Don't worry," said the accountant, "I will." Then he called another debtor, and another, and repeated his generous offer.

What was the crooked accountant doing? Plainly, the man was using the company's capital to build up a reserve of personal favors so that when he lost his job he would be able to find another one. His boss quickly saw what he was doing, too, and he had a most unusual reaction—he praised his accountant's ingenuity and shrewdness!

Now neither Jesus nor the boss ever praised deceitfulness, dishonesty or creative bookkeeping. But both of them recognized the accountant's vision. When faced with a serious problem, he did not hide, blame somebody, run to the bottle or jump off a cliff. Instead he faced his problem and came up with a shrewd way to solve it. Jesus commended him because, as soon as he saw his problem, he became solution oriented.

What is so mind boggling about that? Doesn't everybody become solution oriented when faced with a pressing problem? Strangely, no. The longer I work with people, the more I realize that the prevailing tendency is not to try to solve problems but to get stuck on them. A person is going along happily when suddenly he is hit with a big problem—work related, marital, family, relational, financial, spiritual, physical, whatever. His first reaction is to wonder, "Why me? Of all the billions of people on this planet, why did this problem hit me?" He begins to moan and groan about the fact that he now has a problem.

It is not enough just to feel bad about the situation; he is soon calling his friends to see if they will moan with him about his bad luck. He gets on his knees and tells God about the problem in vivid detail, as if God didn't know what was going on. He turns it over and over in his mind like a piece of meat on a rotisserie, eventually sending out formal invitations to a black-tie pity party. Before he knows it, his whole life is revolving around his problem. Paralysis sets in. He has chosen to let his problem define him, and he can no longer either solve it or attend to business in other areas of his life. He *is* his problem.

Amazingly, he has done everything he can about his problem except the one thing he should do—devote himself doggedly and determinedly to finding a solution to it.

All Things Are Possible

The disciples once thought that they had heard Jesus say that respectable, well-to-do, upstanding community leaders could not be saved. If that were true, then their chances of being saved were not very good either. The disciples, who had not yet become visionaries, immediately gave up hope. They saw no solution; salvation was obviously out of reach. Jesus looked at them and said, "Fellas, you're right. With human beings, some problems have no solutions. But with God all things are possible" (Mt 19:26).

Does your problem seem bigger than life, bigger than God himself? It isn't. God is infinitely bigger than any problem you ever had or will have, and every time you call a problem unsol-

vable, you mock God. "With God all things are possible." Visionary people face the same problems everyone else faces; but rather
than get paralyzed by their problems, visionaries immediately
commit themselves to finding a solution. Almost as a reflex reaction to the problem they say, "The situation is bad, all right, but
no problem is bigger than God. And right now, before I get
bogged down, I need to start down the path of solving it." More
often than not, visionaries find a way, with God's help, to deal
with their problems and overcome them rather than surrender
their lives to them.

Vision is a vitally important quality to cultivate, because life is
really just a series of problems, challenges, trials, and disappoint-
ments. If you allow yourself to be overwhelmed by difficulties,
your future is not bright. You will get stuck first on one problem
and then on another. You will spend your whole life spinning your
wheels and cursing the mud. If, on the other hand, you cultivate
vision—if, whenever you are faced with a problem, you immediately explore ways to deal with it—you will not only avert all
sorts of discouragement, but you will also discover just how much
creativity and wisdom God wants to give his children who look
to him for help. How often we underestimate God, doubting his
ability to assist us with the everyday problems of life!

Some years ago a woman talked with me after a church service.
I knew she had been despondent about something for a long
time, and so I probed a little bit until she said, "You know, I am
sick and tired of my job."

"What are you doing about it?" I asked.

"Well, there's just nothing that can be done," she said.

"All right," I said, "let me give you a homework assignment.
Go away to a quiet place. Take a pencil and paper and put down
five possible solutions to your job dilemma." To get her started,
I gave her two of the five off the top of my head. I remember the
look in her eyes as I did this—a mixture of defiance and shock.

This woman had been surrendering to her problem for so long that she had forgotten that she could do something to solve it.

Four Steps toward Problem Solving

"Well," you may say, "obviously Hybels hasn't walked in my shoes. If my problems could be solved that easily, I would have done so right at the beginning." I admit I am not in your shoes. I don't know your boss, your wife, your child, your friend, your doctor. Like you, however, I have some mountain-sized problems that, humanly speaking, are unsolvable. But I don't want pity parties, and I don't want to get stuck on my problems. So by God's grace and with the help of a lot of other people, here is what I do when I face a problem. These four practical steps may also help you when you face problems that look unsolvable.

First, I repeat Matthew 19:26: "With men this is impossible, but with God all things are possible." I have known that text for a long time, but I have to apply it to each new problem that comes my way. When a solution looks impossible, that truth flies right out the window. I have to haul it back and hang on to it tenaciously. God is bigger than my problem.

Second, I go to a place where I can be all alone, and I take another Scripture verse at face value. James 1:5 says, "If any of you lacks wisdom, let him ask God, who gives to all men generously and without reproaching, and it will be given him." I force myself to believe that God will fulfill that promise in my case. If I cannot believe it right away, I pretend. I say to myself, "I'm going to act as if that promise is true." I say to God, "I'm going to take a walk, and I'll keep walking until I have some sense that you've heard my prayer for wisdom, until I know you're going to help me find a solution to this problem." Sometimes the walks are long, but eventually I believe.

Third, I meet with brothers and sisters in Christ who are solution-oriented people. I don't want to meet with people who will just sympathize. "Poor Bill, what a terrible problem he's facing." That does not help me much. It feels good for a while, but the next day I wake up and the problem is still there, big as life. So I meet with people who can tell me how they have solved similar problems in the past.

Fourth, in a spirit of humility, prayer and openness to the Holy Spirit, I list what look like the four or five best possible solutions to my problem. Then by faith I start down the path of one of those possible solutions, trusting God to close some doors and open others, unveil more possibilities or cause something to break in the situation until my problem is solved. I often tremble as I take those first steps, but I would rather move ahead in fear than stay stuck in a bad situation.

No matter what kind of problem you have—relational, marital, financial, spiritual, emotional, vocational—you can find a solution if you are willing to be visionary. Claim the promise that all things are possible with God. Ask him for wisdom. Discuss your situation with wise friends. Put down some options, and head out by faith. It will make a tremendous difference in your life to be on the road to a solution.

Seeing beneath the Surface

Vision is not only for problem solving, of course. A second definition of vision is this: *Vision is the ability to see beneath the surface of people's lives.* Visionary people know that it pays to look beyond the obvious to understand what makes other people tick.

Most of us are amazingly gifted at seeing the obvious in one another. "He's arrogant (or talented, or selfish, or vain)," you say, and your friend says, "I've noticed that too." You smile agreeably at each other and remark about your marvelous mutual insight. But all you have seen is the obvious. Visionary people don't settle for the obvious—that's too easy for them. They look beneath the surface for the other person's uniqueness. They look at the heart, the character, the hopes and the fears that motivate the person's behavior.

Jesus showed vision when he changed Simon's name. All that everybody else ever saw of Simon was his impulsiveness, his aggressiveness, his faintheartedness. But Jesus looked beneath his outer layer and saw a potential that no one else saw. Simon had backbone, a strength that even Simon himself didn't know he possessed. So Jesus renamed him *Peter,* which in Greek means "rock" or "pillar"—something suitable for the foundation of a tall building. "On this rock," Jesus said, "I will build my church, and the powers of death shall not prevail against it" (Mt 16:18). Can you imagine the shock on the faces of the other disciples when Jesus said that? But Peter did indeed become a pillar (Gal 2:9), a respected leader and a founder of the church in Rome. His leadership career goes back to Jesus' vision, his willingness to look beneath Peter's surface-level characteristics to his true self.

I love Proverbs 20:5: "The purpose in a man's mind is like deep water, but a man of understanding will draw it out." There is greatness in the hearts of all people who are created in God's image, but someone with vision has to find it and draw it out.

Visionaries have an important mission to accomplish in the lives of others—looking past the obvious into the shadows, trying to draw out the greatness that God himself put there. We need visionary *parents*—mothers and fathers who will study their children diligently, pray intensely and converse with them perceptively in order to identify and draw out each child's uniqueness. We need visionary *spouses*. Most of us spouses have a stranglehold on the obvious. We need to look beneath the surface and probe around until we find the jewels hidden deep in our mate's soul.

We need visionary *business leaders* who will treat their workers like real people and diligently try to match their unique skills with commensurate responsibilities. In the church, we need visionary *disciplers,* mature Christians who can look past the stumblings and bumblings of baby believers and say, "I see potential there, and I'm going to draw it out." We also need visionary *witnesses* who can look at unbelievers with no time for Jesus and say, "I wonder what Christ's transforming power could do in that person's life?"

This vision that looks past the obvious and sees what's really going on in people's souls can be developed. It takes time—time for meaningful meditation on people's character, thoughtful conversations, persistent prayer for insight and quiet reflection. It also takes courage, for the Holy Spirit may lead you to affirm something in that person that no one else sees.

Seeing As God Sees   *Dec, 3*

I am going to offer a third definition of vision that is more difficult for me to formulate because it is on the cutting edge of my own walk with the Lord. I am not sure how this works, and I do not always know how to activate it, but I know this kind of vision is important. *Vision is the God-given ability to catch a glimpse of what God wants to do through your life if you dedicate yourself to him.*

God once came to Moses and said, "I need a leader to perform a vital, but difficult, task for my people."

Cowering, Moses said, "Here I am, Lord—send my brother. He's the gifted one. He's impressive. He can speak in public." At that point in his life, Moses had no vision of how God could use him.

I have to admit that I share Moses' problem. I look in the mirror and say, "I'm not the kind of guy that God does miracles through." My life is not earmarked for greatness. There is no aura of drama about it. I feel plenty ordinary most of the time, and I often wonder if I matter at all.

But every once in a while—and I won't pretend that it happens often—when I'm in tune with the Lord, the Holy Spirit seems to whisper to me, "Hybels, take your blinders off. Where's your vision? You're not much, but God is. And you matter to him. Why don't you believe what you preach? God delights in using foolish people to confound wise people. He loves to use weak people to amaze strong people. And he'd love to use you, if you'd just believe all things are possible."

At some time in your life you must have sensed God saying to you, "I want to use you in a significant way. It's time to start going in a new direction. I want you to change vocations (go back to school, quit school, start a ministry, strike up a friendship, track down an opportunity, get a job, go to the mission field), because you matter to me. I have great plans for you, and I'm going to work in your life. If you'll just take those blinders off, I'll use you." Just for a moment you felt a flutter in your heart, and you thought, "Maybe that was God's voice." But then instead of looking at stars, you focused on bars. In front of those metallic reminders of reality, you turned off the voice. You quenched God's Spirit. You said, "I think I'll stay in my cell." And God was grieved.

I cannot ask you to do something that I am not willing to do. I want to be more willing to say, "God, here I am. Use me. Lead me. If you have something significant planned for my life, count me in. I'll follow you the best I know how—trembling, but trusting. I want to see stars, not bars. I want to grow in vision."

5
ENDURANCE
Crashing through
Quitting Points

Looking back over the last ten years of your life, what do you wish you had not quit?

Do you wish you had finished high school, college or graduate school?

Do you wish you had kept on taking voice lessons, dance lessons, piano lessons or skiing lessons?

Do you wish you had stayed with that rather low-level job that nevertheless had a great deal of potential for advancement?

Do you wish you had continued to work on your relationship with your first spouse?

Do you wish you had maintained that long-term friendship that dissolved when the going got rough?

Do you wish you hadn't given up on God?

Most of us try not to think about our failures any more than we have to, and Scripture itself advises us not to live in the past (see, for example, Phil 3:13-14). But occasionally it pays to consider the high cost of quitting. So many people live with scars or lingering wounds from having quit on something or someone. So many look back on their lives, shake their heads and ask, "Why did I cash in so easily?"

The answer is obvious: it is infinitely easier to quit than to endure. It's easier to go out and play than to practice scales. It's easier to watch TV after work than to take night classes at the community college. It's easier to walk out of the room during an argument than to stay and work through the conflict. It's easier to read the paper and drink coffee in your bathrobe on Sunday morning than to get yourself and your family up, dress everybody, face the traffic and go to church. It's easier to do what you want to do with your life than to kneel before God, turn the reins over to him, and wait patiently and expectantly and sometimes agonizingly for him to lead you. It's easier to quit following Jesus Christ than to go through the painful process of daily surrender.

We may as well admit it—it's almost always easier to quit than to endure. But quitting exacts a high cost, and many of us have paid dearly for giving up too soon.

Grand Prize: Endurance

Imagine that the Illinois State Lottery, during Easter week when people are supposedly thinking more about Christ than about money, offers a character quality instead of a few million dollars as the grand prize. The ticket lines at convenience food stores are shorter than usual, but still thousands of people pay their dollars and guess at the winning numbers.

When the time comes for the winning number to be announced, eager radio listeners and TV watchers from all over the state hear that a forty-four-year-old, balding store clerk from Joliet has won the fully developed character trait of endurance. And he—we'll call him Herman—comes forward and pretends to be excited, and for about two days he is the object of TV cameras and reporters' questions, and then he goes back to work at K-Mart and is completely forgotten.

Let's check in on Herman ten years later and see how he has fared. Ask him about his grand prize, and see him smile broadly and say, "You know, I wouldn't have believed it at the time. In fact, I was rather angry that the one time I guessed the right numbers, I got a character quality instead of a check for seven million dollars. But I was forty-four years old and still working for minimum wage because I could never keep a job. I guess I always wanted instant promotion and instant money, and whenever a job got tough, I'd quit.

"But ever since I was given endurance, things have been different. I've stayed at K-Mart for ten years, doing my best work wherever I've been assigned, and they've moved me up the ladder several times. Now I'm assistant manager. I went back and finished my high-school education by spending two years at night school. I never could have done that before—I would have quit after the second class. But I kept going because now I have endurance, and I'm real proud of that diploma. And I also put endurance to work in my marriage, which was almost washed up when I won the lottery, and my wife and I have been getting along just fine for several years now. I had just about given up on God, too, but I started my search all over again and I now have an exciting spiritual life. I feel good about myself for the first time in my life, thanks to endurance."

Herman cannot talk much longer because he is being paged over the K-Mart intercom, but he concludes the interview by saying, "Looking back on it, I see that a seven-million-dollar check would have enabled me to keep on quitting whatever I wanted to quit. It probably would have destroyed my dignity and maybe even my life. But this thing called endurance—now that has turned me into a successful, happy person."

The Instamatic Era

James 1:12 says, "Blessed is the man who endures trial, for when he has stood the test he will receive the crown of life."

We spend a lot of energy trying to avoid trials, but we actually ought to thank God for them. Adversity helps us develop endurance, and endurance is a powerful weapon to have in our character arsenal.

But endurance makes my endangered character-quality list along with courage, discipline and vision, because we live in the instamatic era. Nowadays we demand overnight stardom, overnight success, overnight growth, overnight solutions, overnight marital bliss and even overnight spiritual maturity. If our expectations are not met overnight, we have a strong tendency to quit. This is especially true for those of us under forty-five. We were called the "now generation" in the sixties, and things have not gotten any better since. So we quit jobs, educational programs, relationships and spiritual quests—prematurely. Even if we are Christians, we give up on God's mission for our lives before we've really put it to the test. We are fast becoming a weak-willed people, because we don't understand endurance. But endurance is essential for facing life's challenges.

Endurance sustains *courage*. A burst of courage for fifteen minutes is good, but it is not enough to carry you through. Endurance gives staying power to *discipline*. It is important to understand delayed gratification and to make advance decisions, but these are not one-time actions. Endurance turns your *vision* into reality. Without it, visions are no more than pipe dreams. Endurance is one of the most essential character traits of all, but you will never win it in a lottery. You can't buy it, and you can't bargain for it. How, then, can you develop it?

Quitting Points

You build endurance by learning how to crash through quitting points. If you're a runner, you know what a quitting point is. It happens on the twentieth lap when your sides are splitting, your legs are heavy, your throat is burning and your mind is screaming "Quit! Enough! Don't go another lap, another half lap, even another step!" You're at a physical quitting point.

It happens in a work situation when the pressure is mounting as a deadline draws near. You are dizzy from working as hard as you know how, and suddenly the boss comes in and barks yet another assignment. You think, "That's it! I can't stand it one moment longer. I'm going to write out a resignation notice, throw it on his desk, and walk out." That's a vocational quitting point.

It happens in an argument with your spouse for the tenth time over the same thing. The two of you strongly disagree; frustration has been building for weeks. Then your spouse says the magic word that ignites the fireworks. Your emotions go through the roof. Everything in your mind and body screams, "Quit, storm out, call the lawyer—it's not worth it anymore." That's a marital quitting point.

It happens in your struggle to build a good character. You have been wrestling with a particular sin, and someone you care about makes fun of your ideals. Why continue to struggle, you wonder, if nobody else even cares? Why not just cave in to the prevailing morals of the day? That's a moral quitting point.

It even happens in your walk with God. He has been at work in your life, and you have experienced important changes. You know that he is leading you down the right path, but he is making some enormous demands and you don't know if you can trust him—or yourself. "Nobody else is doing this," you think. "Am I the only one crazy enough to trust God down a blind alley?" Then you experience failure, human rejection or scorn, and you say, "That's it, God. I'm not going a step further. You're asking more

— 51 —

than I can give." That's a spiritual quitting point.

Sweet Relief

There are many other kinds of quitting points—educational, emotional, psychological, relational. In almost everything you do, you will reach a point where all you can think of is the sweet relief of cashing it in. In our grandparents' day, quitting was considered disgraceful. But today, it's often praised.

Perhaps endurance does not make good drama, but my blood boils when TV glamorizes giving up. Watch the screen—things are tense at work. The employee is disagreeing with the boss. Nerves are snapping as the background music builds. The camera comes in tight on the employee and shows the veins popping out on his forehead. A moment of silence, and then his voice proclaims, "I quit!" The music crescendoes wildly as he storms out, slamming the door behind him. And while the show's sponsors sing the praises of beer or antacids, viewers across the nation sigh and say, "That's exactly what I want to do to my boss someday. I want to quit in living color, in front of a vast audience, with violins and a drum roll."

Look again—a husband and wife are disagreeing. The tension builds. At the peak of anger, the wife suddenly slaps her husband across the face, just as the cymbals crash, of course. Spinning on her heels, she storms out and slams the door just as the employee did on the last show. And half the wives in America say, "That's what I want to do. Johnny, get the pie tins and we'll go talk to Dad. This time I'm going to tell him to take a walk."

Watching these shows, we do not stop to think that the man is now unemployed, the woman is divorced and little Johnny doesn't have a dad anymore. All we see is the glamour, the sweet relief of cashing it in and walking out. But God's truth pierces through our tinsel-town values. He says it's the other way around. "Blessed is the man who endures" (Jas 1:12). "He who endures to the end will be saved" (Mt 24:13). The lights and music should not be focused on those who quit but on those who, when they think they cannot go one step further, grit their teeth and say, "With God's help I am going to press on." That is when the heavenly choirs break into singing and the spotlight from above shines down. That is when ordinary people like you and me become extraordinary in God's sight.

You may not feel a lot of slaps on the back in those moments. You certainly do not hear the angels sing or feel the burning spotlights of heaven. But if you are walking with the Lord, you hear the Holy Spirit whisper the words, "Blessed are those who draw on God's strength, who endure trials and crash through quitting points—for they shall receive the crown of life."

Crashing Through

If you are at a quitting point right now, count the cost very carefully before throwing in the towel. Quitting is not glamorous. It does not develop your character. God does not call it blessed. In most cases, you will regret it the rest of your life. But when you come to the quitting point and then, drawing on God's strength, crash through it, you build endurance in your life.

You may be at a quitting point in your job. You wanted overnight satisfaction, advancement and fulfillment, and you did not get it. Do you seriously think you will find these things somewhere else? One of my colleagues said to me last week, "I'm sure there have been at least fifty times when I've wanted to leave this place. I'm grateful that, by God's strength, I didn't do it, because I'm now experiencing more blessedness, more fulfillment, more excitement than I ever dreamed possible. I'm glad I stayed."

Or you may be about ready to give up on your marriage. I am embarrassed to admit it, but early in our marriage that sometimes became an inviting option to me—and Lynne was not to blame, believe me. Fortunately, God was gracious. Other people encouraged us to work on our problems, and the Holy Spirit worked overtime inside us. Now our marriage is well worth all the adjustments, pruning, chipping and molding God had to do. Sometimes I look at Lynne and say, "Oh, God, I would have been a foolish man to cash in our marriage!"

Perhaps you are at a spiritual quitting point. You have attended church for a number of weeks, months or even years, and it still is not clear to you who Jesus Christ is. You still wonder why, when you pray, no one seems to be listening. You still wonder why you don't feel what everyone else claims to feel. Yet God's Word says that "he exists and that he rewards those who seek him" (Heb 11:6). "You will seek me and find me; when you seek me with all your heart, I will be found by you, says the LORD" (Jer 29:13-14). Those promises apply to you.

Or perhaps you have walked with God for many years and are tired of struggling, tired of trying to conform your life to Christ's, and tired of the responsibility and the pain of leadership. How attractive it looks to slip back into automatic pilot and become a spectator instead of a leader or a servant. But do you really want to cash in the influence you have on other people's lives, the opportunities you have to serve for God's glory?

You may even be at so many quitting points that you are thinking about ending your life. But suicide is not the answer. God is bigger than any problem you face. The solution is to find out just what path he is going to open up so that your life can take a new course.

Whatever your quitting point, I challenge you to test God's truth and faithfulness by saying, "God, I am going to proceed, trusting you to empower me to crash through this quitting point and come out in one piece on the other side."

Brick or Tissue Paper?

Endurance is a precious quality to me. It has helped me through countless times when I have felt pressed to the wall, tempted to give up my ministry and go back into the marketplace. Because endurance means so much to me, I assign myself extra-credit projects that help strengthen it.

When I run laps at the gym, I always decide in advance how many to run. When I reach my goal, I am usually tired and aching and at my quitting point. That's when I often say, "I'm going one more lap. This quitting point is not made of brick; it's made of tissue paper, and I'm going through it."

When I'm at the beach on vacation, I like to windsurf. I'll go out and back over and over again until my arms are burning, my legs are aching and I'm ready to drop from exhaustion. That's when I say to myself, "I'm going to turn around and go back out just one more time." Again, I want to prove to myself that quitting points are made of tissue paper, not brick.

When I'm working on sermons I sometimes get to the point of saying, "That's it! My mind is scrambled, and I can't come up with one more new thought." That's when I take a walk around the church building and resolve, "I'm going to sit down once more, and that quitting point will prove to be tissue paper."

Every time you break through a quitting point, you prove to yourself that quitting points are not as solid as some people think they are. With God's help you can go through them more often than not. Every time you break through one, a victory is gained in heaven and in your life. Endurance has grown stronger in your spirit. The next time, even if the mountain is higher, you will have more endurance to help you climb it.

Quitting points are painful—Jesus knows that even better than we do. He endured all the way to the cross. Every time the soldiers plucked his beard or someone slapped his face or the whip tore his back open, all hell screamed, "Quit!" When the nails went through his hands, bystanders ridiculed him and he couldn't feel his Father's presence anymore, his whole soul screamed, "Quit!" But by strength from above and by his own resolve, Jesus Christ the Savior crashed through his quitting points and died the death that makes salvation possible for every human being.

I'm glad we follow a Savior who "for the joy that was set before him endured the cross" (Heb 12:2). I'm glad that endurance, even though it will never be offered by the state lottery, can be developed. And I'm glad the Holy Spirit says to us every time we come to a quitting point, "Crash through it—I'll give you the strength. It's made of tissue, not brick."

6
TENDER LOVE
Walking in Someone Else's Moccasins

A huge plant in our living room got a disease, and my wife, worried that it would infect other plants in our house, decided to dispose of it. One morning while the children were at school she hacked all the branches off and loaded them in garbage bags. She left the big pot with the plant's stump in the living room so that, when I got home, I could carry it out to the garage.

In the afternoon our kids went into the living room and saw the pot. Our son, who was then six, burst into tears. "Why did you do such an awful thing?" he asked Lynne. "Did you have to kill the plant? Did it hurt when the plant died? Did it bleed? Couldn't you have called a doctor?" It took half an hour for Lynne to explain the situation and put him back together again.

Meanwhile our daughter, age nine, said disgustedly, "Todd, it was only a sick old house plant. Don't worry about it. I'm glad Mom chopped it down and put it out of its misery. Are you going to chop down any more, Mom? Do you need any help?" Two children born of the same parents, raised in the same family with the same levels of love—but one was being a lot more tender than the other.

Some friends of mine had a dog that had been a loyal, faithful member of the household for thirteen years. But the pet's health had deteriorated so much that the only kind thing to do was to put her to sleep. The family agonized over having to do that. They postponed the evil day repeatedly. Eventually all the members of the family except the dad had to go out of town for some occasion, and he decided to take the dog to the vet. He told me, "I picked the dog up and carried her out to our car. As I drove to the vet's office, she crawled up on the seat, put her head on my leg and nuzzled me. It was terribly hard to take her into the office. After the vet put her to sleep, I went back out to the parking lot and sat for a while before I could go back to work."

The man and his brother worked together. When he walked into the office, his brother asked where he had been. "Well, you know, today was the day," he said. "I had to take the dog to the vet to be put to sleep."

His brother responded incredulously, "You paid a vet to put the dog to sleep? You should have brought it to me. I would have knocked it over the head and taken care of it—no problem." Two brothers with the same parents and similar upbringing, but one is tenderhearted and the other is very tough in spirit.

Some Tender, Some Tough

Paul says in Ephesians 4:32: "Be kind to one another, tenderhearted, forgiving one another, as God in Christ forgave you." For many of us, that is not an easy command to follow. Tenderness seems to be a reflex reaction to some people, but for others it is alien and difficult. You see this in public places like airports and shopping centers. An elderly woman is struggling with luggage or packages, and a steady stream of able-bodied people pass her by. Some even scowl and say, "Get a move on, Grandma." And then a tenderhearted person comes along and takes time to help her.

In the parable of the good Samaritan, Jesus pointed out that being religious is no guarantee of being tenderhearted (Lk 10:30-37). The priest and the Levite passed the injured traveler on the other side of the road because they did not want to get involved. But an irreligious man, a Samaritan, gave assistance because he had a tender heart.

There are many reasons why some people are tender while others are tough. Part of it can be explained as God's workmanship. He makes us all different. Part of it is due to family heritage, the individual's temperament and the kind of experiences he or she has had. Both tenderness and toughness are important character qualities; both are necessary sides of love.

I offer this chapter to the Rambo clones—people who, like me, are naturally on the tougher end of the continuum. I want to show you that some softening has to happen in your life, that you need to learn to be kind and tenderhearted if you want to have a character like Christ's. But the next chapter is dedicated to the gentler Christians who need to learn about tough love—speaking the truth even when it hurts, making waves in relationships that should not stagnate, rebuking people before they shipwreck their lives. The tough need to learn tenderness, and the tender need to learn toughness. Both are important aspects of Christ's love.

The Tough Guy's Dilemma

If we harder-hearted Christians are honest, we have to admit that our tough approach can do damage. We kid people that we shouldn't kid, and when they get hurt we say, "Can't you take a joke?" We don't listen to other people very well. Usually while they are talking to us we are either making unrelated plans or mentally responding to what they are saying. We wonder why many people are so weak and timid. We use people and dispose of them unceremoniously when they have served our purposes. Although we may not realize it, others tell us we act superior. We love to be right, to compete and especially to win. If the truth were known, we secretly view tenderhearted people as emotional weaklings or psychological misfits. We don't understand them.

But in our moments of quiet reflection, which come semiannually, if that often—and usually only when we've been brought low by a financial setback, an accident, an illness, a divorce, or some other crisis—we don't like what we see in our souls. This is especially true if we are in a saving relationship with Jesus Christ. During my own rare times of introspection, I have asked myself, "How can my heart be so hard? I've experienced the personal love of Jesus Christ firsthand. His love has marked my soul and changed me. I know the Holy Spirit resides in my life and is working me over from the inside out, trying to make me a more loving man. I know that God has graciously put me in charge of a community of brothers and sisters who are growing in their attempt to become more loving people. But I'm still too callous and cold. What more is required for me to become tenderhearted? What practical steps can I take to relate to people in a more tender fashion?"

Distorted Vision
Shortly after becoming a Christian, I realized I needed a lot of softening. I needed help in becoming kind, gentle and tenderhearted toward others. One day while reading the Bible, I ran across an episode in Jesus' life in which he healed a blind man. Usually when Jesus healed people, he just touched them or spoke to them and their ailment was cured instantly. But in the story

told in Mark 8:22-26, the healing had two phases. Jesus touched the man's eyes, and then he asked, "Do you see anything?"

The man replied, "I see men; but they look like trees, walking." Jesus touched him again, and this time he received his whole sight. At last he could see people clearly, without distortion.

In those days I did not understand much about biblical interpretation, but I knew that story spoke to me. I feasted on the words, "I see men; but they look like trees, walking." I thought, "That's my problem too. I don't see men very clearly. People, as far as I'm concerned, are just part of the landscape. They are about as important to me as trees."

I remember saying to myself, "When I look around and see other people, I don't think, 'Wow, this person is a custom-designed creation of the almighty God. He has God's image stamped on him. He is the object of God's greatest affection. Jesus shed his blood for him. The Holy Spirit is seeking him out night and day in order to bring him into a relationship with the Father. He really matters to God.' I don't think like that. For me, people are like trees, walking." And when I realized how far my view of people was from Jesus' view, I knew I needed my vision changed. I needed to learn to see people as they really are.

Seeing with God's Eyes
I know a lot of hardhearted people. They tend to be on the fast track. They are going places and getting things done. The adrenaline races through them. They have goals to achieve, quotas to meet, deals to be cut. What they are doing seems so important to them that they view people primarily in relation to themselves and their own projects and aspirations. People are either necessary means to their ends or unnecessary obstacles hindering the way of progress. To a hardhearted, fast-track person, people are either tools to be used or trouble to be avoided.

Hardhearted people, then, tend to divide the world into

winners and losers, heavyweights and lightweights, survivors and basket cases, sharp and two bricks short of a load. It is hard for them to realize that they have never bumped into just an ordinary person—that every living, walking, breathing human being is an extraordinary treasure in God's eyes. It is hard for them to grasp that losers and basket cases matter to God every bit as much as winners and survivors; that Russians, Cubans, Libyans and Palestinians are just as important to God as Americans; that God loves prisoners, homosexuals and bag ladies as much as he loves stockbrokers, dental students and seminarians.

All human beings are God's beloved creations, and all are invited to receive forgiveness at the cross. Because God has invited everybody into his family through Christ, every person we meet is a potential brother or sister. When we grasp this truth and begin to see people for what they mean to God, we begin to soften up and treat people tenderly.

Hardhearted people, pay attention. Next time you're rude to someone because he or she is only a waitress, only a parking lot attendant, only the butcher or baker or candlestick maker—stop! There are no "only's" in God's eyes. These people may be doing humble work, but each one is extraordinary to God. Each one matters. Employers, if you have to give an employee a pink slip, don't just "sack" her. Remember that she matters to God. Single people, if you feel you should break up with the person you are dating, don't just "dump" him. Remember that he matters to God. Drivers, next time someone shakes his fist at you in traffic, don't snarl back. Remember that even hotheads matter to God. And God's treasures should be treated tenderly.

Feeling with God's Heart

To learn tenderness, then, we hardhearted people need first to begin to see as God sees. Second, we must make ourselves walk a mile in the other person's moccasins. Tenderhearted people have a natural tendency to empathize with others, to feel what they are feeling. Hardhearted people, by contrast, can look at people who are hurting, broken or upset and say, "They seem to be having a problem." It is much easier for them to analyze other's problems than to feel with them.

A few years ago, Lynne and I went to see *Sophie's Choice,* a rather heavy psychological drama, a part of which was set in a World War 2 extermination camp. I was a barrel of laughs that evening. Feeling like a teen-ager on a date with the prettiest girl in school, I bought popcorn, put my arm around my wife and settled back to enjoy the movie.

About three-quarters of the way through, the movie started to get intense. Holding her two children in her arms, Sophie was having to decide which one to hand over to the Nazi officer for sure incineration. "This is pretty heavy drama," I thought. "But it's getting a bit long. I wonder if the popcorn stand is still open? I'd like another box." As I turned to look, I noticed that Lynne was sobbing. I decided to get popcorn some other time, and she cried through the rest of the movie.

As we walked back to the car, I could tell that it was no time for cracking jokes. So we drove home quietly and went to bed without saying a word. I did not know what was wrong with her until a day and a half later when she was finally able to bring herself to talk about it. "I want to tell you why I was so upset," she said. "I was picturing having Todd in one arm and Shauna in the other, and having thirty seconds to choose which one was going to live and which one was going to die. How in the world would I ever make that choice?" Lynne had not only put on Sophie's moccasins; she had crawled into her socks, her dress and her bonnet. She became Sophie for a while.

This did not happen to me. I stayed outside the characters' skins and watched the drama unfold; in fact, I did not immediately understand why my wife was so powerfully affected by the movie. Empathy does not come naturally to us hardhearted people. We have to slow down and make a determined effort to put ourselves in other people's shoes. We need to ask ourselves how it would feel to be in their situations.

How would it feel to be handicapped, unable to stand up, walk, dress yourself, drive or even find a good seat in church because there is no room for your wheelchair?

How would it feel to be unemployed, to have mortgage and car payments you cannot make and to have children you cannot provide for?

How would it feel to be Black in a White community that is not particularly sensitive to minorities?

How would it feel to be divorced, to be widowed, to lose a child or a parent?

How would it feel to have cancer, multiple sclerosis, Alzheimer's disease or AIDS?

When we take the time to empathize, to walk a mile in someone else's moccasins, a few cracks begin to appear in the concrete that surrounds our hard hearts.

Treating People As Christ Treats Us

Of course, tenderheartedness has to go beyond feelings. It's vital to start seeing people as God's treasures. It's important to learn to empathize with them. But how should these feelings be expressed? Should I slobber all over people? Should I give away the store? Should I sell my house and join the Peace Corps? What does a tenderhearted Christian do?

In a nutshell, Scripture says to treat people the way Jesus Christ treats you. When you pray, the Lord listens attentively to every word you say. Why not treat your spouse, your children, your friends and your coworkers the same way? Slow down, turn off the television, close out any distractions and say, "I'm going to listen, because I really want to hear what you have to say." When you make a mistake, Jesus lifts you up, forgives you, and continues to treat you with love and respect. Why not do the same for the people with whom you live, work and worship? When you feel lonely and insecure, the Holy Spirit stays by your side, comforts you and assures you of God's love. Why not give comfort and support to the people you love when they are going through difficult times?

No believer ever has to doubt God's affection. Open the Bible and find evidence of it on every page. "You are precious in my eyes, and honored, and I love you" (Is 43:4). "I have called you friends" (Jn 15:15). "I am with you always, to the close of the age" (Mt 28:20). "As a father pities his children, so the LORD pities those who fear him" (Ps 103:13). If God does not want his children wondering whether or not they are loved, why not express your own affection regularly so that your family, friends and coworkers know how you feel about them?

What will happen if we hardhearted people begin to see people as they are in God's eyes, walk in their shoes and treat them the way Christ treats us? The results will be unbelievable. After their initial shock, our spouses and children will go wild with joy. Our coworkers will shake their heads and say, "The whole atmosphere around here has changed—I wonder what has happened to old Harry Hardheart?" Our superficial friendships will deepen into warm brotherly or sisterly relationships. Our churches will multiply in effectiveness as people discover they can find love where Christ is worshiped.

Thank God for people who are naturally tenderhearted. Without them our lives would be barren and unfulfilling. Thank him also that we can all grow in tenderness—even those of us who are naturally tough.

7

TOUGH LOVE

Insisting on Truth in Relationships

Who said the following harsh words?

"Woe to you, teachers of the law and Pharisees, you hypocrites!"

"You blind guides! You strain out a gnat but swallow a camel!"

"You clean the outside of the cup and dish, but inside they are full of greed and self-indulgence."

"You are like whitewashed tombs, which look beautiful on the outside but on the inside are full of dead men's bones and everything unclean."

"You snakes! You brood of vipers! How will you escape being condemned to hell?"

You probably recognize these words of Jesus, the gentle Shepherd, the tenderhearted, meek and lowly Savior (Mt 23:13-33

NIV). How could he talk so tough to people he claimed to love? Why did he say these hard words?

Jesus said these things because they were true. His words were upsetting, difficult to receive, tough to swallow—but true. Quite often the truth must simply be told straight out, with no room for confusion or misinterpretation, to avoid the greater damage of living by lies. Jesus had an overwhelming concern for the people he was addressing. He loved them, and he wanted them to come to grips with the truth before they shipwrecked their lives and jeopardized eternity. Jesus was demonstrating *tough love*—a kind of love that is usually painful but very potent.

I've received my share of hard words over the years:

"Billy, head on down to your room. There's no supper for you tonight. Mistakes are one thing, but lies are another."

"The next time you talk to your mother like that will be on the way out the door to shop for an apartment."

"You know I love you, but I'm not going through with this wedding. You aren't mature enough."

"Do you call this a marriage? I call it a joke, and I'm not going to let you continue to treat me like yesterday's mail."

"Why do I feel I can't disagree with you? Are you always right?"

I could go on and on. There comes a time when the truth must be told, and it must be told straight. Fortunately, some people have loved me too much to allow me to continue to act in a rebellious, deceitful or arrogant fashion. So they rolled up their sleeves, took me to the woodshed and made me face some un pleasant things about myself that were damaging my character and jeopardizing our relationship. That's what I mean by tough love—and I love those people for using it on me.

Tender People and Tough Love

Tender love is badly needed in this hardhearted world. We need compassion, sensitivity, affirmation and encouragement. But without its counterpart, tough love, tender love can rapidly degenerate into a sniveling sentimentality that paves the way for deception and, eventually, the disintegration of the relationship.

To tenderhearted people, tough love sounds unnatural, frightening and maybe even unchristian. It admittedly comes easier to those of us who are by nature tougher hearted. When we see a problem in the life of someone we love, we do not hesitate to go to work on it. We easily say, "What we need here is surgery. So let's lay this guy out and, with a scalpel or a dull butter knife—it doesn't matter which—let's hack through his surface-level excuses and get right to the heart of the matter. And if it causes a little bleeding, that's okay as long as the problem gets fixed. We'll stitch him back up later. If he survives the surgery, he'll thank us later."

Tenderhearted people who read that last paragraph already have their stomachs in their throats. They are saying to themselves, "Surgery? Scalpel? Blood? I never want to see that happen to anyone, let alone do it myself. All I want is peace and harmony. Maybe with enough hugs, the problems will solve themselves and the pain will go away." To you tenderhearted people, God would say, "I understand your tender spirit—I made you that way. But if you're going to learn how to really love, you're going to have to learn about tough love."

Who Needs Tough Love?
One of my colleagues is a true-blue charter member of the tender hearts club. He says he knew nothing about tough love until recent years when some of his Christian brothers demonstrated tough love to him in a lot of ticklish areas in his life. Several months ago, hearing I was preparing a sermon on tough love, he wrote me this note: "Tell those tenderhearted people that if my brothers hadn't demonstrated tough love to me, I wouldn't have a growing relationship with my wife, an effective ministry, a dis-

ciplined walk with Christ, a righteous hatred of sin, respect for the people I lead, my debts paid and money in the bank. But because of tough love, I have all those things. Everybody needs tough-love lessons."

Everywhere I look I see people who need to experience tough love—precious people who really matter to God but who are running around and around in circles, dizzied by deception. I see married couples on the edge of serious trouble, young people pushing their luck to the limits, all kinds of people wandering aimlessly in the wastelands of destructive pleasure seeking. Too many of us who see these people destroying themselves simply chew our nails and wring our hands, saying nothing because we do not understand tough love.

But somebody has to get close to these people and tell them they're on a merry-go-round going nowhere. Somebody has to shake them and say, "God has a better way for you. Get off the merry-go-round and look to him for direction." Somebody has to say, "I love you too much to watch you shipwreck your life, your marriage, your family, your job, your soul. So sit down and listen to me, because I'm going to say some hard things to you. I don't like doing this, but I must because these things are true and because I love you too much to stay silent when I see you hurting yourself."

In order to understand tough love and express it effectively, a person must have two fundamental convictions. First, he or she must believe that *truth telling is more important than peace keeping.* Second, he or she must realize that *the well-being of the other person is more important than the current comfort level in the relationship.*

Truth Telling or Peace Keeping

Tenderhearted people will go to unbelievable lengths to avoid any kind of turmoil, unrest or upheaval in a relationship. If there's a little tension in the marriage and one partner asks the other, "What's wrong?" the tender one will answer, "Nothing." What he or she is really saying is this: "Something's wrong, but I don't want to make a scene." In choosing peace keeping over truth telling, these people think they are being noble, but in reality they are making a bad choice. Whatever caused the tension will come back. The peace will get harder and harder to keep. A spirit of disappointment will start to flow through the peace keeper's veins, leading first to anger, then to bitterness and finally to hatred. Relationships can die while everything looks peaceful on the surface!

Peace at any price is a form of deception from the pit of hell. When you know you need to tell the truth, the evil one whispers in your ear, "Don't do it. He won't listen. She won't take it. It will blow up in your face. It will cause too much hurt. It will only make things worse. It's not worth it." If you believe those lies, there is a high probability that you will kill your relationship sooner or later.

The Lord gives a command in Ephesians 4:25 that makes tenderhearted people tremble to their bones: "Therefore, putting away falsehood, let every one speak the truth with his neighbor, for we are members one of another." First, we are to stop lying to each other. Second, we are to speak the truth—"in love," Paul says in verse 15. It takes courage to speak the truth when we know that doing so will make waves and rock canoes. But any approach other than truth telling, over time, will undermine the integrity of our relationships. A relationship built on peace keeping won't last. Tough love chooses truth telling over peace keeping and trusts God for the outcome.

Counterfeit Peace

In the early years of our marriage, both Lynne and I chose peace keeping over truth telling. I was starting up a church and I had a lot of upheaval at work—no money, no people, no buildings and plenty of disagreement among those who were involved with the project. Lynne had troubles of her own at home. She was pregnant; we had two boarders living with us who took a great deal of her time; and she was teaching flute lessons to help make ends meet. So with upheaval at home and upheaval at work, we had a common understanding whenever we got together— "Don't make any more waves." Nevertheless, inside us the frustrations were building up.

God began to work on Lynne's heart. Before long, my tender-hearted wife started meeting me at the door saying, "Sit down, I have to tell you something. I haven't been truthful with you. I am sick and tired of being tenth on your priority list. You don't show me much affection. I don't like the way this marriage is heading, and I'm not going to stand for it."

I did not respond very well. I did not say, "I'm glad to hear what's on your heart. I'll change my schedule and start thinking about your needs as well as my own." Instead I yelled, "With all the problems I have trying to start this church—and you lay this trip on me! What do you want, anyway? Here, take some blood."

In spite of my reaction, Lynne stuck to her guns. She knew our marriage needed work, and she decided to fight until I saw the light. Over the years God used Lynne's tough love until I faced the truth about myself and allowed him to do a lot of surgery on me.

But then, once I started listening to Lynne and working on my problems, I began seeing some things in her I did not want to live with anymore. Having learned the value of truth telling, I decided to open up. "Sweetheart," I said, "I see a streak of self-centeredness in your life that bothers me."

Sweet, softhearted Lynne did not say, "Thank you for sharing your feelings." Instead she ran away sobbing, "I can't believe you'd say that!" and slammed the bedroom door. But I stuck to my guns, and we had several more rough months. Eventually she made some changes, just as I had had to do, and our marriage became peaceful once again. But this time there was a difference. This was not a counterfeit peace based on avoiding the real issues. This was the peace of the Lord—based on truth, real and lasting.

Well-Being or Comfort

To love as Jesus loves, then, you have to put truth telling ahead of peace keeping. You also have to put the other person's well-being ahead of the comfort level of your relationship.

Imagine a mother looking out the living room window at her three-year-old son, who is riding his Big Wheel in the driveway. Her heart spilling over with love, she goes to the kitchen, pours a glass of lemonade and takes it out to him. After he drinks it, she picks him up and hugs him and tells him how much she loves him. The little guy feels wonderful. But while Mom is going back into the kitchen to rinse the glass, he gets back on his Big Wheel and cruises right into the street where he was told never to ride. Mom looks back out the living room window just as a Chevy screeches to a stop and then carefully eases its way around her precious son. She flies out the door, rushes into the street and picks up the boy, Big Wheel and all. As soon as they are back in the safety of their own yard, she starts yelling at him and spanking him.

The child wonders what is wrong with Mom. He suspects schizophrenia, but he doesn't want to say anything. His reaction is not the point, however—his life is at stake. Mom's behavior is saying, "That happy time five minutes ago with the lemonade and the hugs is a distant memory right now, because we are dealing with life and death. Your well-being is far more important than warm fuzzies."

One of the best definitions of tough love I know is *action for the well-being of the beloved.* We need more people who love others with such devotion that they will risk their current comfort level in the relationship and say whatever needs to be said in order to protect the other person's well-being.

"I love you so much that I can't stand by silently while you work yourself to death."

"I love you so much that I'm not going to pretend to be happy while you ruin your body by eating wrong, never exercising, drinking too much or smoking."

"I love you so much that I have to warn you you're not going to find what you're looking for in bars."

"I love you so much that I'm going to have to say you can't stay in this position in my firm any longer. It seems to be destroying you as a person, and I can't let that happen."

I went to a close friend one time when I saw his life taking a bad turn. I took him to a restaurant and said, "I'm not trying to run your life, but I'm concerned about the direction it's taking." He was so angry that he came close to leaping over the table to punch my lights out. So, man of valor that I am, I looked him in the eye and said, "Sorry, I'll never mention this again." I didn't, either, and he shipwrecked his life. I still see this friend occasionally, and many times I've said to him, "I failed you. I should have been on you like a shirt. I should have said, 'Leap over that table and deck me, if it will make you feel any better, but I'm going to tell you again that I'm concerned about your future.' " Maybe God would have used me if I had been a little more tenacious.

Whenever you take action on behalf of another person's well-being, you are taking a big risk. The comfort level between you may drop precipitously. Over time, however, the outcome of speaking the truth in love—especially when the relationship is basically mature and healthy—is usually positive. The obstacle in your relationship turns into a building block, and the two of you reach new understandings, make new commitments and establish deeper trust. But we all know that it is much easier to write and read about tough love than actually to sit down and have a heart-to-heart talk with someone. Confronting people can be frightening.

Beware the Banana Room

My dad owned a produce company in Kalamazoo, Michigan. We had a large payroll: tough dockworkers, hard-drinking truck drivers, smooth salespeople and efficient managers. As could be expected with such an assortment of people, we had our share of relational problems.

I don't know how it all began, but even when I was a little boy I noticed that, whenever a problem had to be worked out between two employees, they would go into the banana room. Sometimes my dad or one of the other owners would say to someone, "I need to see you in the banana room." Sometimes a foreman would grab a dockworker and they would disappear in there.

The banana room was a temperature-controlled room containing up to 800 cases of bananas. It was completely enclosed and had a four-inch steel door, so no one outside could hear what was going on inside. Maybe that is why, when a summons to the banana room came, everybody quaked. "Oh no—not the banana room!" No one ever died in the banana room, and a lot of times after a discussion in there, people would come out smiling with their arms around each other. Still, people feared the banana room. They were terrified of the face-to-face, heart-to-heart discussions that always accompanied trips there.

Most of us prefer to avoid confrontation. We have a strong aversion to the very vehicle God has appointed to restore true peace between people! In Matthew 18:15, Jesus says, "If your brother sins against you, go and tell him his fault, between you and him alone. If he listens to you, you have gained your brother." Don't shove your feelings into a closet. Don't internalize your frustration. Instead, be tough. Schedule a heart-to-heart talk, and try to work out your differences.

Prepare to Be Tough

But before making an appointment to get tough with somebody, it is important to prepare yourself. First of all, *clarify the issue.* What exactly is causing the tension in your relationship? Is it a mountain or a molehill? Is the problem temporary or lasting? Is the difficulty avoidable or unavoidable? Take out a pencil and paper and write down what you think is the root cause of the conflict you feel in this relationship.

Second, *cleanse your spirit.* Jesus said in Matthew 7:3-5: "Why do you see the speck that is in your brother's eye, but do not notice the log that is in your own eye? Or how can you say to your brother, 'Let me take the speck out of your eye,' when there is the log in your own eye? You hypocrite, first take the log out of your own eye, and then you will see clearly to take the speck out of your brother's eye." In other words, if you feel critical, angry and judgmental—if you can hardly wait to go in and wreak havoc—be careful. A heart-to-heart talk conducted with that attitude will not restore peace. Before calling your friend, surrender your spirit before God. Say, "God, I'm not ready yet. I'm too charged up. I have to cool off and get things in perspective. I need your Holy Spirit so I don't hurt somebody."

Third, *carefully select a time and place for your meeting.* For example the wife of a football fanatic should not plan on meaningful dialog during half time of the Super Bowl. Likewise, a husband should not expect his wife to listen eagerly while she is fixing dinner, the baby is crying and the two older children are fighting to the death in the next room. Plan to meet when you are both physically fresh, when you won't be hurried and where you can enjoy privacy.

Fourth, *pray*. God does amazing things when we ask him.

Tough Does Not Mean Insensitive

When you prepare properly for a confrontation, you have won half the battle. You win the other half when you conduct the heart-to-heart talk sensitively. Here are three steps that will help you present your concerns clearly. They won't guarantee heartfelt thanks and warm fuzzies all around, but they will give you the best possible chance of being listened to and respected.

First, *begin with a sincere statement of commitment to the relationship*. If you're talking to your spouse, tell him or her that your marriage is the most important relationship in the world to you and that you want it to get even better. If you're talking to a friend, tell him or her how much you appreciate the friendship. If you're in a work situation, tell your supervisor that you enjoy working for her, or your employee that you're glad he's on your team. In all cases let the person you're talking to know that you're not issuing ultimatums—you're just trying to work on a problem.

Second, *make a careful, nonaccusatory explanation of the issue as you see it*. Avoid saying "you always" or "you never." When you say, "You're never home, Frank," Frank will answer, "You're wrong. I was home two years ago on February 4. You have blown this all out of proportion." But if you say, "I feel alone so much, Frank. I feel neglected. I feel frustrated and confused," Frank is more likely to listen. You may be crazy for having certain feelings, but he can hardly deny that you're having them. State the problem as carefully as you know how, using "I feel" statements whenever possible.

Third, *invite dialog*. After you have spilled your heart on the matter, ask, "Am I out to lunch on this? Do I have my facts straight? Am I missing something? Am I overly sensitive?" As a pastor, I am frequently challenged and confronted. When I sense in the challenger an open invitation to discuss the point, usually something can be worked out. But if someone finishes off an accusation by saying, in effect, "So there—I will allow you one phone call before I sentence you to an untimely death," I feel defensive. It is hard to reconcile with a person who has an attitude like that.

The Results of Tough Love

Knowing the value of tough love, you have carefully prepared for a heart-to-heart confrontation, and you have conducted it with wisdom and restraint. What possible outcomes can you expect?

I wish I could guarantee that the person you love will say, "Thank you very much for bringing this to my attention." But it is not likely. You might get a slammed door, a pink slip or an earful of angry words. You might end up in big trouble. But if your relationship is built on deception, you are in big trouble already. So take the risk, make some waves and see what God does.

Most probably, the person will eventually take your words seriously, and your relationship will once again stand on firm ground. It is hard to resist someone who is humble and vulnerable. This may not happen immediately, however. Sometimes it takes several confrontations before the process is complete, and sometimes a relationship gets worse before it gets better. Some people excuse continuing hostilities by saying, "Well, I tried to patch it up once, and the other person wouldn't listen." But if your relationship has been disintegrating over months or years, reconciliation may take many attempts. It is unrealistic to expect one hour to undo the work of ten years.

Unfortunately, despite your best efforts, sometimes the person refuses to listen and your relationship seems to be worse off than before. In that case, try mediation. Bring in someone you both trust and respect, and let this person help you communicate. Your church may be able to help you find a mediator—the pastor, perhaps, or members who have dedicated themselves to this task, or maybe a small-group leader or elder. Or you may wish to discuss your problems with a professional counselor. I especially recommend this when alcohol or drug abuse is involved. Mediation may bring good results you cannot obtain on your own.

But we might as well face the facts—in some cases, tough love brings on permanent division. Paul says, "If possible, so far as it depends upon you, live peaceably with all" (Rom 12:18). But sometimes it isn't possible. For whatever reasons, sometimes the two of you will separate and go your own ways. When relationships are terminated, it breaks God's heart. But sometimes that is life in this sinful world; when it happens, we confess our sins, pick ourselves up and, by God's grace and with the help of our friends, we go on.

Too many of us, however, give up without a fight when a relationship begins to disintegrate. We scrap and claw and even go to court to protect our property, but all we do is cry a little when relationships die. This is backward thinking. Relationships are worth fighting for. Love needs to be tough enough to hang on.

Jesus' love for us is the tenderest love we will ever know. He died to heal our sins and to give us eternal life with him. He guides us, protects us, comforts us and nourishes us with his Word. But Jesus' love is also the toughest love we will ever face. He knows our hearts and does not hesitate to tell us when he finds sin there. He insists on truth no matter how painful it may be. He loves us too much to allow us to continue unchecked down a path of self-destruction.

Real love is always both tender and tough. May God give us the sensitivity to know when to show each kind of love and the courage to do whatever love demands.

8
SACRIFICIAL LOVE
Giving without
Giving Out

A lot of strange things are said about love. It's a many-splendored thing, a flower, a rose, a free-floating feeling of benevolence and good will toward all people, a scintillating opportunity to meet someone's need that will result in miraculous bonds of mutuality. In the contemporary view of love, what is important is not what I give to a relationship but what I get from it.

In today's view of love, the parable of the good Samaritan does not sound much like a love story. With a few modifications, however, it has real possibilities. Change the wounded traveler into a curvaceous blonde standing helplessly by her red Porsche, which has been incapacitated by a flat tire. In this retold story, you—the Samaritan—are able to change the tire without ever getting your hands or your three-piece suit dirty. The woman, of course, hovers nearby marveling at your skill and strength. Once the tire is changed and the tools put away, she hands you five crisp $100 bills, plants a wet kiss on your lips and says, "I don't know how I can thank you enough."

Somehow, though, love never works out that way for me. For some reason, real life more closely resembles the original parable. One January, for example, during a twenty-degree-below-zero Arctic blast, I was driving home from my workout at the gym when I noticed a middle-aged woman in a dirty Toyota pulled off the road in a snowbank. I fully intended to pass her by. I had things to do, people to see and places to go; not to mention wet hair, deck shoes, and no hat and gloves. But I felt the convicting voice of the Holy Spirit saying "Love," and I reluctantly turned around and went back.

The woman's trunk was full of books and clothes, and I had trouble finding the jack. When I finally found it, I was baffled about how to work it. Once I figured it out, my freezing hands stuck to it. And by the time I got the car off the ground, I discovered that there was no lug wrench in the trunk. Fortunately, the woman had a friend who lived only three blocks away. We were able to drive that far, and while she went in for hot chocolate, I stayed out in the unheated garage and finished the job. She thanked me and drove away, and I dragged my frostbitten body into my car and drove home, saying to myself as my brain thawed out, "Where is this many-splendored thing they sing about? If I ever find it, I'll kill it."

Love Is Sacrifice

I have found that love is a lot more closely related to work than to play. It has a lot more to do with being a servant than with being a hero. When I set about the task of loving, I usually end up giving instead of receiving. Love inevitably costs me something, usually the three commodities most precious to me—my time, my energy and my money. I do not easily part with these resources, because I have them in limited quantities.

Tell me how to show love without spending time, energy or money and I will gladly sign up. Tell me that love means sacrifice, however, and I become reluctant to commit myself. Maybe that is why some Christians emphasize the fun, fellowship and fulfillment aspects of Christianity without ever mentioning the sacrifice. It is high time to strip away the false glamour that the world—and sometimes the church—puts on loving. It's time to tell the truth: *true love is sacrificial.*

The most famous verse in the Bible, John 3:16, gives the biblical definition of love: "God so loved the world that he gave his only Son, that whoever believes in him should not perish but have eternal life." Because God was concerned with the well-being of people who were precious to him, he *gave*—he sacrificed—his only Son; and when you are concerned about the well-being of others, you usually have to sacrifice too. You may have to expend your time, your energy or your money for them. You may have to give up your plans, your independence or your privacy. To love as God loves, you may have to part with whatever is most precious to you for the sake of other people.

Sacrificial love is a difficult concept to grasp, because our culture teaches the exact opposite. We are constantly bombarded with books, articles, radio and TV shows, commercials and ads shouting, "You are number one. Take care of yourself. Don't let others steal your time. Save your energy so you can enjoy leisure moments. Stockpile financial resources so you can spend more on yourself. If you protect your time, conserve your energy, and amass your resources, you will be happy."

I did not realize how much I had bought into today's misplaced values until, during my junior year in college, I was shocked awake by a professor's statement: "True personal fulfillment never comes through self-gratification."

"That is the boldest, most radical, most countercultural statement I have ever heard," I thought. "It flies in the face of everything I've been taught." But, I began to realize, it does not fly in the face of Jesus' teachings. "If any man would come after me," Jesus said, "let him deny himself and take up his cross and follow me. For whoever would save his life will lose it; and whoever loses his life for my sake and the gospel's will save it" (Mk 8:34-35). "Whoever would be great among you must be your servant . . . for the Son of man also came not to be served but to serve, and to give his life as a ransom for many" (Mk 10:43-45).

The world writes books with titles like *Think and Grow Rich*. If Jesus were writing for today's market, he might call his book *Love and Give Everything Away*. Paradoxically, when you give yourself to God and serve his people in sacrificial love, you find a fulfillment and satisfaction the world never experiences.

Sacrificial Love in Marriage

Let's get specific. How does sacrificial love operate in marriage?

According to the world's wisdom, a good marriage enhances the life of each spouse, making it fuller and more satisfying than it would be if the marriage did not exist. Marriage, then, should not inhibit either spouse from living up to his or her full potential. One spouse should not put the other's needs above his or her own; this will lead to loss of personhood. In a marriage like this, if either spouse discovers he or she is giving more than he or she is getting, a power struggle is likely to ensue. If reciprocal rights cannot be agreed on and guaranteed, the marriage is often dissolved.

The world's view of marriage emphasizes maximum pleasure with minimum sacrifice. It does not take into account possibilities such as incapacitating illness, emotional disturbance, financial reversals or even the arrival of a helpless but demanding baby. That is why this view of marriage is not working, why the divorce rate has soared almost beyond comprehension. Love has never been able to operate for long without sacrifice.

God's wisdom is completely different from the world's. In a biblical marriage, each partner looks the other in the eye and says, "I love you, which by definition means I commit myself to serve you, to build you up, to cheer you on. I know full well this is going to cost me lots of time, energy and money, but I want to put your interests ahead of mine. I'll stand at the back of the line; you go first."

In a biblical marriage, there is no power struggle with each partner trying to gain the upper hand. Instead, there is a serving contest in which each is trying to outlove, outbless and outserve the other. My wife knows how to love sacrificially. One night recently I took her out to dinner, and she said to me, "I've been noticing that the demands on your life are increasing. Maybe I should quit writing and concentrate on making your life smoother."

Although I was tempted to say, "Great! And while you're at it, will you give me a backrub?" I held back, because I knew she was offering me one of her dearest treasures. "No," I said, "I really want you to develop your potential. Don't quit writing. Maybe I should say no to more things so you can continue to grow and flourish." And right there in the restaurant, we got into an argument—not the kind that destroys, but the kind that builds up.

Sacrificial love is the backbone of lasting marriages, even when it leads to impasses in restaurants. It is also the backbone of strong friendships.

Expending Yourself for Your Friends

The world does not understand the Christian concept of brotherhood and sisterhood. The world says to find friends among like-minded, like-incomed people who vote like you and have about the same golf handicap. These are safe people; they won't start asking for counseling or financial assistance. If you keep a healthy distance from them, the relationship won't get muddied up with commitments or expectations.

These friendships work until the bottom falls out of your life. You face a pressing problem, a tragic loss or a serious illness, and suddenly you realize that no one cares much about you. You made no investment in anybody else's life, and so now when you need to make a withdrawal, there's no money in the friendship bank.

Christian friendship is different. You find a few brothers and sisters and decide at the outset that you are going to expend yourself for them. You invest time, energy and often money in them. Because you meet regularly and talk, you get into each other's lives. You encourage, counsel, challenge and rebuke each other. You make sacrifices. Some time ago, a close brother wrote me a letter that began, "This letter is in part to tell you formally that whatever I have is yours. If you and your family ever need any kind of help, just say the word." A colleague once told me, "I know I could go to the phone right now and call five friends who would give me a car, a hand, a place to live if I needed it. This is one of the greatest blessings of my life."

Such sacrificial love is the foundation of true friendships and strong marriages. It also has many other applications. In the business world, for example, it can change the way we treat our colleagues, employees and customers. In our communities, it can reach out to many people and make their lives better.

My father always ended his letters to me with the phrase, "Love those people who need love the most." He put his words into practice in Kalamazoo, Michigan, where he helped a blind man start a restaurant, worked on providing safe shelter for vagrants in the downtown area and, when Vietnamese refugees flooded the country, adopted four or five families and found housing, cars and jobs for them. In addition to his heavy work responsibilities, every week for twenty-five years on Sunday afternoons my father led a hymn sing and Bible study for a hundred mentally retarded women at the state hospital. That is sacrificial love, and today's world desperately needs more of it.

Burnout!

Sacrificial love has just one problem. If you really commit yourself to it, you will quickly find out that it is extremely exhausting. After a certain amount of giving and serving and expending, you may begin to feel numb, as if you have nothing left to give. You are running on empty.

Some people with strong moral fiber and good self-discipline say, "Even though I'm all out of love, I'm going to keep on giving. It's the action that matters, not the feelings." Although they are entirely right about that, they still eventually come to the point of being not only empty, but angry. Angry at people who matter to God, maybe even angry at God himself.

People become problems to be avoided. Phone calls become intrusions. Letters, even from friends, are simply obligations to attend to. Unexpected guests are invaders. Everyone who is on the front lines of loving others knows the feeling: "I can't handle another heartache, another need, another hurt—another person. I want to run away, build a wall around myself, and become a hermit." At that point the great temptation arises to give up altogether on loving people. I frequently hear people say, "I used to be actively involved with others. I used to have relationships and be in ministries. But I burned out, and now I stay away from commitments to people." That is one way of handling burnout, of course. But there is a better way.

It is possible to run completely out of love and then refill the tank. It is possible to love people not only sacrificially but also steadfastly. This is what God calls us to do—not to run the hundred-yard dash in loving people but to run the marathon. In order to do that, we have to learn how to refuel ourselves when we run out of love.

Spiritual Refueling

In 1 Samuel 30 we find a little-known episode in David's life before he becomes king, while he is still an outlawed rebel leader. David has been loving and leading and helping and serving people until he is nearly out of love. His tank is almost dry when an opposition force ambushes the camp and carries off the wives and children of David and his men. The men, outraged, talk of overthrowing David and even killing him. David can't take any more. He feels like pitching his leadership position. He would like to spit on the ground and leave the people. He's sick of them, and he's exhausted. What can he do?

The answer is found in an amazing little phrase, "David encouraged himself in the LORD his God" (v. 6 KJV). He left the people with their incessant demands. He turned his back on still more opportunities for service. He took time out, got away by himself and had a long talk with God. For a little while he basked in God's love for him. He remembered that "God is our refuge and strength, a very present help in trouble" (Ps 46:1). He spent time in solitude with God until his spiritual energy supply was replenished.

Jesus did the same thing after long periods of loving, serving, healing, counseling and teaching. "After he had dismissed the crowds, he went up on the mountain by himself to pray" (Mt 14:23). "Great multitudes gathered to hear and to be healed of their infirmities. But he withdrew to the wilderness and prayed" (Lk 5:15-16). He needed time alone with the Father to replenish himself. It goes without saying that, if David and Jesus needed spiritual refueling from time to time, so do we.

Somehow we must learn to slow down, get off the treadmill,

seek out solitude and encourage ourselves in God. One way to do this is through a daily time of solitude, perhaps before the events of the day rush in. Talk with the Lord and read his Word. Allow him to regenerate your spiritual energies. Some people find spiritual refueling by listening to Christian music tapes. Sometimes when I'm driving to an appointment, feeling stretched to the limit, I turn off the news with its catastrophes and commercials and put in a worship tape. After a half-hour on the road, my spirit is refreshed by the Spirit of the Lord.

I know a man who takes fifteen minutes of his lunch hour to spiritually refuel. Almost every day he closes his office door and reads promises from God's Word. Other people take walks every night, worshiping God as they walk, while still others play musical instruments, read Christian books or sing choruses to the Lord. There's no one right way to encourage yourself in the Lord; the possibilities are endless. Experiment until you find a way that's right for you, because when you learn to do this, you will be well on your way toward loving sacrificially and steadfastly.

Emotional Refueling
It is important to watch your spiritual fuel gauge, though that is not the only indicator that may register empty. You also have to watch your emotional fuel gauge as well. It is possible to keep your spiritual reserves replenished and still feel all out of love.

Major life changes can drain you emotionally: the death of a spouse, divorce, personal injury or illness, loss of employment, change of residence. Even happy events, such as family holidays or the birth of a child, can leave you emotionally spent.

A friend of mine recently had five extremely difficult conversations in one day. When he left the office that evening, he was doing great spiritually—but he was emotionally depleted. Similar experiences happen often in the marketplace. You must fire somebody or reorganize something. Your supervisor makes you redo a major project. The computer goes down for the day. Emotional depletion also happens at home. The sink backs up and the plumber is busy until the end of the week. Chicken pox attacks the children one by one. You learn that your teen-aged son has a drug problem. When your emotional tank is empty, you are likely to feel uninterested in the well-being of others, no matter how full your spiritual tank is.

How do you replenish yourself emotionally? There are basically two ways. First, *relaxation*. Some people cannot accept that. They like the fast track, and if they need emotional refueling, they prefer to get it from a pill or an injection. But there is no quick solution. To fill up your emotional reserves, you need to wind down, take a break, put your feet up, take deep breaths and hold the phone calls. Let nature take its course and restore you to your usual emotional strength.

The second way to replenish yourself emotionally is *recreation* Some activities seem to inspire you, to re-create your enthusiasm for life For my wife, it's reading, writing and playing the flute. For me, it's sailing. For you it may be walking the dog, playing racquetball or weeding the garden. You may have to experiment for a while to find what works best for you. When you find it, you'll know. A couple of hours of the activity, whatever it is, will refuel you emotionally and make it possible for you to go back to loving others sacrificially and steadfastly.

Physical Refueling

If your spiritual and emotional reserves are full and you still feel like hiding under your desk whenever you hear footsteps in the hall, you may need to check your physical fuel gauge.

One Wednesday night before Thanksgiving, I went to a rather lengthy meeting at church before driving with my family to Michigan. Although we did not get to bed there until five in the morning, we had to get up early and start visiting with the relatives. I was in fine shape spiritually that Thanksgiving morning and in reasonable shape emotionally. But physically I was shot.

Every conversation was like hard labor for me. Someone would tell a joke and I would think, "Don't be a jerk, Bill—laugh!" Relatives came to me, hoping for some input about a major decision they were making. But as I talked with them a little voice in my head was saying, "Why don't you handle your own problems? I didn't come here to do counseling. I came for turkey and football. If you want an appointment, call my secretary. I'm sure there's an opening in June." I tried hard to hide how I really felt, and I doubt that any major family damage occurred. But not until late Friday, after I had had time to recuperate physically, did I feel like myself again.

A lot of people these days are chronically run down physically. Most have no idea how much their physical condition undermines their attempts to love other people. They fail to realize that it takes physical energy to listen, to serve, to confront, to rebuke. Not only are physically run-down people short on energy; they also tend to be easily irritated, critical, short fused, defensive and negative. It is hard for them to love others and it is equally hard for others to love them.

How do you stay physically fit? You know the three rules. Eat right, sleep enough, and exercise. Most Americans eat far too much sugar and fat; consequently, many of us are overweight. It is also why we suffer from sugar highs and sugar lows, and it has a lot to do with our high rate of heart disease. It is impossible to maintain good physical reserves on a junk-food diet.

In addition, many of us are careless about sleep. If you do not wake up reasonably refreshed, maybe you are not spending enough time in bed. Or maybe the time you spend there is less than refreshing because the coffee you drank all day or the pepperoni pizza you ate at midnight is keeping you awake.

And for far too many of us, our major form of exercise is

walking down the hall to the photocopy machine. We say we don't have time or energy to exercise, yet experts have medically proven that exercise replenishes the energy supply and actually decreases the need for sleep.

If you are spiritually and emotionally on track, but still feel burned out, check your diet, your sleep and your exercise. A few simple changes in your daily habits might be just what you need to refuel your tank and refit you for steadfast, sacrificial loving.

The Rewards of Sacrifice

Real loving is not easy. It will cost you more than you can imagine. After you have spent all the time, energy and money that you can spare, you will have to take time out for refueling in order to keep on spending your resources. But sacrificial loving will reward you more than you ever dreamed.

The Bible tells about a time when Peter began to wonder if all his sacrifices were worth it. "Then Peter said . . . 'Lo, we have left everything and followed you. What then shall we have?' Jesus said to them, 'Truly, I say to you, in the new world, when the Son of man shall sit on his glorious throne, you who have followed me will also sit on twelve thrones, judging the twelve tribes of Israel. And every one who has left houses or brothers or sisters or father or mother or children or lands, for my name's sake, will receive a hundredfold, and inherit eternal life' " (Mt 19:27-29).

If you give yourself to God and to others, God will register your sacrifice in heaven's ledger sheets. He will pour out a return so bountiful that, over a period of time, you will marvel at how full your life is. You will find yourself breaking out in spontaneous bursts of worship. You will hear yourself singing, "You satisfy my soul. You give me life in all its fullness." Today's imitation love offers no such rewards. As my professor said, "True personal fulfillment never comes through self-gratification." Instead, it comes through sacrifice.

9
RADICAL LOVE
Breaking the Hostility Cycle

We have looked at love from several angles. We have seen that it needs to be tough as well as tender, and it almost always requires us to sacrifice. Jesus shows us yet another angle on love in Matthew 5:39-41, part of the Sermon on the Mount: "I say to you, Do not resist one who is evil. But if any one strikes you on the right cheek, turn to him the other also; and if any one would sue you and take your coat, let him have your cloak as well; and if any one forces you to go one mile, go with him two miles."

I think that when Jesus preached these now-familiar words, he was trying to startle his disciples into taking the next step in their understanding of Christian love. He was saying to them, "Fellas, you are making reasonable progress in understanding what it means to follow me, but when it comes to understanding the kind of interpersonal relationships I want you to have, you need some straightforward, practical, eye-opening information. So listen closely to a few down-to-earth, everyday illustrations about what it means to love as I love."

A Slap in the Face

Consider how Jesus' illustrations must have sounded to the disciples:

Picture yourself walking through the busy streets of Jerusalem. You happen to notice some men standing on a corner discussing politics. You know a few of them and so you amble over and begin to listen to what they're saying. Then someone asks you to explain your views on the Jerusalem political scene. You enthusiastically comply, offering a few well-thought-out suggestions that would solve Jerusalem's problems, knowing full well that some of them are rather bold. Out of the corner of your eye you notice that one of the men is getting red-faced with anger. All of a sudden he squares off in front of you and, with all the pomp his indignation can muster, gives you a backhanded slap across the face.

In the culture of first-century Jerusalem, receiving a slap in the face was considered the ultimate degradation. Even today when we are insulted we say, "That was a real slap in the face." There's no doubt about it—you have been publicly humiliated by an arrogant, opinionated ignoramus. You can still feel the sting of his slap on your face. Your adrenaline is flowing; your anger level is skyrocketing. Your *honor* is at stake. You know you could knock this guy into the middle of next week if you wanted to. And inside your head, voices are saying, "Rocky, Rocky, Rocky . . ."

The moment of truth has arrived. What are you going to do? In the Sermon on the Mount, Jesus commands his followers to show *radical love.* Don't slap him back. Don't scream at him. Don't kick him in the shins. Don't curse him under your breath. Instead, look the man straight in the eye and remind yourself that, in spite of his arrogance and anger, he matters to God. Even at that moment God is trying to reach out to him. In fact, he is looking for someone through whom he could love this guy. So dig down deep into the foundations of your faith and love him. Do something radical that will mark his life. If turning the other cheek to him for a second slap will make a mark on the man's soul, turn the other cheek.

Can you imagine how hard it must have been for the disciples to hear Jesus' challenge? Born and raised in a revenge-oriented culture, they knew all about male honor, bravado and machismo. Turn the other cheek? What a crazy idea!

Beyond Legal Rights

Jesus' second illustration requires a brief explanation of the Middle Eastern wardrobe in New Testament times. People wore an inner garment of a soft fabric next to the skin. Most people had several sets of these. Over the inner garment they wore a heavy, warm, loose-fitting outer garment that served a dual purpose. During the day it was like a suit coat or sport jacket, but at night it functioned as a blanket.

In that climate a man without an outer garment for warmth at night was in a bad way. So important was the outer garment in fact, that it was protected by law. During trading and bartering sessions, it was common for men to hold each other's garments as collateral until the deal was consummated and the good delivered. Usually the inner garment was demanded, because even a poor man would have an extra one. Ordinarily the outer garment was not used, because it was illegal to keep another man's outer garment overnight, even if the man reneged on his part of the deal. The cloak had to be returned at sunset, because without it he would have nothing to protect him from the night's chill.

In view of the importance of the outer garment, Jesus' command is amazing. If you are making a deal with someone and for some reason can't come through with your end of it, and if that man demands an inner garment as overnight collateral, give it to him, of course. But go a step further. Offer him your outer garment as well. Look him in the eye and say, "I know what's right. A deal is a deal, and I have not fulfilled my part. So please take my outer garment, even though by law I am entitled to keep it. It is important to me to be known as a trustworthy trader, and I can get by for a night without my cloak. And, by the way, is there any other service I can render to your family?"

According to Jesus, the demands of radical love often exceed those of any written law. Love never seeks to get away with doing the bare minimum. It goes beyond law keeping and offers outrageous service.

The Second Mile

This leads to Jesus' third illustration, one that cuts to the very souls of his listeners because it had to do with a practice they all absolutely detested—*impressment.* In those days Israel was ruled by Rome. Governors were stationed throughout the empire, and soldiers occupied the various provinces. A Roman soldier had the legal right to approach any civilian at any time of the day or night and impress—that is, coerce—him into service. The soldier could force the civilian to make meals, do laundry, provide lodging or whatever else the soldier thought needed to be done.

The Jews particularly hated it when a Roman soldier made them carry baggage. Whenever troop assignments were shifted, soldiers would appear, tap Jewish men on the shoulder with spears, and say, "Carry that suitcase and that duffel bag, and do it quickly." No matter what the civilian was doing—sleeping, plowing a field, selling his wares—he would have to quit and do as the soldier said. There was a limit, however. The Jews hated this practice so intensely that apparently the Roman officers instructed their men to restrict their demands. They could force a Jewish man to carry baggage for no more than a mile at a time.

So suppose a Roman soldier grabs you by the scruff of the neck, pushes a heavy suitcase into your stomach and says, "Carry this, pal." He walks leisurely along beside you, eating grapes, while you stumble and strain to carry his suitcase. How does Jesus say to respond? When you get to the end of the obligatory mile, instead of slamming the suitcase to the ground hoping to break something fragile inside, instead of shaking the dust off your robe and spitting on the ground to show your contempt for this pagan soldier and this detestable practice, show him radical love.

When you get to the end of that mile, say, "Sir, could I be of further service to you in any way? God has put love in my heart for all his creations, and that includes you, whether you are aware of it or not. You matter so much to him that it would be a privilege for me to be able to serve you. So if you want to go another mile together, I'll go with you."

Understanding the Stories

As Jesus clearly taught, the highest priority in the life of every believer should be to love God with all our hearts, souls and minds (Mt 22:37-40). Our second-highest priority should be to love people, all of whom matter to God, in a radical, nonretaliatory, second-mile way.

For two thousand years people have read and reread Jesus' Sermon on the Mount, asking the Spirit of God to help them understand and apply these three illustrations. Believers have drawn a wide range of conclusions from them, and I still have a lot of questions about their implications myself. But these stories have some general applications that are as plain as can be. There's no mystery about them.

One obvious principle taught by these stories is that retaliation is a dead-end road. Revenge only perpetrates and escalates animosity. Somebody has to stop the senseless escalation—and God wants that someone to be me.

Another clear implication of these stories is that male honor is not the most important thing in the world. I have to learn how to absorb some everyday slaps—being cut off in traffic, having someone push in line in front of me or being interrupted in a conversation. I need to become less defensive, and learn how to absorb some shots instead of returning them.

Finally, the stories plainly point out the secret power of the second mile. When we exceed the barest minimums of service, when we go beyond the call of duty, it has an effect on people that they do not soon forget.

Jesus' way of loving was radically new. Old Testament laws carefully preserved justice—"an eye for an eye and a tooth for a tooth"—but Jesus went far beyond justice in these three illustrations. Why did he want his disciples to be radical, nonretaliatory, second-mile lovers?

Breaking the Vicious Circle

First, God knows it takes a radical lover to break the cycle of interpersonal hostility. The day "Cain rose up against his brother Abel, and killed him" (Gen 4:8), this cycle was set in motion, and it has continued unabated ever since.

A friend of mine is a paramedic in Humboldt Park, a Chicago neighborhood notorious for its gangs. "You know how it goes," he told me. "It starts with a little misunderstanding. It escalates when someone gets his feelings hurt and uses a little sarcastic language. His sarcasm provokes a smart-aleck response, which elicits a threat and then a challenge. Now the male bravado and honor get going. And then come the fists and the clubs and the knives and the guns. The blood flows and the flesh tears, and when it's all over and people are lying in piles, they call us and we come in and pick up the pieces."

I know how it goes. It's been going that way for thousands of years. Granted, in a "sophisticated suburban" environment most of our hostilities do not end in hand-to-hand combat. They end in cold wars: detachment, distrust, alienation, bitterness, name calling, mudslinging, separation, isolation and lawsuits. Although we rarely fight with our fists, we can do a great deal of damage without ever soiling our three-piece suits.

But the cycle of hostility must be stopped if there is ever going to be relational harmony in this world, and it will take radical, nonretaliatory, second-mile lovers to stop it. Somebody has to take a blow, insult or slap instead of returning it. Somebody has to absorb an injustice instead of inflicting another one on somebody else; somebody has to pull the plug on continued cruelty. God says, "You can do it, if you're willing to become a radical lover."

In your marriage, are you willing to be the one to break the icy silences when feelings have been hurt? In the workplace, are you willing to say, "I apologize—let me help with one of your projects so your load will be easier"? In school, are you willing to complete your assignments cheerfully and then offer to do more, even—especially—if the teacher or professor is unpleasant and demanding? God is looking for radical lovers who will report for duty.

Radical Love As Evangelism

The second reason why God challenges us to become radical, nonretaliatory, second-mile lovers is that nothing leaves a deeper mark on the lives of spiritually hardened men and women than seeing radical love in action. If you know the love of Jesus Christ in a personal way, you may sometimes lie awake nights thinking of ways to make a mark on people's lives so that they too will come to enjoy what you have found. Should you wear a little lapel pin? Put a bumper sticker on your car? Display a large Bible in your office? Tell people that you don't go to movies or buy sexually explicit rock albums? Jesus says, if you really want to make a deep, lasting mark on someone, demonstrate radical love. There is so much compelling power in that kind of love that it makes callous people's heads spin. They cannot figure out why you are giving up your rights and letting someone take advantage of you.

Jesus showed radical love all his life. At the end he took slaps without saying anything. He absorbed beatings without cursing anyone. When nails were pounded into his hands and feet, he did not turn to the people doing the pounding and say, "You're going to rot in hell for this!" No, he said, "Father, these men matter to you. Don't charge this crime to their account. Forgive them, if that's possible."

As Jesus died, a Clint Eastwood kind of man, a hardened Roman officer, broke down and cried, "Surely this was the Son of God!" I doubt if the army man had ever heard any theology, but he was broken by the power of Jesus' radical, nonretaliatory, second-mile love.

A Gateway into Christ's Presence
A third reason God asks us to show this kind of love is that it knits the soul of the radical lover to the heart of God.

I know a man who has an unusual rapport with God. He was not born that way; he drew close to God through practicing radical love. Some years ago, he and his father were missionaries in a faraway land. Representatives of another religious sect asked the father if they might pray with him. He readily agreed, and a date was set. When the time came, a man arrived, and the two of them went into a private room to pray. Suddenly my friend heard a great deal of commotion. Rushing into the room, he discovered his father bleeding on the floor. The visiting man, instead of praying with him, had stabbed him to death.

The younger man, in spite of his grief, decided to dedicate himself to reaching the very religious sect that had arranged for his father's murder. No one would have blamed him for leaving the ministry. But rather than leaving, he actually expanded the work his father had begun—and in the process of radically loving his father's killers, he learned to feel Christ's presence and power as he had never felt them before.

When you take slaps, give up your legal rights and carry baggage a lot farther than you need to, you find yourself out in deep water with Christ. Realizing that the ground is not solid beneath your feet, you cling to him. You feel his support in ways you would normally never notice. Most people never leave the harbors of love. They are afraid to venture out on the high seas of radical, nonretaliatory, second-mile love. But that's where the action is. That's where God's presence manifests itself in a far greater way than shorebound people could ever imagine. That is where people are startled into taking a closer look at Jesus Christ, the world's only perfect example of radical love. That is also where hostilities die and lasting peace begins.

Radical love does not make sense. It is not easy. But it is something that the world desperately needs, now more than ever.

10

The
CHARACTER
of Christ

A friend of mine once asked me to teach a class of fifth-
and sixth-grade campers. After a session with the children during
which I gave them a simple message on how to receive Christ,
a boy of about ten approached me and said, "You talked about
asking Jesus into your heart. Before I do that, can you tell me what
he's like?"

Realizing he was looking for a three-minute answer, not a sem-
inary course, I opened my Bible and turned to John 10. This is
what we read together: "The thief comes only to steal and kill and
destroy; I came that they may have life, and have it abundantly.
I am the good shepherd. The good shepherd lays down his life
for the sheep. He who is a hireling and not a shepherd, whose
own the sheep are not, sees the wolf coming and leaves the

sheep and flees; and the wolf snatches them and scatters them. He flees because he is a hireling and cares nothing for the sheep. I am the good shepherd; I know my own and my own know me, as the Father knows me and I know the Father; and I lay down my life for the sheep" (vv. 10-15).

Jesus is a great teacher. Knowing that most people think in pictures, he gives a picture of himself as a good shepherd. Realizing that most people have misconceptions about why he wants to come into their lives, he begins revealing his character by telling who he is *not*.

Not a Thief

"I am not like a thief," Jesus says. A burglar's basic aim is to break into your house and find something of great value that will get good money on the market. You hardly ever hear of a thief who makes off with four dishtowels, two throw rugs and a tube of toothpaste; thieves look for jewelry, family heirlooms, paintings and electronic equipment. That's the character of a thief—to find what is precious and steal it.

Jesus is the exact opposite of a thief. He does not come to rob but to give. He does not break into anyone's life; he stands at the door and knocks. If invited in, he wanders around the house placing precious objects on the mantels, on the shelves and in the cupboards. He fills up the person's life with everything life is worth living for: purpose, fulfillment, meaning, love, peace, confidence, security and even freedom.

A lot of people don't understand that about Jesus. They fear he wants to break into their lives and rob them of the joy of living. They are sure he wants to limit their freedom and make them live in confinement. They suspect he wants to take away fulfillment, put an end to adventure and stop the fun. Sometimes these people come to me and say, "I sense that God wants greater control of my life, and I don't want to let him in. I'm fighting him."

I usually tell them, "Don't worry—you'll win. You can keep God out. Slam the door, put bars on the windows and close your mind. You can stop him." But I also tell them that they don't understand who Jesus is. He is not a thief but an anti-thief. He knocks patiently until you open the door, and then he fills up your house with a whole truckload of life's most precious commodities.

Christ is an altruistic lover: he loves us for what he can give us, not for what he can get from us. If you tear down the bars on the windows, unbolt your doors and fling them wide open so that he can come in, he will fill your house with everything it needs in order to be warm, and beautiful and pleasant to live in.

Two Kinds of Shepherds

Jesus, then, is a shepherd, not a thief. But there are two kinds of shepherds—owners and hired hands. A hireling makes a daily or hourly wage in exchange for doing what the owner asks. He tends to do whatever is necessary to earn his paycheck, but not a bit more. For a hireling, there is no emotion, no compassion, no fulfillment, no overtime and no extra mile.

While I was going to college, I was a hireling. I worked for a butcher, chopping up chickens. It was a job, but that was all. Sometimes the boss would say, "Bill, we're going to have a special sale tomorrow. Do you think you could stay a little later tonight?" I tried to answer politely, but inside I was thinking, "I don't care if this building burns down; I'm out of here at five o'clock." That's the attitude of a hireling.

An owner has a very different attitude. When my father's produce company had a load of vegetables that had to be halfway across the continent by a certain deadline, he sent my brother or me, not a hired driver, to deliver it. If there was a field that had to be plowed at exactly the right time for planting, he sent my brother or me, not hired field hands, to plow it. We were owners, and we cared!

Every day of the week I drive down a road lined with privately owned businesses. Monday through Friday the parking lots are always filled. On Saturday mornings, however, only one car is usually parked in front of each business— and it looks very much like the owner's car. Why? Because the business belongs to him. He probably built it up from nothing, and he wants to keep a close watch on the statistics, the cash flow, the deposits and the statements. He cares about it in a way his employees can never understand.

Jesus is a caring owner. We are his sheep, not someone else's, and he will walk miles to lead us to green pastures. He counts and recounts us. He protects us from impending danger, and he even laid down his life for our sakes. Because he owns us and loves us, Jesus monitors every step we take. He knows every hurt we feel, every crushing disappointment we experience. He is in love with us, and he will do whatever it takes to keep us safe in his flock.

Sons and Daughters, Not Slaves

Because Jesus is our shepherd, we can become personal friends of his. "I know my own and my own know me," he said, "as the Father knows me and I know the Father" (Jn 10:14-15). In other words, the relationship between us and our shepherd can be as close as the relationship between Jesus and his heavenly Father— what a mind-stretching thought!

To help us understand the depth and permanence of such a relationship, Scripture uses another picture to describe it. In Romans 8:14-17, Paul writes, "All who are led by the Spirit of God are sons of God. For you did not receive the spirit of slavery to fall back into fear, but you have received the spirit of sonship ["adoption," KJV]. When we cry, 'Abba! Father!' it is the Spirit himself bearing witness with our spirit that we are children of God, and if children, then heirs, heirs of God and fellow heirs with Christ."

Jesus does not want us to relate to him out of fear, as a slave relates to a master. Over a century has passed since the Emancipation Proclamation, and we may not be able to feel the degradation of being a slave. Most of us have never belonged to a human master with total power over us, including the authority to injure us, kill us or break up our families. But we still have employers to relate to, and we still know what it means to be fearful.

A few years ago, on a plane bound for Los Angeles, I sat next to a person who worked for a well-known international conglomerate. This man said to me, "We do our work on a quota basis. If we come through with sales that meet or exceed the quotas, there's a future for us in the company. So far, for the eleven years I've been with the company, I've been able to do it. But they upped my quota last quarter, and I don't think I'm going to make it. That means my job is in jeopardy."

Eleven years of faithful work for the company and if he falls short of one quota, he's out! That employee could hardly miss the message—his value is tied to his performance; the performance must always improve and mistakes will not be tolerated. Jesus Christ says, "I want none of that. I don't want my people to be terrified slaves. I don't want them to think I love them because of what they can do for me. I want them to know I love them for who they are—the adopted sons and daughters of God, my brothers and sisters. And I don't want them to fear being thrown out on the street for whatever reason; I want them to know they are in my family forever."

Our Adoptive Father
A few years ago, Lynne and I took in an eight-year-old boy and

a three-year-old girl who, because of their parents' alcoholism and divorce, had been passed from home to home. For several months they lived with us, and we grew to love them. I had bought the boy a model car that he really enjoyed putting together. He had worked on it for two weeks and was just putting the finishing touches on it when I had to tell him that the next day the authorities were transferring him to another home. Tears came to his eyes, and then he got angry. He took his little fist and hit the model right on its top, shattering it into a million pieces. "I feel like a football," he said.

All human beings long for family permanence, but most of us quickly learn that it will not be found in an earthly family. A parent dies. A couple gets divorced. Grandparents move far away. Our families do not fill our yearning for a home and family that endures. Christ recognizes that need and meets us by adopting us into his family. He gives us his name: we are called Christians. He gives us his inheritance: life eternal.

I know couples with hearts full of love who yearn to focus that love toward some little one, but no little one arrives. When these couples find children to adopt, they are absolutely thrilled. They don't warn the children that they had better come up to expectations if they want to remain with them. They don't tell thim that they are allowed three mistakes, and then it's back to the agency. They accept them with open arms and joy-filled hearts because they love them, and they take them into their homes forever, give them the family name, and make them legal heirs. That is exactly how God acts when he adopts us into his family.

Just as a husband and wife who decide to give birth to or adopt a child begin to plan for that child long before it is born, God has arranged to take us into his family long before we realize our need for him. As Paul says in his letter to the Ephesians 1:4-5, "He chose us in him before the creation of the world to be holy and blameless in his sight. In love he predestined us to be adopted as his sons through Jesus Christ" (1:45 NIV).

God is saying to us, "My heart is so filled with love that I want to take you in and make you a permanent part of my family. Anybody—of any race, color, creed, background or hang-up—is welcome in my adoptive family." When we sincerely say, "Lord Jesus, I want to be a part of your family," the transaction is consummated and our adoption becomes legally binding and permanent. From then on, we no longer have the spirit of slavery. We are sons and daughters of God.

Confidence in the Spirit

In today's culture we thrive on legal documents. When you get married, you get a marriage license. When you buy a home, you get a title. When you buy a car, you get registration papers. In a transaction as important as adoption into God's family, some form of evidence that the transaction has taken place is important, and the evidence God has given us is more important and more binding than any piece of paper—it is the daily and hourly announcement of the Holy Spirit to our own spirits that we belong to God.

God does not want us to wonder how we stand with him. That is why "the Spirit himself bear[s] witness with our spirit that we are children of God" (Rom 8:16). The inner witness of the Spirit is mysterious. I cannot explain it or always describe it, but I can testify that it is real. When people say to me, "I don't know if I'm a Christian or not. I think I might be. I hope I am," I get worried, because the Bible clearly states that when you give your heart to the Lord, he becomes real to you and you know you belong to him (see, for example, 2 Cor 1:22; Eph 1:13-14; 1 Jn 3:24; 4:13). The Holy Spirit lives inside you and repeatedly whispers, "Have confidence—you are part of God's family."

The Spirit's witness shows how Christ loves us—not as statistics in the heavenly census records, not as voices in the vast heavenly choir, but as individual, significant human beings. He does not want us to be timid or fearful, to live under the constant threat of condemnation. He wants us to be aware of the gift he has given us and secure in his love. He loves us as a brother would love us, because that is exactly who he is.

Fellow Heirs with Christ

Some people think of the Fatherhood of God and our adoption into Christ's family as a lovely metaphor, a divinely inspired figure of speech that helps us understand the depths of God's love for us. This is true, but it does not go far enough. God has *literally* taken us into his family: the proof is that he offers us a share in the estate. If we are children, says Paul, we are heirs—"fellow heirs with Christ" (Rom 8:17). Along with Christ, God's beloved Son, we will receive part of the inheritance!

Paul adds, however, "provided we suffer with him in order that we may also be glorified with him" (v. 17). When Christ came to earth on our behalf, he did not get any glory. The only time he was ever lifted up in any way was when he was nailed to a cross. The throngs cheered for him, but only when they mistakenly thought he was going to overthrow the Roman Empire. Everyone in Jerusalem knew he died like a common criminal; only a handful knew he was raised from the dead and ascended into heaven. This Jesus, who invites us to join him as brothers and sisters in God's family, also calls us to join him in obscurity and suffering: "If any man would come after me," Jesus said, "let him deny himself and take up his cross and follow me" (Mt 16:24).

Being Jesus' brother or sister, then, means sharing everything with him. It means joining him in obedience and suffering as well as in his glorious reward. "Whoever does the will of my Father in heaven is my brother, and sister, and mother," Jesus said (Mt 12:50), and this made perfect sense to his first-century listeners who knew that you could not contest the patriarch's authority and still consider yourself part of the family.

Needed: Character

What does it take to do the will of the Father? It takes *courage* to join a family that is misunderstood by the world. It takes *discipline* to accomplish the tasks God has set out for his children. It takes *vision* to overcome inevitable problems and to see what God is doing in the lives of his children. It takes *endurance* to stick with your brothers and sisters when it would be so much easier to go your own way. Above all, it takes *love* to hold God's family together and to reach out and invite others to join it—tender, tough, sacrificial, radical love.

In a word, it takes *character* to do God's will—and, wonder of wonders, Christ's character is what God offers us when we timidly say we would like to be part of his family. Paul writes that those whom God chooses for his family members he makes "conformed to the image of his Son" (Rom 8:29)—he gives them character qualities like those of their elder brother, Jesus.

He does this through the work of the Holy Spirit, his representative in our hearts. "We all . . . beholding the glory of the Lord, are being changed into his likeness from one degree of glory to another; for this comes from the Lord who is the Spirit" (2 Cor 3:18). The Spirit writes Jesus' own character traits on our hearts: "love, joy, peace, patience, kindness, goodness, faithfulness, gentleness, self-control" (Gal 5:22-23).

After adopting us and making us like Christ, God invites us to claim our inheritance—the same glorious reward claimed by the triumphant Jesus after his resurrection. Jesus is eager to share his inheritance with us: "The glory which thou hast given me I have given to them" (Jn 17:22), he said of his disciples. He will not take the spotlight alone. Instead, "when Christ who is our life appears, then you also will appear with him in glory" (Col 3:4). When Jesus Christ reveals himself in glory to the whole world, he will bring us—his brothers and sisters—with him to share his glory eternally.

The more I learn about Jesus Christ, the more I love him. I realize he is worthy of all my adoration, devotion and praise; he is worthy of my whole life's service. He is a giver, not a thief; an owner, not a hired hand; a father, not a taskmaster. He wants to make me part of his family and give me the character qualities I need in order to live obediently, successfully and happily, now and forever. He wants to have a personal relationship with me that will last eternally, because his heart overflows with love for me.

If you do not know this side of Jesus Christ, God longs to reveal it to you. He wants to adopt you into his family. All you need to do is say, "Lord, I am a sinner who could never earn entrance into your family. But because your perfect Son Jesus died for me, I am eligible for adoption. I want to be part of your family. Thank you for taking me in."

If you do that, God will take you into his family immediately. He won't say, "Wait a few years until your character is more like my Son's," because he knows that character qualities develop best inside the family, not outside it. He will take you just as you are; and with infinite love, patience and gentleness he will begin shaping you. He will send you the Holy Spirit as a living adoption certificate, and you will know that your status as God's child is legal, permanent and binding.

Many secular thinkers know that character development is one of the most important tasks facing this generation. Without it, our nation, our families and millions of individuals are in grave danger; with it, strength and success are still possible. But character development is a difficult, even grim, task when undertaken with no more than firm resolution and gritted teeth.

Character qualities are more easily caught than taught. Like young plants, they develop best in a warm, nurturing atmosphere.

That is exactly what God offers: the best possible example of character, Jesus Christ; and the best possible school for character, the fellowship of his own family. Today is not too soon to take that first small step of courage and say, "Yes, Lord, I want to be like Jesus. Please take me into your family and love me into your likeness."

Neuberger&Berman Management Inc.

A Few Words from our President

Every payday, you're moving one step closer to securing a comfortable retirement for yourself. That's because you made the smart decision to join your company's 401(k) plan. If you're like other 401(k) plan participants, you know how painless it can be to have a small portion of your paycheck automatically deducted and invested for your retirement.

Stanley Egener
President
Neuberger&Berman Management Inc.

I am sure that you have read a few of the many stories that have appeared in newspapers and magazines about the financial difficulties that many Americans will face during their retirement years. Clearly, our Social Security system will have to be changed. Most likely, these changes will result in lower benefits for most people. Additionally, we have the lowest savings rate of any industrialized country in the world. The bottom line? When you look in the mirror each morning, you're looking at the person most responsible for your retirement.

That means that your 401(k) plan is not just a convenience. It is a necessity. Your 401(k) plan will probably be the major source of your retirement funds if you are currently 50 years of age or younger. I believe that the most important concept to understand while building a retirement fund for yourself is this one simple fact: you cannot avoid risk. If you invest your money very conservatively in fixed-income funds only, you run the risk of inflation severely reducing the purchasing power of your savings.

Neuberger&Berman Management Inc.℠

On the other hand, if you invest too aggressively, you run the risk of your savings being subject to severe market volatility.

So you have to take charge of your financial future — and that's where this book, *Building Your Nest Egg With Your 401(k)*, comes in. This investment primer is yours, compliments of Neuberger&Berman Management. This book is just one way Neuberger&Berman Management is working to keep you informed. If you would like to request any of our educational booklets or consult with one of our Shareholder Services Representatives, please call us at **800-877-9700**.

On a more personal note, I would like to share with you the thoughts of my partner, Roy Neuberger, the founder of Neuberger&Berman. On the following few pages, you'll find excerpts from *Roy Neuberger's Almanac* — a collection of wit and wisdom from one of Wall Street's legendary value investors.

Sincerely,

Stanley Egener
President

Falling In Love

One should fall in love with ideas, with people, or with idealism based on the possibilities that exist in this adventuresome world. In my book, the last thing to fall in love with is a particular security. It is after all just a sheet of paper indicating a part ownership in a corporation and its use is purely mercenary. The fact that a number of people have been extremely fortunate in the past by falling in love with something that went their way is not necessarily proof that it will always be that way. Stay in love with a security until the security gets overvalued, then let somebody else fall in love.

"Stay in love with a security until the security gets overvalued, then let somebody else fall in love."

&

Watching the Kettle Boil

A sizable part of the Wall Street community has in recent years developed an obsession. It appears to be over-zealous in finding out what is happening minute by minute to corporate earnings. The fever has spread as well to corporation executives, who appear to worry excessively over reported quarter-to-quarter earnings. The greatest game among a number of research firms seems to be to determine the next quarter's earnings before someone else does. This focus on short-term earnings appears to ignore the significance of longer-term trends in earnings. Corporations often must make current expenditures, with an effect on current earnings, to build for the future. If the goal of immediate reported earnings gains becomes dominant, it can become detrimental to a company's future. Gains in earnings should be the result of long-term strategies, excellence in management, good exploitation of opportunities and so on. If these things fall in place properly, short-term earnings should not be of major importance.

Another trouble with over-attention to each quarter is the upset when a favorite stubs its toe. Then the unexpected causes a stock price drop which can be both precipitous and shocking.

General Philosophy

Over a period of time the market seems to have long waves of advances lasting about two years; it has waves of declines lasting a shorter period, perhaps one half the period of the upswing. During the down cycle, there is extreme irregularity in most individual securities, affording institutions and people great opportunities for enhancement of wealth. If one is not too fearful in bad times and not too optimistic in good times; if one accepts a small loss because of poor judgment; if one is willing to pay the taxes because of enormous gains when securities become overvalued, then one can generally gain by investing in so-called Wall Street, which now stretches across the country.

Neuberger&Berman Management Inc.℠

A Closer Look at Neuberger&Berman Management

Like you, all of us at Neuberger&Berman, L.P., take our retirement planning seriously. Our partners and employees — together with our families — consider an array of investment options, just as you do. After all is said and done, we have chosen to invest over $100 million of our own money in the Neuberger&Berman Funds.

Which tells you something about how much faith we have in our practices and principles. Since Roy Neuberger introduced one of the nation's first no-load mutual funds in 1950, our portfolio managers — all experienced professionals — have sought to provide consistent long-term performance through bull and bear markets alike.

For most of our equity funds, we reduce risk primarily by using a value-oriented investment approach. To select stocks, our portfolio managers work closely with our experienced team of industry analysts and interview top executives of over 400 hand-picked corporations that visit Neuberger&Berman, L.P., each year. On the basis of such exhaustive research, they identify the stocks that are selling for less than their perceived value.

Once investors realize the worth of these undervalued securities, the stocks have the potential to appreciate. Even when they do not, we believe the downside risk has been reduced, since the securities were bought at attractive prices. When we pursue value, therefore, it is because we believe investors can benefit from both the upside potential and the downside protection.

Individuals seeking high current income or total return are also attracted to our limited-risk approach to fixed-income investing. Instead of pursuing bonds with the longest maturities, many of our portfolio managers prefer to buy intermediate-term securities, offering highly competitive yields at a considerably lower level of price volatility.

We invite you to find out more about the funds that we invest in ourselves. Whatever your investment goal, you can choose from our diversified family of no-load funds. Our knowledgeable Shareholder Services Representatives would be pleased to discuss the Funds you want to consider. Call us at **800-877-9700** today. We'll send you a free Information Kit, including a prospectus. Please read it carefully before you invest.

Neuberger & Berman Management Inc.℠

"**If we don't invest in our funds, why should you?**"

– Roy Neuberger,
Partner & Founder,
of Neuberger & Berman, L.P.

Forty-four years ago, I became the first Neuberger & Berman mutual fund investor. Today, my partners and I, together with our employees and their families, have over $100 million of our own money in our no-load funds. I invite you to call now and find out about joining us as a Neuberger & Berman investor. I think you'll decide that's a smart idea – even if you're not an employee. **1-800-877-9700, ext. 3600.**

Neuberger & Berman Funds℠

Three questions to ask before you buy your next mutual fund...

1. Does the fund's investment objective match your own?

Whether you're seeking high income for today or long-term capital growth for a comfortable retirement down the road, you can turn to our diversified family of no-load mutual funds. Simply call **800-877-9700**, and we'll be pleased to review our funds with you.

2. Who manages the fund?

Today's financial market is simply too complicated and volatile for you to place your hard-earned money in inexperienced hands. So it's reassuring to know that Neuberger&Berman, L.P., the sub-adviser of our funds, has been managing money for over half a century.* Our oldest fund, Neuberger&Berman Guardian Fund, has delivered consistent performance since its founding in 1950 (though, of course, there is no guarantee this trend will continue).

3. Does the company invest in its own funds?

If a company doesn't invest in its own funds, why should you? At Neuberger&Berman, L.P., our partners, employees, and their families believe so strongly in our principles and practices that they have over $100 million invested in the firm's mutual funds.

Please complete and return the attached card or call us toll free:

800-877-9700

Neuberger&Berman Management Inc.℠

For more complete information of any of the Neuberger&Berman Funds, including management fees and expenses, obtain a free prospectus by calling Neuberger&Berman Management at **800-877-9700**. Please read it carefully before you invest or send money.

*Neuberger&Berman, L.P. and Banque Nationale de Paris formed a partnership known as BNP-N&B Global Asset Management L.P. This venture is the investment adviser of our International Fund's portfolio.

Please Send Me Information On...

NEUBERGER&BERMAN
INCOME FUNDS
- ❏ Cash Reserves
- ❏ Government Money
- ❏ Ultra Short Bond
- ❏ Limited Maturity Bond
- ❏ Government Income

NEUBERGER&BERMAN
MUNICIPAL FUNDS**
- ❏ Municipal Money
- ❏ Municipal Securities Trust
- ❏ New York Insured Intermediate***

COLLEGE PLANNING
- ❏ *9 Tips for College Savers* Booklet with Worksheet

NEUBERGER&BERMAN
EQUITY FUNDS
- ❏ Focus
- ❏ Genesis
- ❏ Guardian
- ❏ International
- ❏ Manhattan
- ❏ Partners
- ❏ Socially Responsive

RETIREMENT PLANNING
- ❏ *Taking Charge of Your Financial Future* Booklet
- ❏ Retirement Worksheet
- ❏ IRA/Rollover

** *State & alternative minimum taxes may apply.*
*** *Available only to residents of New York and Florida.*

Name

Address   Suite/Apt.

City   State   Zip

❏ Call Me   ❏ Do Not Call Me

Daytime Phone

Evening Phone

Best Day(s) and Time(s) to Call

BUSINESS REPLY MAIL

FIRST CLASS MAIL   PERMIT NUMBER 2857   NEW YORK, N.Y.

POSTAGE WILL BE PAID BY ADDRESSEE

NEUBERGER&BERMAN MANAGEMENT INC.

605 THIRD AVENUE

2ND FLOOR

NEW YORK, NY 10157-1578

BUILDING YOUR NEST EGG WITH YOUR 401(k)

**A GUIDE TO
HELP YOU
ACHIEVE
RETIREMENT
SECURITY**

© 1995 by Investors Press, Inc.
All rights reserved under International and Pan-American Copyright Conventions.
Published in the United States by Investors Press, Inc.
Library of Congress Cataloging-in-Publication Data
    Investors Press, Inc.

    Building Your Nest Egg With Your 401(k)

        ISBN 1-885123-09-4

        I. Building Your Nest Egg With Your 401(k)
Printed in USA
10 9 8 7 6 5 4 3 2 1
Jacket art ©1995 by Wendell Minor
Cover and book design by Silver Communications Inc., NYC

PREFACE

Investors Press takes great pleasure in publishing **Building Your Nest Egg With Your 401(k)**, an important new book that gives you the confidence and knowledge you need to manage your 401(k) account.

This book doesn't tell you how much money to save or which investments to choose. Those are decisions only you can make for yourself.

What it does tell you is why it's critically important for you to contribute the maximum amount you can to your 401(k). It explains everything you need to know in order to make that decision sensibly:

> ➤ how each type of investment works;

> ➤ how different investments can be combined to provide the return you need without taking on more risk than you can live with;

> ➤ how to create an investment strategy for your retirement that's truly easy to implement.

Lynn Brenner, its distinguished author, is a personal finance columnist for *Newsday*, a Times Mirror newspaper with more than a million readers. Her work has appeared often in *The New York Times, Corporate Finance, Financial World, CFO* and numerous other respected national publications. She has been a 401(k) participant, and manages her own Individual Retirement Account (IRA) and Simplified Employer Pension (SEP).

Building Your Nest Egg With Your 401(k) continues IP's commitment to provide informed, independent information that helps each employee learn and understand more about the benefits of participating in his or her 401(k) savings and retirement program.

TABLE OF CONTENTS

INTRODUCTION 7

PART ONE: THE ONLY INVESTMENT CONCEPTS YOU REALLY NEED

What You Need To Know To Use Your 401(k)

1 The big three asset classes:
cash equivalent, fixed-income, and growth investments 14

2 Understanding the different kinds of investment risk 26

3 Reducing investment risk through diversification,
asset allocation, and dollar cost averaging 30

4 The magic of compounding: why saving as early as possible—
even on a very small scale—has such a powerful positive impact
on your retirement account 37

5 Six reasons not to panic when the market falls 38

PART TWO: YOUR FINANCIAL SELF-PORTRAIT

*What You Need to Know About Yourself in Order to Find An Investment
Mix That's Right for You*

1 Your time horizon: how much time do you have to save and invest before you retire? . . 42

2 Your life expectancy in retirement 44

3 Your personal circumstances: how likely is it that you'll have to use some
of your retirement account to pay for a few major expenses before you retire? 45

4 If there is an emergency and you have an unexpected need for money,
do you have any source of available cash outside your 401(k) account? 46

5 Do you have any other savings and/or investments that you can use when
you retire in addition to your 401(k) account? If so, how are they invested? 46

6 Does your spouse invest in a retirement plan at work? If so, how is it invested? ... 47

7 How much do you want your account to be worth when you're ready to retire? ... 47

8 What is your risk tolerance? 48

PART THREE: YOU'RE WITHIN FIVE YEARS OF RETIREMENT

What You Should Be Thinking About

1 What financial decisions should you make as you approach retirement? 53

2 What does retirement mean to you? 54

3 Should you move? 55

4 What are your distribution choices when you
take your money out of your 401(k)? 58

5 Investing in retirement: should your approach
to investing change after you retire? 62

6 What should you know about Social Security and Medicare? 66

7 Buying private health insurance 72

PART FOUR: ANSWERS TO THE MOST COMMONLY ASKED QUESTIONS

What Plan Participants Want to Know About 401(k) Plans

CHAPTER:

One	How does a 401(k) plan work?	74
Two	401(k) contributions	78
Three	Employers' obligations for 401(k)s	83
Four	Tax rules	87
Five	Which is better for me: 401(k) or IRA?	90
Six	Taking my 401(k) money when I change jobs	94

PART FOUR:

Seven   Rules on 401(k) distributions 98

Eight   How safe is my money? 102

Nine   Do I control my 401(k) account? 108

Ten   How can I take money out of my 401(k)? 111

Eleven   Borrowing from my 401(k) 115

Twelve   More important information on my 401(k) 119

PART FIVE: WHAT ARE YOUR INVESTMENT CHOICES?

Understanding Your Plan's Investment Options

1 How does a mutual fund work? 122

2 What investments does my plan offer? 123

3 What are the main advantages and disadvantages of each of these investments? . . 124

4 What should I look for in a mutual fund prospectus? 134

5 How can I get more information about the funds I've invested in? 136

6 If I decide to invest in a stock fund, how can I tell when the market is
likely to move up or down so I know when it's a good time to buy
and when it's a good time to sell? 136

PART SIX: FOR YOUR QUICK REFERENCE

An Easy Way to Find the Information You Need

Glossary 138

Subject Index 146

Index to the Most Commonly Asked Questions 148

List of Illustrations 147

Suggested Additional Reading 154

Worksheet 156

Order Form 160

Your decision to participate in your company's 401(k) plan shows that you understand how important it is to take charge of your financial future. You've made a smart decision and you should feel good about it.

But if you're like most plan participants, your heart probably sinks a little as you wade through that big package of brightly colored brochures, handbooks, forms and support materials distributed by your employee benefits department.

You may feel that you're drowning in information about 401(k) plan features and options, but can't relate any of it to your own particular situation. Perhaps you feel that you're ill-prepared to cope with what seem to be confusing investment choices. Perhaps you feel that you have no real control over your own money because you don't understand enough about investing. And perhaps you feel that in a more perfect world you wouldn't be forced to make decisions like these because your employer would make them for you.

If so, don't worry. You're not alone.

People as intelligent and financially responsible as you are, at all income levels, often feel totally unqualified to invest their own money, no matter how competently they handle everything else in their lives.

Building Your Nest Egg With Your 401(k) was written specifically for people like you—plan participants who want to invest their money intelligently without making it their life's work.

This book doesn't explain modern portfolio theory, discuss the inner dynamics of financial markets, or give you a crash course in economics. You don't have the time or the inclination to learn all that. *And you don't need to.*

The basic rules of investing are much simpler and easier to follow than most people think. You don't need a working knowledge of high finance. You don't need an MBA or a BA, or even an aptitude for arithmetic. All you really need are the fundamental principles explained in this book, and a little common sense.

Most of us don't feel knowledgeable enough to make our own investment decisions because we reach adulthood without having had any formal education in personal finance or investing. Managing money is as essential a skill for an adult as driving a car, but unlike Drivers' Ed., personal finance isn't a required course in high school. It's not part of the core curriculum in college, either.

One result of that gap in our practical education is that a great many people who successfully negotiate the purchase of a house—the biggest single investment they'll ever make—are utterly unnerved by the choices offered in a small menu of relatively simple financial investments. People who automatically spend a few hours studying back issues of *Consumer Reports* before they go shopping for a washing machine, or devote a whole week-end to comparing a dozen paint-chips before selecting a new color for their living room, don't spend as little as fifteen minutes reading a brochure that describes their retirement investment choices.

Why? Because they're so sure they won't understand it.

The only information about investing and finance that we're all exposed to is provider sales material, and that incomprehensible nightly sound-bite: "The Dow Jones average closed up (or down) X points today and trading was light (or moderate, or heavy)." Small wonder so many Americans are convinced that the financial markets are capricious, complicated and impossible to understand.

As recently as ten years ago, this widespread lack of knowledge didn't matter very much. Anyone who had a pension plan at work didn't need to know how to invest for retirement. The traditional pension plan guaranteed the employee a specific retirement income, based on salary and years of service. The employer was entirely responsible for funding the pension plan and for deciding how to invest the money.

It was nice while it lasted. But the security these old plans offered really belongs to the vanished U.S. economy of the 1950s, a time when it was not unrealistic to think that you would spend thirty years working for the same company. What's more, today's longer life expectancy has made the guaranteed retirement income a much smaller security blanket than it used to be. Your retirement is likely to last two decades or more—and the buying power of a fixed benefit will shrink drastically during twenty years of inflation.

Traditional pension plans currently account for fewer than 20% of all existing retirement plans. Although they cover more than 35 million Americans—and you may be one of them—even the dwindling number of employers who can afford to maintain their old pension plans have limited their future growth and supplanted them with new ones, usually 401(k) plans.

The 401(k) plan is designed for the harsher economic reality of the 1990s. It has important features that don't exist in traditional plans:

Your contributions reduce your current income taxes. You can often borrow from your account for major expenses like the down payment on a house or the cost of a college tuition. Most important, anytime you leave a job, you can take your retirement account with you.

This portability is a significant plus in a world where a new college graduate can expect to change jobs seven to eight times during his or her career. In a traditional pension plan, you don't qualify for a retirement benefit unless you stay on the job for at least five years. The job-hopping that is now common substantially reduces retirement income from traditional pension plans.

A 401(k) plan gives you an unprecedented degree of control over your own financial future, and the freedom to pursue career opportunities without necessarily reducing your pension.

But a 401(k) plan offers no fixed, guaranteed retirement benefit. *You* fund the plan and *you* make the investment decisions. *Your retirement income depends on what you save and how well you invest it.* The message is clear: it is now crucial that you learn about long-term investing.

The good news is that this doesn't have to take a lot of your time, and it doesn't have to be painful.

You already know much more about investing than you realize. When you're shopping for a house, you don't walk into a real estate broker's office and say "I've got about $50,000 to invest, what house do you recommend I buy?" You tell the real estate broker what you're looking for, based on your needs and priorities. You know what's most important to you, and what trade-offs you're prepared to make to get it.

Shopping for financial investments isn't any different. First, you determine your own needs and priorities. Then, you look for the investments that will best meet them, and you make a few sensible trade-offs in the process.

Choosing your investments in a 401(k) plan isn't nearly as exhausting or time consuming as house hunting because most plans offer just three to five basic investment choices—and they have been preselected to fit a wide range of participant needs and preferences.

If you can choose the house that best fits your family's needs, if you can pick which of five vacation spots is most likely to please you and your spouse, you're more than capable of choosing an appropriate 401(k) portfolio.

This book will show you how.

Lynn Brenner

PART ONE

THE ONLY INVESTMENT CONCEPTS YOU REALLY NEED

*What you need
to know to use
your 401(k)*

WHAT YOU NEED TO KNOW TO USE YOUR 401(k)

Joining a 401(k) plan is one of the smartest things you'll ever do. It's the blue ribbon pension plan of our time. There is no easier, simpler, or faster way to save a lot of money for your retirement—and you're going to need more money than you think to retire comfortably.

It takes a very big nest egg to overcome the major obstacle to a secure retirement: the impact of inflation on the buying power of your money. (For a sobering look at how quickly inflation can shrink the value of a dollar, take a look at the chart on page 21.)

Most Americans who retire at 65 can now expect to live another 20 years or more. That's a very long time to support the ordinary comforts of life without a paycheck, let alone pay for the additional travel, recreation, study and hobbies you'll have time to enjoy when you aren't working—and two decades of inflation is a serious threat to the buying power of your savings.

Your 401(k) plan gives you the tools you need to overcome this danger to your retirement security and take control of your financial future. You also get an immediate financial reward: every dollar you save reduces your current income tax bill. If your employer matches a part of your contribution, you have an additional bonus—you get an instant, risk-free return on your money.

But without a basic understanding of investment concepts, you can't take full advantage of your 401(k) plan and make your nest egg grow to its greatest potential. So here they are: the only investment concepts you really need.

Investing is a much simpler and more straightforward process than most people realize. You're halfway there if you know:

1. what your own goals are, and

2. roughly how much time you've got before you'll reach them.

The first investing mistake most people make is to look around for "the best" investments without first determining their own financial objectives. That's like trying to pack a suitcase for a trip to an unknown destination.

Naturally, we all want investments that will provide high yield, safety and enough growth to beat inflation by a handsome margin.

But that wish list isn't an investment strategy any more than a craving for riches and fame is a career plan. You can't plan an itinerary unless you know where you're going. **To create an investment strategy, it's essential that you set down real dollars and cents goals—and the more specific they are, the better.**

For example, do you know:

➤ How much you want to have saved in 15 years?

➤ What amount you can afford to invest every month?

➤ What investment return you need on your money to reach your goal?

➤ What kinds of investments have historically provided the return you need over a 15-year period?

➤ How bumpy a year-to-year ride it has been to hold those investments?

➤ Can you accept that bumpy a ride in exchange for the long-term return? Or would you prefer to settle for a slightly lower long-term return in exchange for a somewhat smoother year-to-year ride?

Your time horizon is also very important. The longer you have to build your nest egg the better, for two reasons. The first is that the more years your money has to compound, the smaller the amount you'll need to contribute

to reach your goal. (See chart, page 37, The Magic of Compounding.) The other reason is that when you have lots of time, you can ride out short-term price fluctuations—the main drawback of high-return investments.

Unless you plan to die the week after you retire, don't think of your anticipated retirement date as the end of your time horizon. You may spend nearly one-third of your life as a retiree.

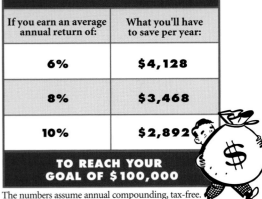

INVESTMENT TIME HORIZON & GOAL

15 YEAR TIME HORIZON

If you earn an average annual return of:	What you'll have to save per year:
6%	$4,128
8%	$3,468
10%	$2,892

TO REACH YOUR GOAL OF $100,000

The numbers assume annual compounding, tax-free.

The average person who retires at age 65 now lives into his or her 80s. That means PG. 62 if you're 40 years old, you have a 40 to 50 year investment horizon ahead of you. (See pages 62-65 on investing after you retire.)

Making the right investment decisions is simply a question of picking the investments that best fit your particular goals and your time schedule.

This, too, is much less complicated than it may sound. Every 401(k) plan offers its own investment options. But as a plan participant, you don't face the equivalent of choosing between 31 Baskin Robbins flavors. The selections available to you will consist of investments that fall into just three asset categories, or classes—the vanilla, chocolate and strawberry of the financial world: 1) cash equivalent investments, 2) fixed-income investments, and 3) growth investments.

To design an investment strategy that fits your needs and risk tolerance, you need to know how you can expect each of these three very different asset classes to work for you.

You may spend nearly one-third of your life as a retiree!

THE BIG THREE ASSET CLASSES: CASH EQUIVALENT, FIXED-INCOME AND GROWTH INVESTMENTS

Forget about the complexity of the financial markets. When you get right down to it, *there are only two ways to invest your money.*

1. You can *lend* it to a borrower—a bank, or a corporation, or the U.S. government, for example—that will pay you interest for its use. That's what you do when you deposit money in a bank savings account or buy a corporate or government bond or shares in a bond mutual fund.

2. You can *buy* something whose value may increase over time, and later sell it at a profit. That's what you do when you buy stock in a corporation, shares in a stock mutual fund, a house, a painting or a collection of gold coins.

When you invest in cash equivalents and fixed-income assets, you are a *lender.* When you invest in growth assets, you're an *owner.*

Which kind of investment is better for you—cash, fixed-income, or growth? That depends entirely on your goals and time frame. There is no one-size-fits-all investment. Each of these three basic asset classes has its own advantages and disadvantages.

The key to successful investing is matching their different characteristics to your own goals. As soon as you do, you'll realize that just as there's no one-size-fits-all investment, there's no investment that's "safe" or "risky" in every situation. In fact, how "safe" or "risky" any investment is depends in large part on what you're trying to accomplish and how much time you have in which to accomplish it.

CASH EQUIVALENT INVESTMENTS

When you invest in a cash equivalent, you're making a short-term loan to a very high-quality borrower — in other words, a borrower considered extremely able to repay the loan. Cash equivalents include bank Certificates of Deposit (CDs) and Treasury Bills (T-Bills) — both backed by the full faith and credit of the U.S. government — as well as commercial paper, the IOUs of corporations with the highest credit ratings. (We're talking about really short-term loans here. Commercial paper maturity ranges from overnight to 90 days.) Money market mutual funds, which buy bank CDs, commercial paper and T-Bills, are also cash equivalent investments.

An investment that's comparable to a CD, but available only in a retirement plan like a 401(k), is the Guaranteed Investment Contract or GIC, which is issued by an insurance company. (The guarantee in a GIC comes from the issuing insurer, not from the federal government.) A GIC pays a fixed interest rate for a fixed term, typically one to five years. Many 401(k) plans offer a GIC fund, often called the stable value fund or the insurance contract fund, which buys GICs from many different insurers.

Both cash equivalent investments and GICs give you stability of principal. In a money market fund, for example, your investment is converted into shares with a fixed value of $1, each of which you can redeem for the same $1 value. Cash equivalents also offer great liquidity, which means that you can turn your investment into cash quickly and easily. A house, by contrast, is a very illiquid investment; it might take months or even years to sell. GICs offer less liquidity than cash equivalents like T-bills and money market funds because your money is tied up for the term of the contract.

But remember, an investment inside your 401(k) plan isn't as liquid as the same invest-

TIME IS MONEY $$$

INTEREST RATE %	YEARS TO DOUBLE YOUR MONEY
1	72.0
3	24.0
5	14.4
7	10.3
9	8.0
11	6.5
13	5.5
15	4.8

The column on the right tells how long it will take to double your money if you can find an investment paying the interest rate listed on the left.

ment held outside a retirement account. There are penalties for taking money out PG. 111 of your 401(k) account before you reach age 59½. The best place for an emergency account is outside your 401(k) plan. (See Questions 66 - 81, pages 111-117.)

A money market fund pays fluctuating interest because the fund is constantly making new loans. As rates rise and fall, so will your yield from the fund. GICs offer fixed rates of interest that are somewhat higher—approximately what you'd earn in an intermediate-term bond—because your money is invested for a fixed term. But GIC investments mature relatively quickly, so you don't lock in a specific yield for very long.

Your risk of losing your principal in a cash equivalent investment is low[1], because the borrowers are credit worthy and loans are so short—typically one year or less. The trade-off is that for the same reasons, your yield from a cash equivalent investment is also low.

Cash equivalents are very risky when used as your main long-term investment.

HOW CASH EQUIVALENT INVESTMENTS STACK UP AGAINST DIFFERENT GOALS AND TIME HORIZONS

Cash equivalents are an excellent short-term investment. Stability of principal and liquidity are important features for an emergency account, for example, because they assure you that you can tap your investment anytime without worrying about a temporary dip in its value.

These characteristics make cash equivalents, and to a lesser degree, GICs, a good investment for any money you plan to use in less than five years and don't want to take any risks with—your savings for a big vacation, or a down payment on a house, or college tuition that's due in just a few years, for example.

As a medium-term investment, cash equivalents are less attractive. If you know you won't use this money for eight years, for example, you may be less willing to accept a lower yield in exchange for liquidity and stability of principal.

Cash equivalents and GICs are very risky when used as your main long-term investment. The reason is that they don't provide any real growth to keep up with inflation. As you can

see in the illustrations on pages 19 and 29, (The Growth of $1 Invested from 1926-1994 and How Different Investments Have Performed Over Time), cash equivalents have proved to be terribly vulnerable to inflation over a long period of time.

---

[1] Money market funds are a very low risk investment, but they aren't risk-free. In 1994, a dozen money market funds had portfolio losses. In every case but one, their managers made up those losses themselves so that investors didn't lose any money. The exception was Community Bankers U.S. Government Money-Market Fund, a small Colorado fund that closed, paying its shareholders 94 cents for each dollar invested.

FIXED-INCOME INVESTMENTS

Like cash equivalents, fixed-income investments are loans. But this resemblance can be very misleading. Fixed-income investments are much more complex than cash equivalents. They offer greater potential return and they also involve greater risk.

Fixed-income investments are longer-term IOUs than cash equivalents. The borrowers include the federal government and federal agencies, as well as corporations and municipalities. The maturity, or term, of these loans ranges from two years up to thirty years.

When you consider a fixed-income mutual fund, you should look at the credit rating of the issuers whose bonds it buys, as well as at the average maturity of its bond portfolio. *Short-term funds* usually own bonds with an average maturity of less than three years. *Intermediate-term funds* own bonds with an average maturity of three to ten years. *Long-term funds* usually buy bonds with a maturity of ten years or longer.

A bond rating gives a rating agency's opinion of the borrower's ability to repay a loan. The bond ratings of Standard & Poor's, for example, start with AAA (excellent), AA (very good), and A (good). The next tier of S&P bond ratings is BBB (adequate), BB (speculative), B (very risky), and B minus (very, very risky). The last tier is CCC, CC, C, and D—all of which denote bonds whose issuers S&P believes are about to go into default or are already in default.

An "investment grade" bond is one whose issuer (the borrower of your money) has a credit rating of BBB or higher. A "junk" bond is one whose issuer has a credit rating of less than BBB.

A fixed-income investment provides higher income than a cash equivalent partly because you're making a longer term loan, and partly because the borrower's credit quality may not be first-rate. The lower the borrower's credit quality, the higher the interest you'll receive on the bonds it issues. That's why "junk" bonds can be called "high yield" bonds.

The longer the bond's maturity, regardless of the issuer's credit quality, the higher the yield. A 15-year bond pays higher interest than a 5-year bond. The reason: the longer the term of the loan, the longer your principal will be exposed to "interest rate risk," the risk that your

The value of your principal in a fixed-income investment isn't fixed at all.

BOND PRICES VS. INTEREST RATES

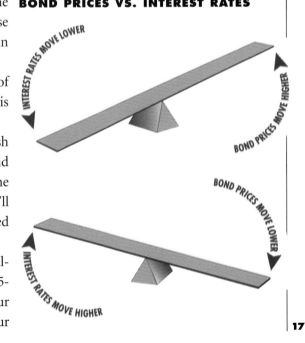

INTEREST RATES MOVE LOWER

BOND PRICES MOVE HIGHER

BOND PRICES MOVE LOWER

INTEREST RATES MOVE HIGHER

	INTEREST RATE	BOND INTEREST PAYMENT	BOND COST OR VALUE	
AT TIME OF PURCHASE	10%	$100	$1,000	Initial cost of bond ($100 payment = 10% on $1,000)
IF RATES FALL TO	5%	Remains $100	$2,000	New value of bond ($100 payment = 5% on $2,000)
IF RATE RISE TO	15%	Remains $100	$666	New value of bond ($100 payment = 15% on $666)

investment will lose value because the prevailing interest rate has changed.

The value of your principal in a fixed-income investment isn't fixed at all. On the contrary, the actual dollar value of your principal fluctuates with each change in interest rates. (See chart, page 17.)

Let's take a $10,000 bond paying 10%, for example. You receive fixed 10% interest payments; if you hold that bond to its maturity date (and the issuer doesn't default), you get back your $10,000. But between the time you buy it and the time it matures, your bond won't always be worth $10,000. Its value—the price you'd get if you sold it—changes every time the prevailing interest rate changes.

If interest rates rise to 11%, your $10,000 bond immediately becomes less valuable. This may sound confusing, especially if you instinctively see that an increase in interest rates must mean bond yields will go up. But think about it for a moment: if the prevailing interest rate is 11%, nobody is going to pay full price for a bond that only yields 10%. If you need to sell a $10,000 bond that pays 10% at a time when people can buy newly issued bonds that pay 11%, you'll get less than $10,000 for it.

By the same token, if interest rates fall, your bond's value shoots up. If the prevailing rate drops to 9%, buyers will pay a premium for an older bond that yields 10%. You could sell it for more than $10,000. If you conclude that the most profitable time to invest in bonds is during a period of declining interest rates, you're absolutely right!

To sum up, in a fixed-income investment the value of your principal has the potential to grow or to shrink, depending on which way interest rates move. *That's why it's a big mistake to judge a bond or a bond fund only by its yield, the way you would judge a money market fund. What counts in a bond is your total return: the yield, plus or minus any change in the bond's price.*

Total return is an especially important concept to understand when you invest in a bond mutual fund in your 401(k) plan. Buying shares in a bond mutual fund is not the same as buying individual bonds because mutual funds don't hold bonds until they mature.

When you invest in a bond fund, you're buying a share in thousands of different bonds in an ever-changing portfolio. That means 1) that the income you receive from a fixed-income fund isn't fixed, but fluctuates as the mutual fund buys and sells bonds. And 2) the market

> Buying bonds in a mutual fund is not the same as buying individual bonds because mutual funds don't hold bonds until they mature.

value of your principal in the fund also fluctuates, depending on whether the fund is selling bonds at a loss or a gain.

The longer the maturity of the bonds owned by the mutual fund, the more dramatically your principal will gain or lose value as interest rates change.

The yield on a long-term fixed-income mutual fund looks especially tempting when prevailing rates are very low. But the yield is high because the risk is high, too: when the prevailing interest rate is very low, it's likelier to rise than to continue falling. And when interest rates rise, 30-year bonds lose a greater percentage of their value than 10-year bonds.

All too often, 401(k) investors buy long-term government bond funds for their yield, assuming that any government bond is "safe," unaware of the fact that if interest rates go up, they will lose money.

HOW FIXED-INCOME INVESTMENTS STACK UP AGAINST DIFFERENT GOALS AND TIME HORIZONS

A short to intermediate-term bond fund invests in bonds that mature in ten years or less. It is a good investment for anyone who needs a dependable stream of relatively high income. These bond funds offer a higher yield than cash equivalent investments. At the same time, they're less vulnerable to interest rate risk than long-term bond funds.

Fixed-income investments also can be very useful as a form of insurance in a long-term retirement account because there have been some economic periods when fixed-income investments have performed well and growth investments have performed badly.

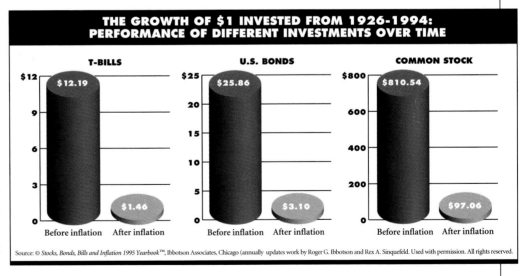

Source: © Stocks, Bonds, Bills and Inflation 1995 Yearbook™, Ibbotson Associates, Chicago (annually updates work by Roger G. Ibbotson and Rex A. Sinquefeld. Used with permission. All rights reserved.

But fixed-income assets alone have not been a good long-term investment because they don't provide enough growth to beat inflation. As you can see in the illustrations on pages 19 and 29 (The Growth of $1 Invested from 1926-1994; and How Different Investments Have Performed Over Time), fixed-income investments don't hold up very well to inflation over long periods of time.

GROWTH INVESTMENTS

When you invest in a growth asset, you're buying something that you hope to sell one day at a profit. You don't *want* stability of principal in this kind of investment. On the contrary, you want your principal to grow. Growth investments include stocks and stock mutual funds, real estate, and precious metals and collectibles.

Growth investments offer the highest potential return of the three asset classes, and are your best chance to outperform inflation. Here's why:

When you invest $1,000 in a stock mutual fund, the best case scenario is that you'll eventually sell your shares for a lot more than $1,000, perhaps for a very high multiple of $1,000. By contrast, when you lend $1,000 to a bank, a corporation, or a government agency, the best case scenario is that you'll eventually get back the same $1,000.

Unfortunately, by the time you get the $1,000 back, it may buy much less than it did when you originally invested it. (Take a look at the illustration on page 21 for a reminder of how drastically inflation can cause prices to rise.)

Over long periods of time, the stock market is the only investment that has consistently outpaced inflation. Since 1926, inflation has risen at an annual compound rate of 3.1%. Stocks have earned a 10.2% compound annual return, as measured by the Standard & Poor's 500 Index, which tracks the average performance of 500 widely held common stocks.

When you buy shares of stock in a company, you're buying a share in a business, in its earnings and in its assets. You get a proportionate share of profits the corporation pays out in dividends, and you benefit from increases in the company's value which are reflected in its share price. Your total return from a stock investment is the dividends it pays, plus or minus changes in its share price.

Profitable companies don't always choose to pay dividends. Rapidly growing companies, for example, often prefer to reinvest profits to expand their business, which of course also benefits their shareholders. A mature company is a likelier source of dividends.

Stock dividends aren't a predictable source of income because companies pay dividends

Fixed-income assets alone have not been a good long-term investment because they don't provide enough growth to beat inflation.

only after paying all their other bills like payroll, rent, taxes and interest to their bondholders. A corporation that's strapped for cash is always free to reduce or eliminate dividends. But historically, companies have cut their dividends only as a last resort. In fact, many companies periodically raise their dividends.

The stock market's total return over time includes both price changes and reinvested dividends, and the reinvested dividends have accounted for a very big chunk of that return.

If you had put $100 into the S&P 500 stock average on the last day of 1925 and kept it there until June 30, 1990 but spent all the dividends, you'd have earned $2,806 on your investment, says Ibbotson Associates of Chicago. But if you had reinvested all the dividends instead of spending them, you'd have $55,091. (See The Magic of Compounding, page 37.)

PG. 37

Just as fixed-income investments come in a variety of maturities and credit qualities, there are several important categories of common stocks.

BIG CAP STOCKS

A company's capitalization (market value) is determined by multiplying its total number of shares outstanding by their current market price. In general, big cap stocks are the stocks of companies with market values of more than $10 billion. Typically, these companies are mature corporations with a long track record of steady growth and good dividends.

Mid cap stocks are generally those of companies with market values of between $500 million and $10 billion. Mid cap companies tend to grow faster than big cap companies, and are less volatile than small cap companies. (A very volatile investment is one whose value can change quickly and dramatically, in either direction.)

Small cap stocks are usually those of companies with market values of less than $500 million. Small cap companies are often the potential stars of tomorrow: Apple Computer was once a small cap stock, to cite just one example. But while small cap companies can grow much

HOW INFLATION SHRINKS THE VALUE OF A DOLLAR

	1968	1988	% INCREASE
CORN FLAKES	24¢	$1.16	383%
1/2 GALLON OF MILK	45¢	.93	107
1 LB. BACON	69¢	1.79	160
McDONALDS HAMBURGER	15¢	.65	334

Source: Statistical Abstract of the United States

faster than bigger companies, they're also more volatile and they fail far more frequently.

The S&P 500 Index reflects performance of big cap and mid cap stocks. Small cap stock performance, which historically hasn't moved in the same cycles as big company stock performance, is reflected in the Russell 2000 Index.

Within each of these size categories there are two basic types of stock:

➤ **Growth stocks** are stellar performers: fast-track companies whose earnings are expected to grow very rapidly.

➤ **Value stocks** are ugly ducklings: out-of-favor companies that nevertheless promise a good long-term return. A value stock is a bargain: its selling price is cheap relative to the company's assets and future earnings potential.

Historically, growth stocks and value stocks have tended to perform well in alternating cycles. That's why it makes sense to own some of both, as many stock mutual funds do. There are also mutual funds that specialize in either growth or value stocks. The latter are called growth and income funds.

HOW GROWTH INVESTMENTS STACK UP AGAINST DIFFERENT GOALS AND TIME HORIZONS

Most people think of stock investments as very risky, mainly because a stock price (the value of your principal) can fluctuate literally from day to day, often for no readily apparent reason.

Any growth investment is subject to price swings based on changes in its perceived value in the marketplace. (The market value of your house changes constantly, too.) The price of XYZ Company's stock may rise or fall for any number of reasons: an anticipated increase or decrease in the company's quarterly earnings; the apparent success or failure of a new product line; the market entry or departure of a big competitor; expected changes in the economy, or in interest rates, or in government regulations that might have a positive or an adverse impact on XYZ's industry.

Sometimes the market's perceptions are wrong. That might mean that XYZ's stock is undervalued and therefore a good buy. Conversely, it might mean the stock is wildly overvalued—just a flash-in-the-pan.

If you have a nervous stomach, you may well feel this kind of irrational volatility is an excellent reason not to own shares of XYZ Company, or any other stock, for that matter. And in the short run, you'd be right. Stocks are a very risky short-term investment. The history of the Standard & Poor's 500 Index shows that over a 12-month period, you stand a 29% chance of losing money in the stock market.

Clearly, you wouldn't want to invest your emergency account in the stock market. Stocks are very liquid—they can easily be converted to cash—but they don't give you stability of principal. If you're forced to sell stock investments in a hurry, you may have to sell at a loss.

But there's a big difference between how the stock market performs in the short run—over a one or two-year period—and how it performs over a ten-year period.

In the short run, fluctuating stock prices reflect investors' passing hopes and fears, sometimes on an hour-by-hour or even a minute-by-minute basis. But in the long run, stock prices reflect the steady growth of the U.S. economy and of American business corporations. In a ten-year period, your risk of loss in stocks drops to just 3%. In a twenty-year period, your risk of loss falls to zero. The S&P 500 Index has *never* had a negative 20-year return.

History shows that if you're investing for less than five years, very little of your money should be in stocks. *But if you're investing for more than ten years, most of your money should be in stocks.*

Why? Because for a goal that's more than a decade away, your first priority isn't short-term price stability, it's beating inflation. And since 1926, over periods of ten years and longer, the stock market has almost always outpaced inflation.

To see how stocks are a much safer *long-term* investment than cash equivalents or fixed-income investments, look at the chart on page 29 (How Different Investments Have Performed Over Time). Since 1926, common stocks have earned a 10.2% compound annual return, medium-term government bonds have earned a 5.1% compound annual return, and Treasury Bills have earned a 3.7% compound annual return. The compound annual inflation rate was 3.1%.

Remember, these compound returns are untaxed. To understand how dramatically stocks have outperformed bonds and Treasury Bills as long-term investments, you'd have to subtract taxes, as well as inflation, from these returns.[1]

---

[1] ©*Stocks, Bonds, Bills and Inflation 1995 Yearbook*™, Ibbotson Associates, Chicago (annually updates work by Roger G. Ibbotson and Rex A. Sinquefeld). Used with permission. All rights Reserved.

BUT WHAT IF HISTORY DOESN'T REPEAT ITSELF?

All the information we have about how stocks, bonds and cash investments perform over long periods of time is based on past experience. But as mutual fund prospectuses always warn you, past performance is no guarantee of future performance.

Isn't it possible that bonds will outperform stocks in the future?

Sure it is. No investment performs best all the time. At some point it's virtually inevitable that bonds will outperform stocks, perhaps for a sustained period of time. That certainly has happened in the past. (Bonds were a better investment than stocks from 1928 to 1937, for example.) That's why you should consider owning both bond and stock investments.

What about the possibility that the best days of the U.S. stock market are in the past? Many people today fear that the future profitability of U.S. business is threatened by foreign competitors that don't have to comply with stringent U.S. safety and environmental laws or pay their workers American salaries and benefits packages. These fears have increased in the past few years in the face of massive lay-offs at major U.S. companies.

No one can deny that our economy is undergoing profound changes as we adjust to a post-Cold War world. And no one can guarantee that the U.S. stock market will continue to grow in the next twenty to thirty years at the same pace that it has grown in the past.

That's one of the reasons that many investment professionals believe that between 10% and 20% of a long-term portfolio should be invested in foreign stocks and bonds. The best way to protect yourself in an uncertain future is to diversify your retirement portfolio. (See page 30.)

PG. 30

SMART PILLS

- The secret of successful investing is selecting investments whose risk and reward characteristics fit your financial goals and time horizon.

- There are three basic types of investments: cash equivalents, fixed-income, and growth. Each one has different advantages and disadvantages. Each is better suited to some goals and time horizons than to others.

- Cash investments and GICs give you stability of principal but no growth. They're best for short-term goals.

- Fixed-income investments, like bonds, pay a higher yield than cash investments but don't give you stability of principal or growth. They're a good provider of steady income stream and a good diversification tool in a long-term stock portfolio.

- Fixed-income doesn't mean fixed value: in a bond mutual fund, both your principal and your interest fluctuate in value.

- When interest rates go up, the value of existing bonds goes down. When interest rates fall, the value of existing bonds rises.

- Never buy a bond fund only because of its yield. Look at its total return: the yield plus, or minus, any changes in price.

- Growth investments, like stocks, are subject to dramatic short-term price fluctuations. But unlike cash and fixed-income investments, in the long-term stocks historically have grown fast enough to outpace inflation.

- Diversification reduces risk. It's safer in the long run to own several kinds of investments that behave differently than to own only one.

UNDERSTANDING THE FIVE DIFFERENT KINDS OF INVESTMENT RISK

Every kind of investment involves risk. Not investing is risky, too—saving your money in a safe deposit box certainly won't keep it safe from the ravages of inflation.

As a 401(k) plan participant, the biggest question you face isn't whether or not you should take risks with your precious retirement savings. It's what *kind* of risks you should take.

Most people worry about only two types of investment risk. The first is risk to their principal: the danger that they'll lose all or part of the money that they invest. For many people, this is the most pressing concern; they feel their primary goal with retirement money is not to lose it.

The second risk most people think about is the uncertainty of investment return.

These two major concerns help explain why so many 401(k) plan participants invest most or all of their retirement money in Guaranteed Investment Contracts. A GIC fund promises stability of your principal. It promises to return your principal on a specific date, and it promises a fixed rate of return so you're in no doubt about how much you'll earn for the term of the investment.

These are indeed attractive characteristics. But it's very risky to invest most of your 401(k) account in a GIC fund if you're more than five years away from retirement because a GIC fund leaves you exposed to a third risk that too many plan participants forget about—the impact of inflation.

If your investment time horizon is longer than five years, your primary goal with retirement money should be to grow it, so that even after inflation, you'll have a nest egg big enough to assure financial security for the rest of your life.

As a long-term investor, you need to understand several different kinds of risk:

1. **Inflation Risk** is by far the most serious danger for any long-term investor. The fact that you don't see how it erodes the value of your principal makes it all the more insidious.

Most people think their money is safe in any investment that guarantees stability of principal, like a money market fund or a GIC fund, because the nominal value of their account in this kind of fund is never less than the amount they originally invested. And what could seem safer than an FDIC-insured bank account where your principal is stable and guaranteed by the full faith and credit of the U.S. Government?

But over time, that apparently stable principal is being invisibly consumed by inflation.

One dollar doesn't buy as much today as it did five years ago. In another 20 years, $1 will buy substantially less than it buys today.

If you're earning 4% in an FDIC-insured account and inflation is running at 4% a year, your real return after inflation is zero. Your real return after taxes is negative.

For a long-term goal, the last thing you want is stability of principal—if your principal doesn't grow, you can't possibly stay ahead of inflation.

As you can see in the illustration on page 29 (How Different Investments Have Performed Over Time), cash equivalent and fixed-income investments have historically provided a very small *real return*—the return that's left after inflation is subtracted—over long periods of time.

When your investment goal is more than ten years away, your biggest single risk is inflation. The best way to reduce inflation risk is to invest in growth assets like stocks.

2. Business Risk is the risk of losing your money in an investment that seemed like a winner but wasn't. Perhaps you buy XYZ Company stock, and management makes a series of disastrous decisions and runs the company into the ground. Or you invest in highly rated Can't-Miss California County Bonds and it turns out the rating agencies were wrong: the county is in a financial hole and you may never get your money back.

The best way to reduce business risk is to diversify. A prudent investor avoids putting all his or her money into a single stock or bond issue. In a mutual fund, for example, you automatically diversify among hundreds of different stocks and bonds, which greatly reduces the impact on your investment of any single business loss.

3. Market Risk is the risk of losing your money in a steep market decline. This is the first risk many people think of when they think of the stock market: you put your life savings into QRX Company stock and two weeks later the stock market crashes for reasons no one ever adequately explains. Suddenly your QRX stock is totally worthless.

There are two ways to reduce market risk. One is to diversify your investments among different kinds of assets: divide your money among cash, fixed-income, and growth investments, for example. (See Asset Allocation, page 32.)

The second way to reduce market risk is to ignore market ups and downs and focus on long-term results. Remember, the people who panicked and sold their stock investments after the October 1987 crash lost money. Those who stayed put saw the market recover within

The best way to reduce inflation risk is to invest in growth assets like stocks.

27

months. The disciplined way to ignore market ups and downs is called dollar cost averaging: by steadily investing on a regular basis, regardless of how well or badly the market is performing, you eliminate the danger of selling at the bottom. (See page 35.)

4. **Credit Risk** is the risk that whoever borrowed your money won't make all their promised interest payments, or won't repay the principal when it falls due. This is the first risk most people associate with the bond market, although it's not the only risk you assume when you buy bonds.

There are two ways to minimize credit risk. The first, obviously, is to make sure you're lending to borrowers who have passed muster with the major credit rating agencies. (See page 17 for more on credit ratings.) The prospectus of a bond mutual fund tells you what credit quality bonds the portfolio manager is permitted to buy. The other way to minimize credit risk is to diversify. The credit problems of any single issuer won't have much impact on the shareholders of a mutual fund that owns hundreds of bonds.

5. **Interest Rate Risk** is the risk that your investment will lose value because interest rates go up.

This is the least understood risk you assume as a bond holder or owner of shares in a bond fund. It applies even to bonds issued by the world's most credit-worthy borrower—the U.S. government. Let's say you buy a $10,000 bond that pays 8% interest. A week later, you open the newspaper to see headlines declaring that the Federal Reserve has hiked the prevailing interest rate. As a result, newly issued bonds with the same credit quality and maturity date as the one you own will pay 9% interest.

Your $10,000 bond is now worth less than $10,000. No buyer is going to pay you $10,000 for an 8% bond when he can invest his $10,000 in a bond that returns 9%. So if you sell your bond, you'll take a loss. And if you keep your bond, you're earning less than the prevailing interest rate.

The best way to reduce interest rate risk is to buy bonds or bond funds with shorter maturities, two to ten years for example, rather than longer-term bonds. Short and intermediate-term bonds lose less value when interest rates rise. A 20 or 30-year bond that pays less than the prevailing interest rate loses a lot more of its value than a two-year bond that pays less than the prevailing interest rate.

PG. 35

PG. 17

THE NO FREE LUNCH RULE

There's one rule about risk that never changes and that applies equally to every type of investment: the higher an investment's potential return, the greater the potential risk involved. Even if that risk isn't readily apparent at first, second or even third glance, it is there.

You never get a high return from a low-risk investment.

"High yield bond," for example, is just a fancy way of saying "junk bond". Junk bonds always pay more than Certificates of Deposit because corporations with bad credit ratings are never as safe a bet to make their interest payments and repay their loans as a borrower guaranteed by the full faith and credit of the United States Government.

This doesn't necessarily mean that you shouldn't buy a junk bond fund. Indeed, you may decide that for a particular goal and time horizon, the potential reward makes a particular risk worth taking. But you should never assume the risk isn't there.

One very quick way to measure an investment's relative degree of risk is to compare its yield with the prevailing rate on U.S. Treasury Bills, considered the world's safest investment. (You'll find the T-Bill rate listed daily in the *Wall Street Journal* and in the business pages of most newspapers.) The higher an investment's yield above the yield for Treasuries, the riskier you can assume that investment is—no matter how it's described to you.

HOW DIFFERENT INVESTMENTS HAVE PERFORMED OVER TIME

COMPOUND ANNUAL RETURN: 1926-1994

Percent

INFLATION	3.1%
T-BILLS	3.7%
LONG-TERM GOVT. BONDS	4.8%
INTERMEDIATE GOVT. BONDS	5.1%
LONG-TERM CORPORATE BONDS	5.4%
LARGE COMPANY STOCKS	10.2%
SMALL COMPANY STOCKS	12.2%

SMART PILLS

➤ There are no risk-free investments.
➤ If your investment goal is more than ten years away, your biggest single risk is inflation.

REDUCING INVESTMENT RISK THROUGH DIVERSIFICATION, ASSET ALLOCATION AND DOLLAR COST AVERAGING

If the bad news is that there are no risk-free investments, the good news is that by choosing and combining your investments with a little care and common sense, it's possible to reduce unavoidable risks to a level you can live with comfortably, and at the same time give yourself a very good chance of achieving the return you need. That's what professional pension fund managers do and there's no reason you can't do it, too.

Does this mean you'll have to learn about dozens of different, complex financial instruments? Absolutely not. You can design a very solid retirement portfolio with just three to five different basic investments.

DIVERSIFICATION

Diversification is a fancy way of saying you shouldn't put all your eggs in one basket, no matter how safe that basket may seem.

There are two important reasons to diversify your investments. The first one, of course, is to protect yourself against a single, devastating loss. If you own several investments, there's less risk that they'll all be clobbered at the same time.

If you own several different *types* of investments, you reduce your risk even more because you increase the chance that some of your holdings will be doing well even when others are doing poorly. An example: you own a stock fund, a bond fund and a money market fund. Interest rates soar, causing your bond fund to plunge in value and sharply reducing or eliminating your stock market earnings. But the interest you earn in your money market fund soars along with the prevailing rate.

The second reason to diversify is to protect yourself against the risk of outliving your money. If you don't diversify into "riskier" assets like stocks and bonds, you run a substantial risk of retiring with too small a nest egg to generate the income you'll need for a comfortable retirement.

In the example above, your money market fund cushioned the short-term impact of higher interest rates on your total portfolio. But your stock and bond holdings are the combination that assures your portfolio's long-term return.

The way you divide your money among the basic asset classes—growth, fixed-income and cash investments—is called asset allocation. (See page 32.)

To further reduce your overall risk, you should also diversify within each asset class. On the simplest level, this means that you don't buy bonds from just one or two issuers, or the stock of only one or two companies. Any mutual fund investment automatically gives you this numerical diversification.

On a slightly more sophisticated level, you also diversify when you invest in more than one kind of bond or stock. You can diversify by investing in both growth stocks and value stocks, for example. (See page 22.) You can diversify by investing in both U.S. stocks and foreign stocks. You can diversify by investing in bonds from different issuers that carry different maturities.

Diversification will reduce your risk; but of course, no diversification can eliminate risk altogether. The U.S. stock and bond markets don't move in lock-step, but it is possible for both of them to bottom-out at the same time. High interest rates and inflation, for example, have a very bad effect on both stock and bond markets. (That's when you remind yourself that high interest rates and inflation are increasing your money market fund yield and the value of your house.)

DON'T FORGET WHAT YOU OWN OUTSIDE YOUR 401(k)

When you decide how to diversify your retirement portfolio, consider *all* your investments—not just those you own in your 401(k) account. Here's why:

Let's say you have $5,000 in various savings and checking accounts and $20,000 in Individual Retirement Accounts that are invested in bank certificates of deposit. You also have $8,000 in your 401(k) account. If you think of your 401(k) money all by itself, investing the whole $8,000 in a stock fund seems very risky.

But look at the bigger picture: your total assets add up to $33,000. More than 75% of that total amount is in cash investments—bank accounts. So if you invested your entire $8,000 401(k) account in stocks, in reality you'd have an extremely conservative portfolio.

As a general rule, it makes sense to keep investments that are heavily taxed, like most stock and corporate bond mutual funds, inside a tax-deferred account like a 401(k) plan or an Individual Retirement Account. Depending on your tax bracket, you may want to use an ordinary taxable account for investments that are tax exempt or liable for fewer taxes—such as municipal bonds (which are free of federal and state taxes for residents of the state that issues them), and Treasury bonds (which aren't subject to state taxes).

You can design a very solid retirement portfolio with just three to five basic investments.

ASSET ALLOCATION: THE KEY TO INVESTMENT SUCCESS

If you're like most people, many of your investing anxieties spring from the fact that you can't predict future financial trends.

You don't know which way interest rates are headed, or how fast the economy is likely to grow next year or what the new Congress is going to do to tax rates. You don't know which particular stock or bond funds are likely to perform best in tomorrow's economic environment. You don't know which way the stock market or the bond market is going to move next year.

Guess what: *it doesn't matter.*

Pension fund studies show[1] that more than 90% of a retirement account's total investment return is the result of asset allocation: how you divide your money between different asset classes.

If you put appropriate percentages of your portfolio into stocks, bonds, real estate and cash, you'll do just fine—even if you don't pick the best-performing funds in each class, or buy and sell at the best times.

Investment selection (choosing the best stock, bond, or cash fund) and market timing account for *less than 10%* of total long-term investment return. Yet ironically, those are the decisions most investors focus on and fret about.

Asset allocation works because different kinds of investments behave differently:

➤ Stocks and bonds sometimes have overlapping cycles, but they don't rise and fall in lockstep. An example: In early 1987 the stock market soared while the bond market plummeted. By the end of 1987 bonds had recovered nicely; they gained 5.8% in the fourth quarter of the year. The stock market crashed in October; it lost 22.5% for the quarter.

➤ Foreign stock and bond markets don't go up and down in absolute harmony with U.S. markets. Again, this diversification isn't perfect. Today, foreign stock and bond markets are more closely linked to U.S. markets than they were in the past. But in the long-term, each country's markets are likely to respond at least as much to their own specific, different environments as they do to broad international economic trends.

➤ High inflation is terrible for the bond market and usually bad news for the stock market. But money market funds, gold funds, natural resources funds and real estate are investments that perform well in an inflationary environment.

[1] "Determinants of Portfolio Performance II: An Update," Gary P. Brinson, Brian D. Singer and Gilbert L. Beebower, *Financial Analyst Journal*, May-June, 1994, pages 40-48.
"The Value of Asset Allocation Decisions," C.R. Hensel, D.D. Ezra, J.H. Ilkiw, *Russell Research Commentary*, March, 1991.

➤ In a recession or a depression, stocks and bonds may fare badly but Treasuries remain totally reliable.

Asset allocation is a personal decision. The best asset allocation for you is the combination of investments that's likely to give you the return you need without saddling you with more risk than you're willing to accept.

When you decide how to allocate your assets, consider everything you own. If you own a house and have an emergency fund whose value is equal to roughly three months worth of your living expenses, you're already invested in real estate and cash. You may want to concentrate on dividing most of your remaining investments between stocks and bonds.

Professional pension fund managers start the investing process by deciding how they want to divide the money they have to invest between different asset categories like stocks, bonds, real estate and cash. The first decision they make is what percentage of total assets to put into each category. Their second decision is how to allocate investments within each category—how to divide stock investments between big companies and small companies, for example.

ASSET ALLOCATION AND MARKET TIMING ARE *NOT* THE SAME THING

The secret to successful asset allocation is *maintaining your investment mix*, regardless of what's happening in the financial markets.

If you've decided that your best allocation is 60% stock investments, 30% bond investments and 10% cash investments, for example, stick with that allocation even when the bond market is soaring and the stock market is in a free fall and all your neighbors are dumping their stocks to buy bonds.

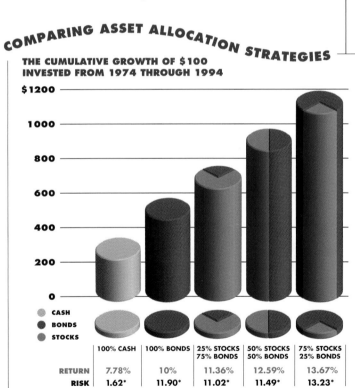

COMPARING ASSET ALLOCATION STRATEGIES

THE CUMULATIVE GROWTH OF $100 INVESTED FROM 1974 THROUGH 1994

	100% CASH	100% BONDS	25% STOCKS 75% BONDS	50% STOCKS 50% BONDS	75% STOCKS 25% BONDS
RETURN	7.78%	10%	11.36%	12.59%	13.67%
RISK	1.62*	11.90*	11.02*	11.49*	13.23*

● CASH
● BONDS
● STOCKS

* This number measures volatility. The higher it is, the more ups and downs you can expect from the investment during the time period considered. Source: Report prepared by Rogers, Casey Investment Advisors, Inc. Cash=90 day Treasury Bills, Bonds=Salomon Long-Term High Grade Index, Stocks=Standard and Poor's 500 Index.

Fixed asset allocation is easy because it relieves you of trying to second-guess what the market is about to do. You don't ask, "Is this a good time to buy stocks, is this a good time to buy bonds?" You simply rebalance your portfolio periodically—once a year is fine—in order to maintain the original allocation percentages.

Here's how you rebalance: Let's say you started with 55% U.S. stocks, 15% foreign stocks, 25% bonds, and 5% cash. At the end of the year, you add up the total value of your portfolio and discover that because your bonds have performed so well, they've risen in value to account for 35% of your portfolio. In the meantime, your U.S. stocks holdings have lost value and they now account for only 45% of your total portfolio.

To rebalance, you'd transfer enough money out of your high-performing bond fund and into your lower-performing stock fund to return to your original allocation percentages.

Rebalancing forces you to sell high and buy low. Sticking with your asset allocation mix guarantees that unlike your market timing neighbors, you'll always follow that good old four-word recipe for investment success: *buy low, sell high.*

Very few people manage to buy low and sell high unless they are automatically rebalancing their portfolios. Human instinct naturally rebels at selling an investment that's earning money like crazy in order to buy one that's been losing value for weeks or months. Instead, most investors do what comes naturally: they sell their funds that are doing badly and buy funds that are doing well. That's why they lose money.

The great thing about asset allocation is that there are no agonizing decisions to make. You don't have to study the financial pages. You don't have to worry about which way the markets are heading, or whether this is the best time to buy or sell a particular fund. You just rebalance once a year.

Will an asset allocation or lifestyle fund do this for you? *Not necessarily.* You have to read the prospectus to find out. Some asset allocation funds do stick with a specified allocation mix and periodically rebalance their portfolios to maintain the mix. But other asset allocation funds keep changing their investment mix to take advantage of current market conditions. That's a form of market timing.

Rebalancing forces you to follow that good old recipe for investment success: buy low, sell high.

NO ASSET ALLOCATION MIX IS POURED IN CONCRETE

Obviously, you can't stay with one asset allocation mix forever. Whenever your financial situation undergoes a material change, you should take a look at your original allocation to make sure that its level of risk and return still fits your goals. What's a material change? Here are just a few of the life events that could change your allocation needs:

> ➤ Marriage
> ➤ Divorce
> ➤ The death of a spouse
> ➤ The birth of a child
> ➤ Buying a house
> ➤ Inheriting a large sum of money
> ➤ Paying college tuitions

It's also very important to reallocate your assets when you're within five years or less of achieving a specific goal or reaching a major anticipated lifetime event. Any money you're planning to use in a couple of years is better kept in a money market or GIC fund than in a stock fund.

DOLLAR COST AVERAGING

Even after you've decided on an investment allocation plan, you may be hesitant about whether this is the best moment to begin implementing it. Is this really a good time to buy? What about short-term market fluctuations? Nobody wants to invest precious retirement savings only to see the market plummet like a stone a week later. If that happened, it could take your nerves even longer than your portfolio to recover from the shock.

DOLLAR COST AVERAGING

MONTH	SHARE PRICE	MONTHLY $ INVESTED	# SHARES PURCHASED EACH MONTH
JANUARY	$5.00	$500	100.0
FEBRUARY	$4.00	$500	125.0
MARCH	$3.50	$500	142.9
APRIL	$3.00	$500	166.7
MAY	$3.75	$500	133.3
JUNE	$5.00	$500	100.0
TOTAL	$4.04*	$3,000	767.9

*Average share price during the six months: $4.04 = ($24.25 ÷ 6 months)
*Average cost for your shares: $3.91 = ($3,000 ÷ 767.9 shares)

When you invest the same amount every month regardless of whether the market is up or down, your money automatically buys more shares when the price is low and fewer shares when the price is high.

Dollar cost averaging is a technique that eliminates this anxiety. Don't worry about timing. Simply invest a fixed amount at regular intervals—every week or every month, for example—paying no attention whatsoever to whether the market is up or down. Let's say you invest $100 a month. It's a *mathematical certainty* that your $100 will buy more shares when prices are down (buy low!) and fewer shares when the prices are up.

Dollar cost averaging is much easier on your nerves and on your money than trying to time the market: trying to buy *before* prices rise, and sell *before* prices drop.

To be a successful market timer, you have to be right twice: at the market peak, in order to know that it's time to sell your investments, and again at the market bottom, in order to know when it's time to start buying.

Let's say you correctly guess when the market has peaked and you sell your holdings before prices start to fall. You still have to figure out when to buy again so that you'll be in a position to take advantage of the market recovery. Market recoveries are easy to miss because the biggest advances tend to be compressed into very short periods of time. The 1980s was a great decade for the stock market, for example, but if you had missed the ten best trading days of the decade, you would have missed one-third of its total return.

Dollar cost averaging protects you against one of the worst risks of market timing: the risk that you won't be invested in the market when it surges forward.

Many studies have shown that over any horizon longer than ten years, hanging on to your investments through market ups and downs pays much better than trying to anticipate those ups and downs by repeatedly selling and buying investments.

One of these studies, by Wharton School finance professor Jeremy J. Siegel, found that investors benefited from hanging onto their investments even in the worst 30-year period in almost 200 years of stock market history—from just before the 1929 crash to 1959. Professor Siegel found that someone who bought stocks just before the 1929 crash and held them for the next 30 years would have earned six times more than if he or she had invested in bonds, and more than ten times as much as if he or she had invested in Treasury bills during the same period.

Dollar cost averaging also protects you from emotional stress. Successful market timing requires more than clairvoyance; it also demands steel nerves. The very best time to buy is the moment when prices have been falling for weeks or months and the market looks truly awful. The very best time to sell is the moment when the market is performing superbly. Not surprisingly, few people can bring themselves to do either.

On the contrary, most people much prefer to put money into a market that has been booming for a reassuringly long time—in other words, a market that is nearing its peak and

Dollar cost averaging protects you against the risk that you won't be invested in the market when it goes up.

will soon tumble. And they tend to sell the investments after the market has been falling for so long there seems to be no light at the end of the tunnel—in other words, when the market has just about bottomed out and recovery is imminent.

THE MAGIC OF COMPOUNDING

Your principal earns interest, and that interest earns interest, and *that* interest earns interest. That's compounding. Its effect is amazing.

The longer your money is invested, the better compounding works for you. Or to put it another way, the earlier you start saving for retirement, the smaller the amount you'll have to save to reach your goal. (See illustration.)

One reason a buy and hold strategy works so well for long-term investors is that staying invested lets you take maximum advantage of the magic of compounding. A recent study of the S&P 500 Index from 1963 to 1992 by Neuberger & Berman Management Inc. is a powerful illustration of what a difference this can make:

THE MAGIC OF COMPOUNDING

In Thousands

Early Investor: Total Investment $12,000
Late Investor: Total Investment $36,000

Years 5 10 15 20 25 30 35 40

THE EARLY INVESTOR SAVES $24,000 LESS AND COMES OUT $50,000 AHEAD!

This example assumes an investment earning 8% interest annually, compounded monthly.

Investor A puts $2,000 a year into the S&P 500 Index for ten years. She makes her annual investment on the worst day of the year. Then she stops investing and just maintains her account. Investor B invests $2,000 a year for the next *twenty* years. He picks the very best day to invest every year.

B has invested $40,000. A has invested only $20,000. But A's portfolio has had twice as long to compound. By 1992, A's portfolio has grown to $264,000. B's portfolio is worth only $256,000.

When you take advantage of the magic of compound interest by investing early, you don't have to take as much investment risk to achieve your goal. Let's say you want to save $100,000. If you have twenty years to do it, you can reach your goal by investing $2,564.58 a year and earning a modest 6% average annual return on your money. To reach the same goal in only ten years, you'd have to put your $2,564.68 annual deposit into investments that returned almost 24% a year! To save $100,000 in ten years in a conservative portfolio that returns only 6% annually, you'd have to save $7,157.35 a year. [1]

SIX REASONS NOT TO PANIC WHEN THE MARKET FALLS

1. Remember that market declines are normal events. They don't last forever. Remind yourself that after the stock market lost 22.5% of its value in October 1987, it was back up 16.5% in 1988, and up another 31.7% in 1989.

2. Remember that market declines are a chance to snap up bargains. Remind yourself that as a dollar cost averaging investor (see pages 35, 36), you're buying at lower prices when the market falls.

3. Remember why you're investing. Your goal is long-term growth. The real issue isn't how much money you have in this account now; it's how much you'll have *years from now*.

4. Don't beat yourself up by comparing your stock fund loss with what you could have earned in the GIC fund. They're totally different types of investments. Remind yourself that your house fluctuates in value too, but when real estate prices fall, you don't kick yourself for not having put your money in the bank instead of in a house.

5. Look at how your entire portfolio is performing instead of staring at one piece of it. Congratulate yourself on how your skillful asset allocation has cushioned your loss.

6. Think in percentages, not dollars. It'll help keep losses in perspective.

[1] Calculation by John McAteer, Holtz Rubenstein & Co., LLP, Melville, New York.

ITS EASY TO APPLY THE BASIC PRINCIPLES OF INVESTING TO A 401(k) PLAN

➤ Your investment menu is pre-selected to offer you choices in each major asset class.

➤ Typically, your choices are mutual funds, so each of your investments benefits from a basic level of diversification.

➤ You're practicing dollar cost averaging without even thinking about it because your 401(k) contribution is a fixed amount, automatically invested in your account at regular intervals.

➤ You're investing for a long-term goal, which gives you plenty of time to take full advantage of the magic of compounding.

When you take advantage of the magic of compounding by investing early, you don't have to take as much investment risk to reach your goal.

S M A R T   P I L L S

➤ To be well-diversified, invest in all three basic asset categories—cash, fixed-income and growth—and diversify within each asset class.

➤ When deciding how to allocate your assets, consider your investments both inside and outside your 401(k) plan.

➤ More than 90% of long-term investment return is the result of asset allocation—how you divide your money between the asset categories. Less than 10% of your return depends on choosing the very best fund in the category, or on when you buy or sell your investments.

➤ A long-term investor is much better off sticking with a fixed asset allocation through market ups and downs instead of trying to time investment purchases and sales.

➤ Rebalance your investment portfolio once a year.

➤ The sooner you start saving, the less you need to save to reach your goal.

PART TWO

YOUR FINANCIAL SELF-PORTRAIT

What you need to know about yourself in order to find an investment mix that's right for you

2

Only you can supply the information that will determine the best investments for your needs.

WHAT YOU NEED TO KNOW ABOUT YOURSELF IN ORDER TO FIND AN INVESTMENT MIX THAT'S RIGHT FOR YOU

The most sensible way to invest your 401(k) account is to divide your money between investments that provide growth, investments that provide income and investments that provide safety. You'll need at least three different funds to do that. (See page 14-23, and Question 89, page 123.)

The crucial issue is getting the proportions right. How much of your total account should go into each type of investment? That depends on your time horizon, your personal circumstances and your risk tolerance. Only you can supply the information that will determine the best investment mix for your needs. You are the best candidate to be your financial planner because nobody else knows your goals as well as you do, has the same instinctive understanding of your risk tolerance or has your best interests as much at heart.

YOUR TIME HORIZON

This is the first thing to consider as you analyze your needs to determine which kinds of investment will give you the best return with the least amount of risk. (See charts, Defining Risk Over the Short Term (1-3 years), and Defining Risk Over the Long-Term (10-20 years), page 49.)

The longer your time horizon, the greater the risk that inflation will shrink the value of your nest egg.

Don't underestimate this danger.

If inflation averages just 3.5% a year, the cost of living will double every 20 years. That means if you plan to retire in 20 years, you'll need $100,000 a year to live the way you can today on $50,000 a year. If inflation averages 5.5% a year, the cost of living will double every 13 years. With inflation at that rate, if you plan to retire in 26 years, you'll need $200,000 to buy what costs $50,000 today.

Scary, isn't it?

Inflation is the bad news. The good news is that the more time you have to invest, the safer it becomes for you to invest in growth assets like stocks, which historically have proven to be more than a match for inflation.

Historically, your risk of loss in the stock market has been 29% in a one-year period, 11% in a five-year period and 3% in a ten-year period. Over a 20-year period, stocks have never had a negative return.[1]

The longer your time horizon, the bigger the piece of your portfolio you should allocate to growth investments. A prudent asset allocation for a 20-year time horizon might be to invest 70% in stocks, 20% in bonds and 10% in cash investments.

The less time you have before you reach your goal, the less you have to worry about the effect of inflation and the more you need to be concerned about short-term price fluctuations, the big drawback of stock investments. For a goal that's only five years away, a more prudent allocation might be to invest 50% of your portfolio in bonds and cash investments.

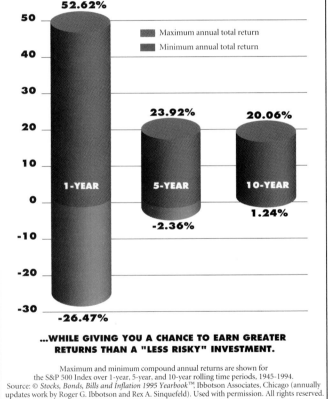

HOW TIME HELPS MANAGE RISK

MAXIMUM & MINIMUM COMPOUND ANNUAL RETURNS OF BIG COMPANY STOCKS 1945-1994

TIME REDUCES THE VOLATILITY OF A "RISKY" INVESTMENT...

...WHILE GIVING YOU A CHANCE TO EARN GREATER RETURNS THAN A "LESS RISKY" INVESTMENT.

Maximum and minimum compound annual returns are shown for the S&P 500 Index over 1-year, 5-year, and 10-year rolling time periods, 1945-1994. Source: © *Stocks, Bonds, Bills and Inflation 1995 Yearbook*™, Ibbotson Associates, Chicago (annually updates work by Roger G. Ibbotson and Rex A. Sinquefeld). Used with permission. All rights reserved.

[1] Ibbotson Associates, Chicago, IL. These numbers refer to the performance of the S&P 500 Index, 1926-1994.

WHAT IS YOUR LIFE EXPECTANCY IN RETIREMENT?

When you calculate your time horizon, don't make the mistake of ending it on your retirement date. Your life won't end when you stop working at a full-time job; in fact, at that point as much as one-third of your life may still lie ahead of you. Your money will have to last all through your retirement years.

How long can you expect to live?

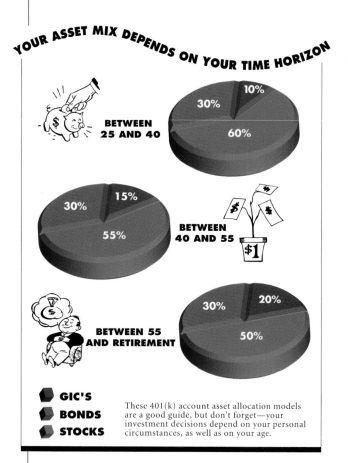

YOUR ASSET MIX DEPENDS ON YOUR TIME HORIZON

BETWEEN 25 AND 40
10%
30%
60%

BETWEEN 40 AND 55
15%
30%
55%
$1

BETWEEN 55 AND RETIREMENT
20%
30%
50%

◆ GIC'S
◆ BONDS
◆ STOCKS

These 401(k) account asset allocation models are a good guide, but don't forget—your investment decisions depend on your personal circumstances, as well as on your age.

Well, the Internal Revenue Service (which can be expected to take a conservative view of this question) uses unisex actuarial tables to give a 65 year-old a 20-year life expectancy. (See table, page 61.) The IRS life expectancy table uses median numbers, which means that the average person has a 50% chance of living longer (or dying sooner) than the IRS numbers indicate.

Most financial planners advise people to add at least five years to the IRS table's estimate of their life expectancy. Mathematically speaking, planning for an additional five years reduces to about 15%—20% the risk you'll outlive your money. To reduce that risk even more, add ten years to the IRS table. In other words, a healthy 65-year-old retiree should plan for a total lifespan of 90 to 95 years.

This means you can't do without growth investments even if you're within a year or two of retiring because you have to think about the effect of inflation on your nest egg *after* you retire. If you spend 20 years in retirement, the cost of living could easily double during that time!

Boston financial planner Jonathan Pond, author of **The New Century Family Money Book**, suggests the following rough rule of thumb to figure out the appropriate allocation between growth and fixed-income investments for your time horizon: multiply your age by 80%. The result is the percentage of your portfolio that you should keep in bonds. The rest should go into stocks. Using Pond's rule of thumb, for example, a 40 year-old would invest 32% of his portfolio (80% x 40 = 32%) in bonds and 68% in stocks.

(Pond's suggested 401(k) asset allocation models are illustrated on page 44.)

YOUR PERSONAL CIRCUMSTANCES

Pond's rule-of-thumb is a useful guideline, but you have to adapt it to your own circumstances. Two people who are the same age, work for the same company and earn the same salary may still have very different investment needs.

A couple of decades ago, it was easier to figure out lifecycle investment needs merely on a person's age. Financial planning manuals made sweeping generalizations: people in their 20s were saving to buy a car, go on a great vacation, for the down payment on a house; people in their 30s were having children, buying a house, starting to save for college educations; people in their 40s were buying a larger house, a second or third car, increasing their savings for college tuitions; people in their 50s had kids in college or were adjusting to life with the kids grown and gone.

Today, these generalizations don't work nearly as well. The baby boom generation has married and had children later than its parents or grandparents did. Divorce and remarriage have changed traditional predictable lifecycle patterns. A 45-year-old who is changing diapers, shopping for day-care, and looking at the cost of pre-schools has a very different time horizon than a 45-year-old who has made the last mortgage payment and is trying to decide what to give the family's youngest child as a college graduation present.

To determine how your circumstances affect your asset allocation, you need to answer the following questions:

1. How likely is it that you'll have to use some of your retirement account to pay for a few major expenses before you retire?

If you expect to have to tap your 401(k) account to pay for major expenses between now and retirement, you need to know your plan's loan provisions. Can you borrow from your account? If not, you should be saving for these expenses outside your 401(k) plan. If you can borrow from your plan, think about how much money you're likely to need, and how soon you'll need it.

If you expect to need money for a specific goal that's only five years away, and your plan does allow you to borrow, you should allocate some of your 401(k) account portfolio specifically for that goal and time horizon.

(When you take a loan from your 401(k), don't forget that that loan is a fixed- PG. 115 income investment for your account. Does that mean your total account is more heavily invested in fixed-income than you'd like? You may want to readjust the rest of your portfolio's allocation. (See Questions 74-81, pages 115-117 for information on loans. See page 34 for rebalancing a portfolio.)

2. If there is an emergency and you have an unexpected need for money, do you have any source of available cash outside your 401(k) account?

The answer to this question has a direct bearing on your investment allocation in the plan.

To see why, let's take Jane and Jim as an example, two people whose personal circumstances look very similar: They're both 25 and single, own apartments in the same building, earn the same income, work at the same company, participate in the same 401(k) plan. Jane has a savings account outside the 401(k) plan. Jim has no other savings account.

The roof of their building develops a leak and all the apartment owners are assessed equal amounts to repair the damages.

Jane draws money out of her emergency savings account to pay the assessment. Jim takes a loan from his 401(k) account. *How* Jim's 401(k) account is invested makes a big difference. If he has the whole account invested in stock and bond funds and the stock and bond markets are both down when he needs his loan, he must sell at a loss to get the cash he needs.

Everyone should have a source of emergency money equal to at least three months of his or her take-home pay. If you have no emergency cash account outside your 401(k) plan, you should allocate for it within the 401(k) plan by keeping that amount in a cash investment in the plan—like a money market fund.

But don't go overboard: you don't need an emergency fund bigger than six months of your take-home pay at the very most. Don't fall into the habit of throwing your 401(k) contributions into your cash allocation until it represents the lion's share of your portfolio.

3. Do you have savings and/or investments outside your 401(k) account? If so, how are they invested? And, **4.** Does your spouse invest in a retirement plan at work? If so, how is it invested?

It's a good idea to consider your 401(k) account as a special retirement fund that you can't draw on for ordinary expenses. But that doesn't mean that you shouldn't consider this account in the context of your whole financial picture, which includes any other investments you or your spouse may have. On the contrary, you can't allocate your 401(k) investments wisely unless you see how they complement the rest of your financial picture.

Once a year you should check your asset allocation by writing down all your household's investments on one piece of paper. List the retirement account investments you and your spouse have in one column; list all of your taxable accounts in another. Then divide the investments in each column into asset classes—growth, fixed-income, cash. Use a pocket calculator to add up your total holdings—retirement and non-retirement—and then figure out what percentage of the total you have in each asset class.

The results will tell you how conservative or aggressive your investment portfolio really is, and show you what kind of adjustments you need to make to achieve a more appropriate mix. (See pages 32-35 on asset allocation and rebalancing.) PG. 32

5. How much do you want your account to be worth when you're ready to retire?

This is a very tough question to answer with any accuracy, especially if you're more than ten years away from retirement.

The conventional wisdom is that most people will need between 60%—80% of their pre-retirement salary to live comfortably in retirement. You should use the high end of that range if you expect to incur major expenses after retirement such as college tuition or the cost of a big wedding for one or more of your children, or if you'll still owe a substantial balance on your mortgage.

It's reasonable to assume you'll spend less on certain kinds of expenses in retirement than you do now. You won't have the expenses associated with working—such as buying and cleaning clothes to wear to the office, commuting and buying lunches away from home. And with any luck, your children will be out of college and your mortgage will be paid off.

PG. 52 But even if all that is true, you'll have other expenses that you don't have now. Your travel and entertainment expenses are likely to increase, at least initially. Your health care costs will undoubtedly rise during your retirement. (To read more about pre-retirement issues you should be aware of, turn to page 52, You're Within Five Years of Retirement.)

The worksheet on page 156 will help you estimate what size nest egg you may need when you retire. Take the time to fill it out. It's better to have a rough estimate than none at all—to be a successful investor, it helps to have a financial goal. PG. 156

But remember, the worksheet is only a guideline.

You can't allocate your 401(k) investments wisely unless you see how they complement the rest of your financial picture.

Don't panic when you fill it out and it tells you you'll need much more than you ever expect to be able to save. Very, very few people are even close to what the worksheet suggests is an appropriate level of retirement savings. Play with the worksheet numbers; see what happens if:

➤ You reduce your goal from 80% of pre-retirement income to 60%.

➤ You increase your estimated return on investments by one percentage point.

➤ You delay your retirement date by a year or two.

➤ You plan to earn extra income in retirement by working part-time. (You may choose to work for its emotional rewards, even if you don't need the money. See page 54.)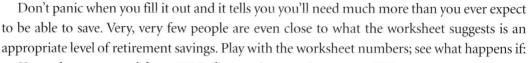

You'll be astonished at how dramatically your worksheet calculations change when you alter any one of these assumptions.

YOUR PERSONAL RISK TOLERANCE

Risk tolerance is partly a function of knowledge. Your risk tolerance is likely to increase along with your understanding of how different investments perform over different periods of time.

Many of your previous ideas about risk may have been based on misconceptions—thinking that stocks are always a high-risk investment or bonds are always a safe investment—or on over-simplifications that ignored essential factors like time horizon. Now you know that time horizon has a major impact on investment risk. (See charts on pages 43 and 49.)

Your risk tolerance also depends on your age. Many people become more conservative investors as they get older and closer to retirement. This shift can be appropriate. The less time you have, for example, the riskier it becomes to invest in stocks. But don't make the mistake of underestimating how much time you have. *If you're 60 years old, your real time horizon isn't five years until retirement—it's a 20 to 30-year life expectancy.* Even after you retire, you still need growth investments like stocks to help you beat inflation.

Finally, your comfort level with investment risk also depends in part on your temperament. New York financial planner Larry Elkin, author of **First Comes Love, Then Comes Money** suggests the following rule-of-thumb for people who are very nervous about the stock market: assume that in an absolute worst-case scenario, the market may temporarily lose half its value. (In fact, the worst one-year stock market loss in 68 years was 43% in 1931.) If you truly can't stand the thought of more than a 15% temporary dip in the value of your 401(k)

The beauty of a diversified portfolio is that it allows you to follow conflicting impulses. With the right asset allocation you can invest for growth, safety and income.

account, says Elkin, invest only 30% of your total portfolio in stocks.

But if you're like most people, your temperament can't be summed up with a single adjective—nervous, impulsive, stubborn, risk-averse, risk-taker. In real life, most of us are a little of all these things, and a lot more besides. The beauty of a diversified portfolio is that to some extent, it allows you to follow your conflicting impulses. With the right asset allocation you can invest for growth, safety and income.

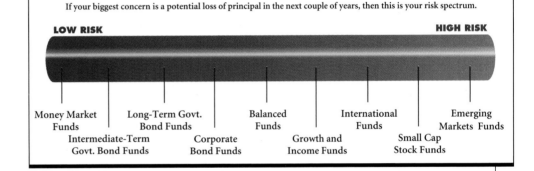

DEFINING RISK OVER THE SHORT-TERM (1-3 YEARS)

If your biggest concern is a potential loss of principal in the next couple of years, then this is your risk spectrum.

LOW RISK   HIGH RISK

Money Market Funds
Intermediate-Term Govt. Bond Funds
Long-Term Govt. Bond Funds
Corporate Bond Funds
Balanced Funds
Growth and Income Funds
International Funds
Small Cap Stock Funds
Emerging Markets Funds

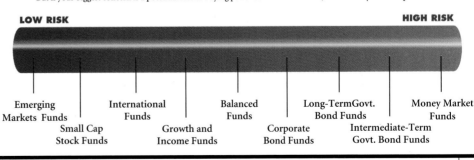

DEFINING RISK OVER THE LONG-TERM (10-20 YEARS)

But if your biggest concern is a potential loss of buying power because of inflation, then this is your risk spectrum.

LOW RISK   HIGH RISK

Emerging Markets Funds
Small Cap Stock Funds
International Funds
Growth and Income Funds
Balanced Funds
Corporate Bond Funds
Long-TermGovt. Bond Funds
Intermediate-Term Govt. Bond Funds
Money Market Funds

SMART PILLS

➤ It's sensible to divide your 401(k) account between investments that provide growth, investments that provide income and investments that provide safety.

➤ Your asset allocation should be based on your time horizon, personal circumstances and risk tolerance.

➤ Your real time horizon for retirement investments is your life expectancy, not your retirement date.

➤ Personal circumstances you should consider in deciding how to invest your 401(k) include whether or not you have other sources of emergency cash and/or other retirement investments.

PART THREE

YOU'RE WITHIN FIVE YEARS OF RETIREMENT

*What you should
be thinking about*

3

Start thinking about your choices several years before your official retirement date.

WHAT YOU SHOULD BE THINKING ABOUT

During most of your working life, it's natural to think of retirement as a final goal. But if you're nearly there, you're probably starting to realize that retirement is really the beginning of a new phase of your life—one that's likely to last 20 years or more.

The quality of your daily life during your retirement will depend in large part on several far-reaching decisions you must make within the next few years.

PG. 61 Some of these decisions—like the payment method you select for taking distributions from your 401(k) plan and other retirement accounts—are irrevocable. (See page 61.) Other choices will have a greater effect on your finances than you may realize. Where you choose to live in retirement, for example, will determine your cost of living and, by extension, your investment allocation in retirement because your ability to live comfortably will depend on whether your nest egg earns enough money to meet your expenses.

You won't be able to make informed choices at retirement unless you've taken time to study the pros and cons of the many options that will be available to you. The best way to do that is to start thinking about these choices several years *before* your official retirement date. There are many resources available to help you evaluate the options ahead: your human resources or personnel department, tax accountant and public library, as well as friends and acquaintances who have already retired.

A stack of scratch paper, a bunch of sharp pencils and a good pocket calculator will also come in very handy.

WHAT FINANCIAL DECISIONS SHOULD YOU MAKE AS YOU APPROACH RETIREMENT?

Your 401(k) account investment mix probably doesn't have to change too much because your real investment horizon is your life expectancy, not your retirement date. You're still a long-term investor.

Certainly, you should reassess your asset allocation to see if you're well-positioned to meet any major expenses that you expect to coincide with your retirement. You want to be able to cover these expenses without having to sell shares in a stock or bond fund whose value might be temporarily depressed, forcing you to take a loss. This may be a good time to increase your allocation to a less volatile part of your portfolio, like a money market fund or GIC fund. (See page 32 on asset allocation and Questions 90-92, pages 124 and 125.)

But the important thing to realize is that the next few years may represent your last chance to sock away money for retirement while you're still earning a full-time salary. You should make the most of it. Here are some suggestions:

1. Accelerate your 401(k) contributions to the fullest extent you can afford.

2. If you can afford it, contribute to a tax-deferred IRA as well, even if your contribution isn't tax-deductible. (See Question 30, page 90 on IRAs.)

3. Make a major effort to pay off any large, outstanding balances on your credit cards. Most people don't realize what a good investment this is. Paying off credit card debt is a superb way to increase your disposable income. If your credit card debt costs 16% for example, paying it off has the same effect on your income stream as putting your money into a no-risk investment that pays a 16% after-tax return!

4. Consider making extra payments against any outstanding balance on your mortgage. This isn't as lucrative an investment as paying off your credit cards because the after-tax cost of your mortgage is much lower. But eliminating the mortgage by the time you reach retirement is one way to lower your future cost of living.

WHAT DOES RETIREMENT REALLY MEAN TO YOU?

After nearly 50 years of working at least eight hours a day, it's hardly surprising if you approach retirement with mixed feelings. Sure, it's exhilarating to think that you'll never have to get up again at the crack of dawn to get to work on time. But it's a little frightening, too. Retirement changes all the daily routines of life; only the very young can experience that kind of change without a sense of dislocation.

The dictionary's multiple definitions of retirement reflect our ambivalence about it. Retirement is initially defined as "leisure, relaxation, rest." But the dictionary goes on to include other, less rosy definitions: "abdication, exile, isolation."

In truth, retirement means leaving your accustomed place in the working world. This presents you with the challenge and the opportunity to create a new place for yourself—a new place that may very well include another job if you want one.

Don't be afraid that you'll have no employment options available to you in retirement. An increasing number of businesses today go out of their way to recruit retirees as part-time workers. (A few years ago for example, a series of "senior power" jobs fairs held around the country attracted 639 companies in 26 states who wanted to hire retirees.) It's no wonder that retirees are desirable employees: they're experienced, skilled, reliable, able and often eager to work flexible hours.

Maybe you'd like to make full use of those strengths by working for yourself. If so, today's technology makes it possible to set up a state-of-the-art home office for just a few thousand dollars.

If you decide to work in retirement, you certainly won't be alone. Depending on how you define "retirement," some 25% to 40% of American retirees work today, often part-time and often for their former employers. This is one trend that is likely to continue. With longer life expectancy, fewer defined benefit pensions that guarantee a monthly income and a probable reduction in Social Security benefits, very few people in the future will be able to afford a "traditional" retirement of traveling, playing golf and clipping coupons.

But there are important emotional and psychological, as well as financial, reasons to keep on working.

Do you really want to spend as much as *one-third* of your life sight-seeing, sitting in airports and restaurants and lowering your handicap? Work provides psychic satisfaction as well as money. Twenty-five years is a very long vacation away from the challenge, structure and emotional rewards of a job.

Long before you reach retirement age, you're old enough to know something that no 25 year-old can ever appreciate: there's nothing more valuable than time. In retirement, you'll have big stretches of free time for the first time since you were a child. No investment allocation decision you make about how to deploy your financial assets can ever be as emotionally rewarding to you as making the right decisions about how to allocate your time in retirement.

Among many other options, retirement gives you an unequaled opportunity to turn an avocation into a second career. If you've always enjoyed carpentry or gardening, consider doing it for money as well as for pleasure. If you think you might like to teach the profession you've practiced, find out what it would take to qualify as a teacher at a local college.

If you've always wanted to be involved in philanthropic or community work but you never had the time, think about how your help can make a real difference, and consider getting involved in hospital or special services activities.

Consider doing your old job on a part-time basis, especially if you work in an industry or profession, like accounting, that has heavy seasonal demand for extra help. Think about getting paid to do the small jobs that people who are working full-time don't have the time to do. Most two-income households today are in desperate need of extra help. Anybody who can relieve the day-to-day pressure of running a household has services to sell. (One woman built a pet watching service for people away on business or vacations into a thriving company with more than 500 clients.)

SHOULD YOU MOVE?

You probably have a strong emotional attachment to your present home. Small wonder, considering the time and money you've poured into it all these years. But does that attachment outweigh the cost of its upkeep and the local taxes that you pay? You'll have to decide whether staying where you live is more important to your future comfort than the financial boost you might achieve by moving.

Your nest egg might support you more comfortably in an area where local taxes and the cost of living are lower than they are where you live now.

Also, selling your house can substantially increase that nest egg. Under current tax law, people over age 55 get a once-in-a-lifetime break on the profit they make from selling a house that has been their primary residence for three of the last five years: the first $125,000 of profit

> There are important emotional and psychological reasons to keep on working.

is tax-exempt. If you move to a less expensive house, you may be able to invest a substantial amount of your tax-free profit and increase your retirement income.

You may want to postpone this decision. But if the current value of your house represents a very big piece of your nest egg, it may make sense for you to sell it sooner rather than later, when real estate values could be lower.

Think about your physical comfort in retirement as well as about the financial pros and cons of moving. Do you want to maintain the plumbing and electricity in a five-bedroom house and snow plow a driveway every winter for another twenty years—or do you find yourself yearning for a small condo in a warmer climate with more freedom and fewer responsibilities?

DON'T BE TOO QUICK TO BUY

Depending on the size of your nest egg, you may want to think about renting rather than owning in retirement. Buying another house or condo may require putting a big chunk of your money into a single, illiquid asset—one that's not easily converted into cash. The greater the percentage of your total assets required by this purchase, the riskier the investment becomes.

Take Rose, who plans to retire in two years at age 65. She has $200,000 in her 401(k) plan account and a house worth $120,000. She plans to sell the house and move to another state. If she uses that $120,000 to buy a new house, she'll be putting more than a third of her total assets into a single investment that doesn't generate income. What's more, any increase in its value won't be easy for her to convert to cash—and it may not increase in value. Contrary to popular belief, real estate values don't always go up. What if the neighborhood goes downhill? What if an interstate highway is built next door? It might make better financial sense for Rose to rent a house or apartment and put her $120,000 to work for her in a diversified portfolio of growth and income investments like a combination of mutual funds and T-bills.

If you decide not to move, the same caveats apply to using a substantial percentage of your nest egg to pay off your mortgage. Ideally, your retirement account should be invested in a diversified combination of investments for liquidity, income and growth. Paying off your mortgage won't give you all that. If you choose to take your 401(k) balance in a single lump sum payment at retirement (see page 58), you should bear in mind that it's unwise to invest all or most of it in a single asset.

PG. 58

DECIDING WHERE TO LIVE

There's a host of factors to consider in choosing where to live in retirement: the cost of living, the climate, the crime rate, the distance from members of your family, the access to good medical facilities, entertainment and cultural events, and the availability of a religious community that meets your needs.

Small university towns are increasingly popular with retirees because of their educational and cultural programs. A college town is likely to offer an excellent library, music and drama departments that give free or low-cost performances and university lecture programs that often attract nationally prominent speakers. Increasingly, colleges and universities also offer special opportunities for continuing adult education.

Another important consideration you shouldn't forget is the availability of public transportation. It may seem inconceivable that a day will come when you no longer want to drive your own car, but retirement lasts a long time. If you find that you're no longer comfortable driving after dark when you're over 75 years old, a lack of alternative transportation could make you feel like a prisoner in your own house.

One good way to check out likely places to retire in is to read back issues of *Money* magazine, available at your local public library. *Money* annually ranks the best cities to live in nationwide, and explains why. The library also provides a shelf full of books about the best retirement spots in the U.S.

Consider spending your vacations during the next couple of years in the places that sound most attractive. If one or two towns make it to the top of your list, take a three-month subscription to the local newspapers. There's no better way to learn everything about daily life there—from the price of movie tickets and fresh vegetables to the political issues. It's definitely helpful to know if the town council in your idyllic low-cost community is having heated nightly debates about whether to double the local taxes to cover the astronomical expense of replacing an obsolete town sewer system.

The library provides a shelf full of books about the best retirement spots in the U.S.

YOUR 401(k) DISTRIBUTION CHOICES AT RETIREMENT

When you reach retirement, you must decide how to take your 401(k) account balance. Rules vary from plan to plan, but in most cases your choices will include:

1. **Taking your entire balance in a lump sum and rolling it over into an Individual Retirement Account (IRA)**

This is very much like rolling your 401(k) balance into an IRA when you change jobs. To avoid withholding taxes, open the IRA account and then ask your employer to transfer your money directly into that account. (See Question 38, page 96.) You don't have to make a hasty decision about how to invest this money; it's quite all right to put the IRA into a money market fund while you're thinking about how to invest it.

An IRA gives you an unlimited choice of investments and total freedom to transfer money among them as often as you like. You can withdraw money as you need it, paying income taxes only on the amount you withdraw. The IRA balance continues to grow tax-deferred. If you can afford to leave it untouched, you won't have to start withdrawing any money at all until after you reach age 70½. (See Question 42, page 99.)

2. **Taking your entire balance in a lump sum, paying taxes on it and investing the remainder in regular taxable accounts.**

Why would you do this? Because under current tax law you may qualify for a special break on a lump sum distribution. You can pay taxes on all this money at a lower rate than your usual income tax rate, if:

> ➤ you take out your entire account balance within a single tax year, *and*
> ➤ you also withdraw the entire balance of any other defined contribution plans in which you participate (such as profit-sharing or employee stock ownership plans), *and*
> ➤ you're older than 59½, *and*
> ➤ you have participated in the 401(k) plan for at least five years.

The government gives you a break on the tax rate in exchange for collecting tax on your entire nest egg in one fell swoop instead of waiting to collect it little by little over many years, as it will if you take distributions from a tax-deferred IRA.

The disadvantage of this choice is that your nest egg's future earnings won't be automatically tax-deferred as they would be in an IRA. You lose the great benefit of tax-deferred compounding. (See chart, page 71.)

3. Leaving your money in the 401(k) plan

This option may be very attractive if you feel the funds offered in the plan give you a good range of choices for investing in retirement.

Bear in mind however, that no 401(k) plan offers as wide a universe of investment choices as you would have if you rolled your money into an IRA. The level of service available to retirees also varies from one 401(k) plan to another.

If you are allowed to leave your money in the 401(k) plan and like the idea, ask your human resources or personnel department what services you can expect in retirement. Find out if it's possible to arrange for automatic monthly distributions from the plan to your bank, for example, as well as how often and how quickly you could change the amount of those distributions if necessary.

4. Taking installment payments from the 401(k) plan

Some companies will pay you a specific monthly amount over a ten or 15-year period. If you die before collecting all of your money, your heirs receive any balance remaining in your account. There are two principal risks with this choice: the value of your fixed installment payments will be eroded by inflation. And you may outlive your money.

5. Taking a lifetime annuity

If this is your choice, your employer uses your 401(k) plan balance to buy the annuity from a commercial insurer. An annuity pays you a fixed monthly income for the rest of your life. If you choose to buy a joint-and-survivor annuity, you'll receive a smaller monthly benefit, but it will last for two lifetimes—yours and your spouse's.

With an annuity, there's no danger of outliving your income unless the insurer fails. But remember that inflation will steadily erode the buying power of a fixed benefit. Your cost of living could easily double or triple over a 20-year retirement. You might consider investing some of your money in an annuity, and investing the balance for growth.

If you decide on this option, it's sensible to comparison-shop before taking the annuity available through your employer. Annuity prices vary widely among insurers and you might get a better deal elsewhere. Don't forget that comparison-shopping includes checking the insurer's financial stability, credit rating and reputation for service as well as its annuity rates.

CAUTION: People who sell insurance often urge retirees who are trying to choose between a single life and a joint-and-survivor annuity to take the larger, single life benefit and use the extra income it provides to buy a life insurance policy on the retiree. They explain that when the retiree dies, the survivor can use the life insurance policy proceeds to buy another annuity to replace the terminated pension income.

This "you can have your cake and eat it too," scenario is called pension maximization or pension max. Unfortunately, pension max typically doesn't allow for the taxes you'll owe on the extra income or for future interest rate changes that unexpectedly may increase the cost of the life insurance policy down the road—perhaps forcing you to drop it and leave your spouse unprotected. People who buy into the pension max strategy very often wind up with less income than if they'd stuck with a joint-and-survivor benefit.

If you're trying to decide which is better for you—a joint-and-survivor annuity or a single life annuity plus a life insurance policy—you owe it to yourself and to your spouse to get a reliable after-tax comparison between these two options from a tax professional who has no vested financial interest in your decision.

MANDATORY MINIMUM DISTRIBUTIONS

No tax deferral lasts forever. You are legally obligated to start taking taxable distributions from your 401(k) plan and other tax-deferred retirement accounts after you reach age 70½. (A rollover from a 401(k) account to an IRA is not a taxable distribution.) The minimum distribution that you must take out every year is based on your life expectancy. (See page 61.)

Once you're over 59½ there's no penalty for taking out *more* than the mandatory minimum withdrawal unless you take out more than $150,000 a year. (See page 62.) But after you turn 70½, there are hefty penalties for taking out *less* than the mandatory minimum withdrawal. (See Question 44, page 100.)

 Whenever you do start taking distributions—at age 59½ or age 70½, or anytime in between—you'll owe ordinary income tax on the money you take out. (The only exception is money that was taxed before you saved it. See Question 28, page 88.)

When you start taking distributions, you must also name a beneficiary and choose a distribution payment method.

These are extremely important decisions because their consequences can't be changed later. Read on.

No tax deferral lasts forever. You are legally obligated to start taking taxable distributions from your 401(k) plan after you reach age 70½.

BENEFICIARY CHOICE

The length of time over which you can stretch out distributions from your nest egg is based on the joint life expectancy of you and the beneficiary you name when you first start taking distributions. If you and your beneficiary have a 20-year joint life expectancy, for example, you have to take all the money out of your tax-deferred nest egg within 20 years. You can take your money out faster—you can take it all out in one day, if you want. But you can't maintain a tax-deferred account longer than 20 years.

You can change beneficiaries as often as you wish. *But your distribution schedule won't change.* You're locked into the first one you choose.

Let's say you name your spouse as beneficiary when you start taking distributions. Together, you have a 20-year joint life expectancy. You can change your mind later and name a grandchild as your beneficiary, but the fact that you and the grandchild have a 50-year joint life expectancy will not change your original 20-year distribution schedule.

PAYMENT METHOD CHOICE

You have two choices here—the *recalculation* method or the *term certain* method.

Take the couple with the 20-year joint life expectancy. If they opt to recalculate their life expectancies every year, their distributions will be adjusted accordingly. (With a 20-year life expectancy, they must take a distribution of not less than one-twentieth of their nest egg. The next year, their life expectancy will be slightly different, and the mandatory minimum distribution will be changed accordingly.) If one of these two people dies, the survivor's future mandatory distributions will be based on his or her single life expectancy.

IRS LIFE EXPECTANCY TABLES

Age	# of yrs the IRS expects you to live	Age	# of yrs the IRS expects you to live	Age	# of yrs the IRS expects you to live	Age	# of yrs the IRS expects you to live
35	47.3	55	28.6	75	12.5	95	3.7
36	46.4	56	27.7	76	11.9	96	3.4
37	45.4	57	26.8	77	11.2	97	3.2
38	44.4	58	25.9	78	10.6	98	3.0
39	43.5	59	25.0	79	10.0	99	2.8
40	42.5	60	24.2	80	9.5	100	2.7
41	41.5	61	23.3	81	8.9	101	2.5
42	40.6	62	22.5	82	8.4	102	2.3
43	39.6	63	21.6	83	7.9	103	2.1
44	38.7	64	20.8	84	7.4	104	1.9
45	37.7	65	20.0	85	6.9	105	1.8
46	36.8	66	19.2	86	6.5	106	1.6
47	35.9	67	18.4	87	6.1	107	1.4
48	34.9	68	17.6	88	5.7	108	1.3
49	34.0	69	16.8	89	5.3	109	1.1
50	33.1	70	16.0	90	5.0	110	1.0
51	32.2	71	15.3	91	4.7		
52	31.3	72	14.6	92	4.4		
53	30.4	73	13.9	93	4.1		
54	29.5	74	13.2	94	3.9		

With the recalculation method, the tax-deferred status of your nest egg can last as long as you do. But bear in mind that when distributions are based on a joint life expectancy and one of the two dies, the survivor's shorter single life expectancy can sharply accelerate the mandatory distribution schedule. The death of one spouse could make the survivor's mandatory minimum distribution schedule change from 20 years to 10 years overnight, for example.

If the same couple opts instead for the term certain payment method, they lock in 20 years of equal minimum annual distributions. That schedule remains unchanged if one of them dies. The risk with this method is that you may outlive your locked-in distribution schedule.

Unfortunately, many people are unaware of the payment method choice. The result is that it's automatically made for them: if you don't elect the term certain payment method, you automatically get the recalculation method by default. Talk to your tax accountant to figure out which method makes more sense for you.

A PROBLEM FOR WEALTHY PEOPLE

You can skip the next two paragraphs unless you expect your nest egg to generate $150,000 or more of annual income.

But if you're among the fortunate few who will retire wealthy, you should be aware that under current tax law, pension distributions that exceed $150,000 a year are subject to a 15% tax penalty in addition to ordinary income taxes. If you're married and file jointly, the IRS generously allows each of you to collect up to $150,000 a year before levying this penalty.

If you think you may fall into this category, you have a special problem: like everyone else, you'll get zapped with additional taxes for taking too little out of your retirement account every year, but you'll also get zapped with additional taxes if you take out too much. Plan ahead by talking to your tax accountant about it now.

INVESTING IN RETIREMENT

Your ability to manage your nest egg investments during your retirement will be critical to your comfort. Your investment earnings will become more important than ever before because they'll replace the salary and annual raises you once relied on. You may be retired from work, but your money isn't—it has to keep working as hard as ever.

You'll have more time to learn how to manage your money after you retire, and you'll *have* to learn more, if only in self-defense. (See page 154 for suggested reading to help you get up to speed painlessly.) Retirees are a favorite target of financial sales-people and unfortunately, many of the most persuasive marketers you meet will be more interested in enriching themselves than in enriching you.

You don't have to learn to decipher every pitch you'll hear—that would be a waste of your time and energy. But you do have to learn to say no—firmly and repeatedly—to eager sales-people who swear they're offering you the investment opportunity of a lifetime.

You'll save yourself a lot of grief by following five basic rules.

Never invest in anything if:

1. It's so complicated you don't understand it.
2. You can't figure out how the company selling it can make a profit.
3. You can't figure out how the salesperson is getting paid.
4. It's described as a no-risk way to get rich.
5. It's being pitched to you over the telephone by a friendly stranger.

YOUR NEW INVESTMENT GOAL

Before you retire, your investment goal is to grow the biggest possible nest egg. After you retire, your investment goal is to ensure that your nest egg lasts long enough to keep you living in comfort for the rest of your life.

But this new goal doesn't necessarily mean that you'll have to make drastic changes in your investment mix.

Your first thought may be to invest your nest egg in bonds or certificates of deposit and live on the interest they pay. That sounds nice and simple. But unfortunately, it doesn't work very well unless you happen to have a very large nest egg and/or a very short life expectancy.

Under those circumstances, you won't have to worry that your interest payments will buy less and less as the cost of living goes up, or that the value of your principal is being gobbled up by inflation.

But if you're like most people, you're going to be around a long time after you retire, buying goods and services whose prices will rise every year. Of course, you will need income-producing investments to pay your bills. But you must continue investing for growth as well, or you run a substantial risk of gradual impoverishment and ultimately, of outliving your nest egg.

History shows that stocks are the only investment that outpaces inflation over the long term. From the end of 1925 to the end of 1994 stocks earned a 10.2% annual compound

From the end of 1925 to the end of 1994, Treasury bills barely kept pace with inflation, let alone with taxes.

TAPPING YOUR NEST EGG IN RETIREMENT

NUMBER OF YEARS YOUR MONEY WILL LAST

Interest rate earned on savings. Table assumes 4% annual inflation.

%	4%	5%	6%	7%	8%	9%	10%	11%	12%	13%	14%
2	50	68	151	∞	∞	∞	∞	∞	∞	∞	∞
3	33	40	52	96	∞	∞	∞	∞	∞	∞	∞
4	25	28	34	42	69	∞	∞	∞	∞	∞	∞
5	20	22	25	29	36	53	∞	∞	∞	∞	∞
6	17	18	20	22	25	31	43	∞	∞	∞	∞
7	14	15	16	18	20	23	27	35	∞	∞	∞
8	13	13	14	15	16	18	20	24	30	65	∞
9	11	12	12	13	14	15	17	19	21	26	40
10	10	10	11	12	12	13	14	15	17	19	23
11	9	9	10	10	11	11	12	13	14	16	17
12	8	9	9	9	10	10	11	11	12	13	14
13	8	8	8	9	9	9	10	10	11	11	12
14	7	7	8	8	8	8	9	9	10	10	11
15	7	7	7	7	8	8	8	8	9	9	10

Percent of capital withdrawn yearly

Source: Alan Kahn, AJK Financial Group, Syosset, New York. All numbers are rounded.

1. Look in the far left-hand column to find the percentage of your nest egg you want to withdraw every year. Let's assume you pick 5%.

2. Look at the numbers across the top of the chart until you find the average annual return you expect the rest of your nest egg will earn. Let's assume 6%.

3. Run your finger down from 6% until you reach the same line you were on in Step number one—you're at 25. This is the number of years your money will last if you withdraw 5% of your nest egg the first year after you retire, increase your withdrawal annually to keep up with a 4% yearly inflation rate, and continue to earn a 6% annual return on your investments.

return, beating the 3.1% annual compound inflation rate in those years by 7.1%. During the same period, intermediate-term government bonds earned a 5.1% annual compound return, beating inflation by only 2%, a margin easily wiped out by taxes. Treasury bills earned 3.7% a year in the same period, barely keeping pace with inflation, let alone with taxes.[1]

Your asset allocation should still focus on growth, income and cash investments in retirement. But you may want to change their proportions—and you may want to change the investment mix within each category.

For example, in retirement your growth investments might emphasize dividend-paying stocks such as those purchased by growth and income funds, equity income funds and utility funds, rather than growth or aggressive growth stock funds which typically don't pay dividends. Owning stocks that pay reliable dividends assures you of a return even in a flat stock market and the dividends cushion your fall in a declining market.

TAPPING YOUR NEST EGG

List all your potential sources of retirement income—Social Security, defined benefit pension, 401(k) plan, rollover IRAs, regular IRAs—and the dates on which you must start taking distributions from them. List any taxable accounts you may have, too. Ideally, you want to spend the taxable accounts first, letting any tax-deferred earnings build up for as long as possible.

There are many ways to draw cash out of your nest egg in retirement. Most mutual fund companies will arrange to send you dividend checks and/or automatically sell shares for you at regular intervals, paying the proceeds directly to you or into a money market account on which you can write checks. To maximize investment growth, you might try to reinvest the

[1] ©*Stocks, Bonds, Bills and Inflation 1995 Yearbook*™, Ibbotson Associates, Chicago (annually updates work by Roger G. Ibbotson and Rex A. Sinquefeld). Used with permission. All rights Reserved.

dividends you earn on your stock funds for as long as possible and spend the interest you earn on your fixed-income funds.

Because this money has to last as long as you do, you must take care not to draw down your capital too fast. The conventional rule-of-thumb is that you can draw out about 5% to 6% of your capital in your first year of retirement, and then increase your subsequent annual withdrawals by the amount of inflation.

If your nest egg is $500,000, for example, in the first year of your retirement you'd draw down 5%, or $25,000. Assuming a 4% inflation rate, you could draw down $26,000 in the second year of retirement, $27,040 the following year, and so on.

Obviously, this rule-of-thumb won't work unless your investments are outpacing inflation over the long haul, constantly replenishing your nest egg. How long your money lasts depends on your average rate of return versus the average inflation rate. If the $500,000 nest egg earns an average 6% annual return, for example, you can increase your withdrawal amounts by the 4% annual inflation rate every year, and your money will last 25 years.

But the scenario changes dramatically if you draw down your capital too fast. If you take out $75,000, or 15% of that $500,000 nest egg in the first year of retirement, for example, and then increase your annual distributions by the same 4% inflation factor, and earn the same 6% average annual return on investments, you'll run out of money in just seven years.

MAKING A MASTER FINANCIAL PLAN IN RETIREMENT

You need professional help to calculate your living expenses, cash flow, the rate of return your investments must earn to cover your expenses and taxes and keep pace with inflation, and how much of your capital you can afford to draw down every year. All these factors will vary depending on your inflation assumptions, your life expectancy, where you decide to live, how you decide to spend your time, which 401(k) pay-out option you select and whether or not you sell your house.

It takes multiple calculations to compare all the different possibilities and their tax consequences and choose the one that looks best to you. Don't try this at home on a pocket calculator. You'll just drive yourself crazy. Instead, pay a Certified Public Accountant—a tax professional—to do the analysis for you. If you work for a large company, someone on the human resources or personnel staff may be able to help you with it, too.

Of course, you can probably get plenty of free advice and analysis from financial planners,

For objective guidance, rely on people who have no vested financial interest in your decisions.

stock brokers and insurance agents. Bear in mind that anyone who earns commissions by selling investment products—no matter how honest and intelligent—has a natural bias in favor of the products he or she sells and will be less familiar with the advantages of other products.

For objective guidance, rely on people who have no vested financial interest in your decisions.

Your goal in retirement is an overall investment return that keeps pace with inflation and lets you maintain the standard of living you want without requiring you to take on more risk than you can tolerate.

How can you measure risk? Look at it this way: any investment promising appreciably more than the stock market's 10% historic long-term annual return is riskier than the stock market.

If you can't earn the return you want without investing your precious nest egg in commodities and options and start-up companies that hope to discover a cure for cancer, you should consider other alternatives—like reducing your expenses, perhaps by moving to a less expensive part of the country, or increasing your income by working part-time.

WHAT YOU SHOULD KNOW ABOUT SOCIAL SECURITY

The first thing you should know is that despite its well-publicized problems and probable future modifications in eligibility rules, Social Security will be there for you when you retire.

The second thing is that your Social Security benefit won't be more than a *small piece* of your total retirement income. (See chart, page 67.)

That's all it was ever intended to be.

Even in 1935, when Social Security was enacted, no one expected this benefit to be the average American's only source of retirement income. Today, Social Security benefits account for about 40% of the average income of people who are 65 or older—but less than 25% of the average income of retirees whose total annual income is $20,000 or more. The average Social Security recipient now collects $698 per month—a little more for men, and a little less for women. The *maximum* benefit for a person who retired at 65 in January 1995 is $1,199 per month.

Although these benefits are modest, Social Security has an important feature not offered by most private sector pension annuities: it's indexed to keep up with inflation. The Social

Security benefit amount you receive increases each January. In fact, far from being short-changed, the average Social Security recipient today lives long enough to collect more in benefit dollars than he or she ever paid into the system in Social Security taxes. Benefits are funded by taxes paid by today's workers.

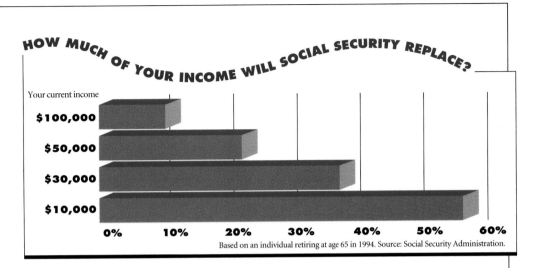

HOW MUCH OF YOUR INCOME WILL SOCIAL SECURITY REPLACE?

Your current income

$100,000
$50,000
$30,000
$10,000

0%   10%   20%   30%   40%   50%   60%

Based on an individual retiring at age 65 in 1994. Source: Social Security Administration.

No one can say for certain how Social Security will be modified in the future. But demographic trends alone make it virtually certain that the benefits will shrink for future retirees, probably in proportion to their retirement income from other sources.

In 1937, when the first Social Security checks were mailed out, there were more than 40 workers paying into the system to support each eligible retiree. Today, there are only three active workers for each retiree collecting benefits. By 2030, the ratio is expected to be just two to one. The inescapable conclusion is that Social Security benefits will have to be reduced, at least for recipients whose other sources of income make their total retirement income relatively high.

This trend is already underway. Currently, people who are single and have $25,000 in total retirement income, or married filing jointly with $32,000 in total income, must pay federal income tax on up to 50% of their Social Security benefit. For single people with $34,00 in income and married couples with $44,000 in income, up to 85% of Social Security is federally taxable. (Your total income for this calculation includes all tax-exempt income such as interest from municipal bonds, as well as half your Social Security benefit.)

Social Security deserves its good reputation for patient and thorough response to consumer questions.

FIND OUT WHAT YOUR BENEFIT WILL BE

Call Social Security at 800-772-1213 and ask for a copy of form SSA–7004. This form is a request to look at your earnings history: the record of what you've earned and what you've paid in Social Security taxes every year. About four weeks after you complete and mail back the form, you'll receive a copy of your earnings record, plus the agency's estimate of the benefit amount you'll collect in retirement.

You can't do an overall retirement budget and investment plan without an estimate of your income from Social Security. But even if your retirement is many years away you should check Social Security's summary of your earnings history periodically, to correct any clerical errors the agency may have made—like inadvertently omitting a year of your earnings.

Your eligibility to collect Social Security in retirement depends on your earnings history. You receive Social Security credits based on the amounts that you earned and on how many years you paid Social Security taxes. Currently, 40 credits are required to collect benefits. If you don't have enough credits because you didn't pay Social Security taxes long enough, you don't qualify for a retirement benefit. There's no partial benefit for fewer credits.

Congress has slowly but steadily been increasing the number of credits needed for retirement benefit eligibility. The most recent rule is that people who reach age 62 after 1990 need 40 credits to be eligible. Anyone who has worked for a decade or more won't have any difficulty meeting that credit requirement.

SPOUSAL BENEFITS

If you're married or a widow or widower, you can collect a retirement benefit based on your spouse's earnings history or a benefit based on your own earnings, whichever is higher. (You also qualify to receive a spousal benefit based on the earnings of a former spouse, provided the marriage lasted ten years and you haven't remarried.)

Once you're 65, your spousal benefit is 50% of whatever retirement benefit your mate collects; you're also entitled to a survivor's benefit equal to 100% of your mate's benefit. If your spouse's benefit is $400 a month, you are entitled to $200 a month in spousal benefit. As a widow or widower, you'll be entitled to $400 a month.

These rules apply equally to both spouses, but the spousal benefit is collected mainly by women. Historically, women have earned less than men, and have worked fewer years because in many cases they left the work force while their children were young. The result is that a woman's spousal benefit is often a bigger amount than the benefit she would collect based on her own earnings.

The good news is that you get whichever of the two benefits is higher—the one based on your own earnings or the one based on your spouse's earnings. The bad news is that you only get one of these benefits—not both. If Anne's benefit, based on her own earnings, is $300 a month, and her benefit as Joe's wife is $200 a month, she will collect $300 a month. She won't collect $300 of her own benefit plus a $200 spousal benefit for a total of $500.

As a widow or widower, you are entitled to a survivor's benefit based on your spouse's earnings. But if the benefit based on your own earnings is higher, that is the amount you will receive. Joe's benefit was $400 per month. Anne's benefit, based on her own earnings, is $300 per month. As his widow, she will collect $400 per month.

WHEN SHOULD YOU START COLLECTING SOCIAL SECURITY?

To apply for Social Security, you'll need to show your Social Security number, your birth certificate (original or certified copy) and proof of how much you earned the year before you apply. Your benefit check can be mailed to your home or the amount deposited directly into any account you designate.

When to apply is a decision you'll want to consider with some care.

Currently, you become eligible to collect 80% of your Social Security benefit at age 62; but if you do, you're locked in to that 80% benefit for the rest of your life. If you start collecting the benefit at age 63, you'll receive about 87%; if you start at age 65, you're eligible to collect 100% of your benefit. If you wait until age 70 to start collecting benefits and you have worked continuously until that point, you're eligible to collect between 115% and 140% of your benefit, depending on your date of birth. Your spousal benefits are also adjusted depending on the age at which you start collecting Social Security.

All these rules are adjusted for your date of birth. If you were born after 1959, for example, you won't be eligible to collect 100% of your Social Security retirement benefit until you're 67 years old. If you opt to start receiving benefits at age 62, you'll be eligible for only 70% of your total benefit.

Most experts say that statistically, you're better off waiting until 65 to collect 100% of your benefit. It's true that if you start at 62, you will collect benefits for three extra years. But by the time you're in your mid-70s, you will have collected about the same total amount,

The good news is that you get the higher of two Social Security benefits—the one based on your own earnings or the one based on your spouse's earnings.

whether you started at 62 or at 65. And thereafter, you'll collect more if you're eligible for 100% of your benefit. Today, the average Social Security recipient lives into his or her 80s.

If you and your spouse are both eligible for Social Security benefits, you should calculate every possibility before deciding on what makes the most sense. Your tax accountant can help you with these calculations, or you can get assistance from the Social Security Administration. Check your telephone book for the agency's local office and telephone number. Social Security deserves its good reputation for patient and thorough response to consumer questions.

DOES IT PAY TO WORK AFTER RETIREMENT?

Again, this depends on your circumstances.

Your Social Security benefit can be reduced by your earnings after you retire. You should factor this into your calculations about how much any salary will increase your income in retirement.

Under current tax law, for example, 85% of your Social Security benefit becomes taxable if you're married, filing jointly and your total annual income is $44,000 or more. For purposes of this calculation, your total income includes any tax-exempt interest you earn, as well as half of your Social Security benefit. If you're single, 85% of your Social Security benefit becomes taxable if your annual income is $34,000 or more.

Other factors to consider: your earnings in retirement are subject to all the taxes you paid before you retired, including Social Security tax. And if you're collecting Social Security retirement benefits, you forfeit some benefit for every dollar you earn.

In 1995, benefit recipients who are between the ages of 62 and 64 must give back $1 in Social Security for every $2 they earn above $8,160. Benefit recipients between ages 65 and 69 have to give back $1 in benefits for every $3 they earn over $11,280. These caps are adjusted annually and disappear at age 70.

On the other hand, if you retire and start collecting Social Security and then decide to start working again, you have the option of temporarily halting your Social Security benefits. You can resume them again later, with a recalculated retirement age that might entitle you to collect a bigger amount.

WHAT YOU SHOULD KNOW ABOUT MEDICARE

If you're eligible for Social Security benefits, you automatically become eligible for Medicare when you turn 65—earlier if you meet specific disability requirements.

Medicare comes in two pieces. Medicare's Part A covers 150 days of your annual hospital bills and pays for skilled nursing care—but not for custodial care such as assistance with daily bathing, dressing or eating meals. Medicare's Part B covers doctors' bills, out-patient surgery, emergency room treatment, X-rays, laboratory tests and some medical supplies.

Medicare pays for 80% of what it deems to be reasonable charges above an annual deductible; there's a list of reasonable charges for every procedure. Needless to say, your doctor may not share Medicare's idea of what constitutes a reasonable charge. If he or she bills you $400 for a procedure Medicare thinks should only cost $300, Medicare will pay only $240 (80% of $300). You'll have to pay the $160 balance. A doctor who "accepts assignment" charges no more than the amount Medicare thinks is reasonable. Medicare will supply you with a list of physicians in your area who take "assignment".

Medicare coverage is also limited to appropriate, medically necessary treatment—you can be denied coverage if Medicare doesn't believe your treatment was appropriate or necessary. If you disagree, you can appeal the decision; Medicare's claim denial decisions frequently are appealed, often successfully. Instructions for how to appeal are enclosed with the form that denies your claim.

Everyone eligible for Medicare automatically receives Part A coverage. But Part B coverage is optional; you have to pay extra for it and can only sign up for it during specific enrollment periods. You should sign up for Medicare during the three months before you reach 65 to avoid any waiting period for Part B coverage.

Before buying a Medigap policy, check how much it pays per day for hospital room and board, and the maximum it will pay for each illness or injury.

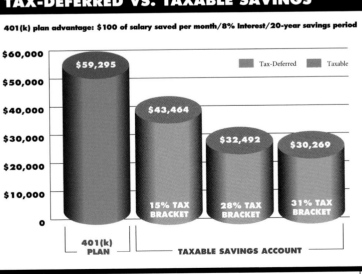

TAX-DEFERRED VS. TAXABLE SAVINGS

401(k) plan advantage: $100 of salary saved per month/8% interest/20-year savings period

Tax-Deferred   Taxable

$60,000
$50,000
$40,000
$30,000
$20,000
$10,000
0

$59,295
$43,464   15% TAX BRACKET
$32,492   28% TAX BRACKET
$30,269   31% TAX BRACKET

401(k) PLAN

TAXABLE SAVINGS ACCOUNT

BUYING PRIVATE HEALTH INSURANCE

Medigap coverage is private insurance designed to plug the gaps in Medicare. But there are some services not covered by Medicare or Medigap policies—such as hearing aids, the extra cost of a private hospital room and most prescription drugs. There are ten basic Medigap policies, each one slightly more elaborate than the others. Before buying a policy, double-check how much it pays per day for hospital room and board, and the maximum it will pay for each illness or injury.

As with any insurance policy, you should comparison-shop, taking into account the insurer's credit rating and reputation for financial stability and service as well as the premium charges. If you have a complaint about a Medigap policy, call the Health Care Financial Administration, which administers Medicare. Its hotline number is 800-638-6833.

PART FOUR

ANSWERS TO THE MOST COMMONLY ASKED 401(k) QUESTIONS

What plan participants

want to know about

their 401(k) plans

HOW DOES A 401(k) PLAN WORK?

When you join a 401(k) plan, you agree to set aside part of your salary in a special retirement account set up by your employer. You don't pay income taxes on your contributions to this account or on their earnings until you start taking money out of the plan.[1] Ideally, this won't be until you retire, when you may be in a lower tax-bracket than you are in now. But even if you aren't, your money will have enjoyed years of tax-free compounding. (For an eye-opening look at the enormous difference this can make to how fast money grows, turn to the chart on page 71.)

Because each 401(k) plan has its own rules, some of your questions about your own plan can only be answered by your company's human resources or personnel department. But all 401(k) plans have a lot in common because they must conform to Treasury Department (Internal Revenue Service) and Department of Labor regulations. Here are answers to some of the most commonly asked questions about them.

1 **How is a 401(k) different from a regular pension?**

The big difference is that you're in control: your 401(k) account is funded with your money and you decide how much to save and how to invest it.

A traditional "regular" pension is funded and controlled by your employer. The traditional plan is sometimes called a defined benefit plan because it promises to pay you a specific monthly income in retirement—in other words, a defined benefit. The amount you get is

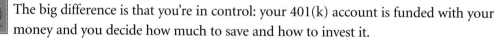

[1] Pennsylvania is the only state that taxes 401(k) contributions in the year you make them.

based on your salary and your years of service with the company. It's up to your employer to put aside enough money to make good on this promise; the contributions don't come from your salary.

Most defined benefit plans are insured by the Pension Benefit Guaranty Corp., a federal agency. The PBGC guarantees to pay retirement benefits if the company doesn't have enough assets to cover them—but only up to a specified ceiling. In 1994 PBGC coverage was capped at $30,681.84 a year for workers who retired after 65, at $19,943.28 for those who stopped working at 60 and at $13,806.84 for workers who retired at age 55.

By contrast, a 401(k) plan is called a defined *contribution* plan because the annual amount that can be contributed to each employee's account is limited. (For more on the limits on contributions, see Questions 7 and 10, pages 79 and 80.) A 401(k) plan is not insured (See Question 47, page 102), and it doesn't promise a defined benefit. Your retirement income from a 401(k) plan *will depend on how much you save and how well your investments perform.*

 2 **How is a 401(k) different from a profit-sharing plan?**
Technically, 401(k) plans are considered profit-sharing plans. But on a practical level, they're usually different in several ways from the classic profit-sharing plan. The biggest difference is that in what we think of as a profit-sharing plan, the employer makes contributions for eligible employees—in some cases, whether or not they also contribute to the plan. In a 401(k) plan, by contrast, eligible employees must choose to participate by making their own contributions, which may or may not be matched by the employer.

Another difference is that in a classic profit-sharing plan, employer contributions depend on the company's profits. In a bad year, the employer may decide not to make any contribution. In most 401(k) plans, on the other hand, your employer's matching contribution depends on your contribution rather than on company profits.

3 **How do I contribute to the 401(k) plan?**
By automatic payroll deduction, which makes contributing virtually painless. Your contribution never shows up in your paycheck, so you don't miss it.

And, because your contribution is untaxed it's worth more to you in the 401(k) plan than it would be in your paycheck, where it would be reduced by income taxes.

PG. 79

With a 401(k) plan, you're in control: you decide how much to save and how to invest it.

When $1 goes into your 401(k) account, you've invested all 100 cents of it.

 How do my contributions lower my income taxes?

The amount you contribute to your 401(k) plan isn't reported as income on your W-2 form to the Internal Revenue Service.

The important thing about this tax break is that it makes 401(k) contributions much more affordable: Let's say Kate earns $25,000 a year. Her marginal federal tax rate is 28%, and her state and local taxes add up to another 4% for a total 32% tax rate. Kate contributes $1,000 a year to the 401(k) plan. That reduces her taxable salary to $24,000 a year. But it also cuts her income taxes by $320 (32% of $1,000). (Does this mean that if you saved enough, you could theoretically reduce your taxable income to nothing? A nice thought, but no. Like all tax breaks, this one is strictly limited. In 1994, the maximum pre-tax 401(k) contribution allowed was $9,240. Under current law, this dollar limit will be increased in $500 increments to keep pace with inflation.)

 A CONTRIBUTION LOWERS YOUR INCOME TAXES

	GROSS SALARY	TOTAL TAXES	TAKE HOME PAY
BEFORE	$25,000	$5,050	$19,950
AFTER	$24,000	$4,630	$19,270*

Source: Edward Slott, E. Slott & Co., Rockville Centre, New York.   * AND YOU STILL HAVE THE $1,000!

Kate has saved $1,000 but her take-home pay isn't reduced by $1,000 a year. It's only reduced by $680.

 Why is the government giving me this tax break?

Because it wants you to save as much as possible for your retirement.

The government has opted to pass up current tax revenue in order to reduce the very real risk that you and millions of other Americans will wind up without enough money to live comfortably in retirement.

Why is that a real risk? Won't Social Security be there for future retirees?

Social Security will be there, but it's not a cure-all. In the first place, Social Security was never intended to be the only source of retirement income; it was supposed to supplement private sector pensions and individual savings. And in fact, that's all it does. The average Social Security recipient now collects $698 per month; the maximum benefit for a person who turned 65 in January 1995 is $1,199 per month. These are not princely sums.

Second, Social Security is grappling with serious problems that no one could have anticipated when it was enacted in 1935. The most obvious one is that people live a lot longer than they did 60 years ago. In 1930 the average American had a 59.7 year life expectancy at birth. Few people lived long enough to collect Social Security. In 1989 the average American had a 75.3 year life expectancy at birth. If you're in good health today at age 62, you may have another 30 years ahead of you.

The bottom line is that the average Social Security recipient today collects more in benefit dollars than he or she ever paid into the system in Social Security taxes. In other words, current Social Security benefits are funded by taxes paid by today's workers.

Given demographic trends, that's a serious problem. In 1950 there were 16 people in the workforce for every one retiree collecting Social Security. Today, there are only three workers for each beneficiary. By 2030 the ratio is expected to be just two to one. The upshot is that no matter how loudly politicians of both parties swear that Social Security benefits are sacred, down the road there simply won't be any choice but to make some changes. Congress will have to reduce Social Security benefits by increasing taxes (on current workers and/or on all but the least affluent benefit recipients) or by redefining the eligibility rules, probably both.

This explains why the government wants to make it easier for you to save for retirement on your own—and why it's critically important for your future security that you do so.

YOUR CONTRIBUTIONS

For many people, the first question about a 401(k) plan is "Where do I find the money to contribute?" Interestingly, this has nothing to do with how much or how little they earn. Surveys consistently show that at every income level the single most frequently cited reason for not participating in a 401(k) plan is that people don't believe they can afford the contributions.

But the truth is that most people can set aside up to 10% of what they earn and hardly notice the difference, especially if it's automatically deducted from their paychecks. When you don't have it, you don't spend it and you don't miss it. If 10% of your income sounds like too much, then start smaller—put in 5% and gradually increase your contribu- tions. If you find you really can't afford to sock away that much, you can always scale back. (See Question 59, page 108.)

It's a mistake to postpone saving in your 401(k) plan until you can afford to put away a larger amount. Take a look at the chart on page 37 to see why. *How soon you start saving is what makes the real difference in the size of your nest egg at retirement.* Even tiny savings can add up to a lot when you have time on your side. Let's say you're 25 years old and decide to save the price of a six-pack of beer a week—about $4.00. Your employer's 50% match brings your total to $6.00 a week, or $26.00 a month. Assuming your money earns an 8% average annual return, in ten years you will have $4,419.81. In twenty years, you'll have $14,277.73. In thirty years you'll have $30,344.36. (Imagine if you save the price of a couple of bags of potato chips, too!)

7   How much can I put into the 401(k) plan?

Most plans allow you to contribute a specific percentage of your pay—it ranges all the way from 1% to 15% of salary—up to a government-imposed dollar ceiling. Under current law, that ceiling is adjusted for inflation in $500 increments. At the current inflation rate, that means an increase every two years. In 1995, the legal limit for pre-tax contributions is $9,240. (In some cases, participants may be limited to a lower maximum dollar contribution. See Question 10.)

There's also a limit on total contributions to all your employer-sponsored retirement plans. Total contributions that you and your employer make to the 401(k) plan and to any other retirement plans the company offers can't add up to more than 25% of your taxable income, or $30,000—whichever is less.

Some plans allow you to make additional after-tax contributions which aren't included in the government limit. (See Question 27, page 87.)

8   How little can I put in?

There's no legal minimum contribution, but many plans establish a minimum equal to 1% or 2% of your pay. Allowing people to contribute any dollar amount they wished would add to the plan's administrative costs, which in some cases are being paid by the plan participants. (See Question 13, page 81.)

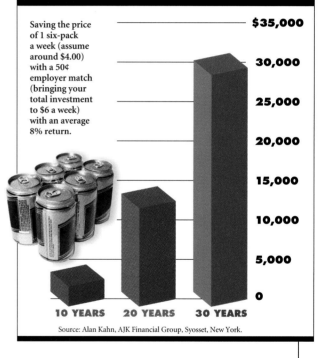

SIX-PACK SAVINGS ADD UP

Saving the price of 1 six-pack a week (assume around $4.00) with a 50¢ employer match (bringing your total investment to $6 a week) with an average 8% return.

$35,000
30,000
25,000
20,000
15,000
10,000
5,000
0

10 YEARS   20 YEARS   30 YEARS

Source: Alan Kahn, AJK Financial Group, Syosset, New York.

9   Are my 401(k) contributions deducted from all the pay I receive, including bonuses and overtime?

It depends on your plan's rules and on how much you earn. Under federal law, you can't make contributions or receive employer contributions for any compensation you earn in excess of $150,000. For example, if you earned $250,000, you'd only be allowed to make contributions from the first $150,000 and you'd only be allowed to receive employer contributions based on the first $150,000 you earned.

As for the vast majority of us who don't have that problem, the rules vary from one plan to another. In some plans, the employer takes a percentage of all your compensation when deducting your 401(k) contribution. In others, he'll count only your base pay. Ask your human resources or personnel department which rule applies at your company.

10 **I've heard that if I earn over a certain amount, my 401(k) contributions are capped. Is that true, and if so, why?**

It's true that your contributions are subject to additional limits if the federal government considers you a highly paid employee. What's their idea of highly paid? In 1995 it is generally anyone earning more than $66,000.

The reason for this distinction is that the government wants to make sure everybody benefits equally from the 401(k) plan—that it's not just an investment vehicle for higher-paid employees.

One of several federal non-discrimination rules prevents highly paid people from saving a substantially greater percentage of their salary in the 401(k) than lower-paid people do.

Your company's plan must pass annual non-discrimination tests after the plan year ends. If there's too big a gap between highly paid employee contributions and lower-paid employee contributions, the plan has to make an adjustment. It can either refund part of the contribution made by the highly paid employees, or the employer can make a special additional contribution to lower-paid employees' accounts.

 NOTE: If your plan permits after-tax contributions, they too must satisfy special non-discrimination tests. (For more on after-tax contributions, see Question 27, page 87.)

11 **What happens to the money I put into the 401(k) plan?**

It goes into the investments you've chosen from a list of investment options supplied by your employer. Most 401(k) plans offer you a selection of at least three different investments. Many plans offer five choices or more. Typical investments include stock and bond mutual funds, a money market fund and a guaranteed investment contract (GIC) that pays a fixed interest rate, as well as your own company's stock. (See Part Five, pages 122-136 for an explanation of these and other 401(k) investment vehicles. See Sections I and II, pages 12-50 for information on how to select the investments that are right for you.)

PG. 12

 12 How do I know how well my investments are doing?

You'll receive a financial statement of your 401(k) account at least once a year that shows the amounts you've contributed and how all your investments have performed. Plans usually report on either a semi-annual, quarterly or monthly basis.

13 What does the 401(k) plan cost—and who's paying for it?

Basically, the plan has two kinds of expenses: administrative costs and investment management fees.

Administrative costs include fees paid to the trustee and the recordkeeper. The trustee sees that the money is properly invested and that all federal laws and plan rules are followed. The recordkeeper is responsible for making sure that your contributions, investment gains and losses, and transfers from one investment to another are properly credited to your account.

Investment management fees are usually charged as a percentage of the total assets under management. These fees might range from 0.2% to 2% of the assets, depending on the investment manager and the type of investment. (In general, investment management fees are higher on stock funds than on bond funds, for example.) If your money is in a mutual fund that has $1 billion in assets and charges a 1% investment management fee, the investment management fee for the whole fund would be $10 million.

Other costs include educational materials (like this book), seminars and information videos that help plan participants decide how to invest their money. Depending on the plan, these educational expenses may be included among administrative fees.

Who pays all these costs? It depends on the plan. Sometimes they're paid by the employer. Sometimes they're divided between the employer and the plan (you and your fellow participants). Sometimes all the expenses are paid by the plan's participants. Your personal share of any charges will be subtracted automatically from your account balance. As a 401(k) plan participant, you will usually pay less for these services than you would pay if you made similar investments outside a 401(k) plan.

Your Summary Plan Description, a booklet that details the plan's provisions and your rights and obligations as a participant, should include some information about plan fees.

The recordkeeper is responsible for making sure that your contributions, investment gains and losses, and transfers from one investment to another are properly credited to your account.

Your human resources or personnel department will give you a copy. They will also be able to give you any information about fees and how they're paid that isn't included in the Summary Plan Description.

14 **If I leave this job, is the money I put into the plan mine to take with me?**
Yes—you take every penny, plus everything it earned. To maintain its tax-deferred status and avoid possible early withdrawal penalties, however, you must roll your 401(k) account into an Individual Retirement Account or into another employer's 401(k) plan. (See Questions 37 and 38, pages 95 and 96, for the right way to do this. There are hefty taxes to pay if you goof.)

WHAT'S MY EMPLOYER'S ROLE?

Your company has a fiduciary responsibility for the 401(k) plan it sponsors. This is a fancy way of saying that your employer is legally responsible for supervising what's done with your money. The law's standard for fiduciary behavior is that the fiduciary must act the same way a "prudent" man or woman would act in similar circumstances, given the same responsibilities. That means that the fiduciary must take all the necessary steps to make well-informed, sensible decisions and avoid taking undue risks.

This "prudent man" standard applies to everything your employer does for the 401(k) plan—and your employer does a lot. As plan sponsor, the employer hires the plan's administrator, trustee, recordkeeper and investment managers, monitors their performance, decides which investment choices the plan will offer and makes sure that you get the information you need to use the plan well.

 15 Does my employer contribute to my 401(k) account?

Many employers do, although they're under no legal requirement to make 401(k) plan contributions.

 16 Why do employers contribute to 401(k) plans if they don't have to?

To stay competitive with other employers and make sure that talented people think of their companies as good places to work.

Employers want to attract and retain valuable employees and a 401(k) plan is a very popular and visible employee benefit. They also want their workers to be able to retire with enough money to maintain a comfortable standard of living. When a company's former employees live comfortably in retirement, its image is enhanced with shareholders and customers, as well as with current and prospective employees.

17 What is a matching contribution?

It's free money. Go for it. An employer "matches" your 401(k) contribution by adding to it. For every $1 you contribute, your employer might add 25 cents or 50 cents, up to a specified ceiling, usually the first 3% to 6% of pay that you put into the plan. Let's say you earn $30,000 and your employer offers a 50 cent match for the first 6% of pay you contribute to the plan. That means that if you make a $1,800 annual 401(k) contribution, your employer will throw in an extra $900.

That $900 is a guaranteed, risk-free 50% return on your investment. You can't beat it anywhere else.

Your employer's matching contribution is a guaranteed, risk-free return on your investment.

18 Is there any other way my employer can contribute?

Yes. Some employers give their matching contribution in company stock, which they may add to the company's Employee Stock Ownership Plan (ESOP) instead of adding cash to the 401(k) plan. Employees cannot sell the company stock they own through an ESOP; they receive its value in cash or in shares when they leave the company or retire.

19 Do my employer's contributions go into the plan at the same time as mine?

Not necessarily. Some employers put matching contributions into the plan along with employee contributions. Others add their match monthly, quarterly or annually.

Depending on the company's annual profits, some employers also offer a 401(k) bonus contribution. The basic match may be 50 cents for example, but the company might add up to 50 cents more in a good year. If applicable, typically the bonus will be contributed in a lump sum after the end of the year.

20 At what point do I own my employer's contributions to my account?

It depends on the plan. In some plans, you're vested in (entitled to) your employer's contributions right away. Others don't vest you until you've been in the plan for five years, or they start vesting you gradually from year three. But in all cases, by law you must be fully vested in your employer's contributions after seven years of service.

Most plans also consider you fully vested after you turn 65, if you die or become disabled, or if the plan is terminated for any reason even if you don't have seven years of service. (See Question 52 page 104.)

21 How are my years of service determined?

Your employer can use one of two methods. In the first, your years of service are determined by the number of hours you actually worked in a 12-month period.

You must be credited with a year's service for any 12-month period in which you worked at least 1,000 hours. This lets you earn a year of service in less than 12 months.

The second way to calculate years of service is the elapsed time method. Your employer counts 12 months from the date you were hired to the date you leave, regardless of how many hours you worked.

Many companies use both methods: the first is often used to determine your eligibility to participate in the plan, and the second is used to decide when you're fully vested in the company's contributions to the plan. (You are fully vested in your own contributions at all times.)

22 What if my company has many different business units and some units have 401(k) plans and some don't? How are my years of service determined if I'm transferred from a unit without a 401(k) plan to a unit that has one?

Your employer is legally required to count all your years of service with the company to determine your eligibility for benefits and for vesting. Your length of service at any particular unit within the company is irrelevant.

23 What information about my 401(k) plan am I legally entitled to have?

A lot less than you actually need. That's why your employer will almost certainly give you more information than the law requires.

Legally, all you're entitled to is a Summary Plan Description, a Summary Annual Report and an annual statement. You may not even be entitled to a prospectus for each mutual fund offered in your 401(k) plan, although you must receive a prospectus or prospectus substitute for any stock in your employer's company that's offered in the plan. (A prospectus is a legal document that contains all the facts the Securities and Exchange Commission believes are necessary for an investor to make an informed decision about whether or not to buy shares in a publicly held company.)

Why are the disclosure requirements so inadequate? Basically, because 401(k) plans are governed by a law that was written before they existed—the 1974 Employee Retirement Income Security Act, better known as ERISA. ERISA didn't anticipate pension plans in which employees would make most of the investment decisions; consequently, its disclosure rules are relatively undemanding.

But don't worry, you probably won't have any difficulty getting much more information than ERISA requires. Employers are strongly motivated to provide employees with all the information they need to use the plan wisely. (To see why, look at Question 16 page 83.)

24 Does participating in a 401(k) affect any of my other benefits?

Not if you make sure the amount you contribute to the plan is added back into your salary for the purposes of calculating other benefits. If you earn $40,000 a year, for example, and contribute $2,000 to the 401(k) plan, your taxable income is reduced to $38,000.

That means that if your group life insurance covers you for twice your salary, you'll have only $76,000 of coverage—unless the 401(k) contribution is included in the calculation. Talk to your human resources or personnel department about it.

25 How long do I have to wait after being hired to join the 401(k) plan?

It depends on the company. Your employer can legally exclude any employee who has less than one year of service. Many companies do. The reason is that employee turnover tends to be highest in the first year of employment; companies want to avoid incurring 401(k) administrative costs for employees who may not stay long.

Your employer is also allowed to exclude anyone under age 21. Many companies with a large number of employees under 21 do exclude them. The reason is that very young employees tend not to participate in a 401(k) plan when given the choice. If they're eligible to join the plan, their lower participation rate can reduce the amount other employees are permitted to contribute because of federal non-discrimination rules. (See Question 10 page 80.)

TAX RULES

401(k) plans are regulated by both the Internal Revenue Service and the Department of Labor, and unless you happen to be a CPA the tax rules governing these plans can seem quite complex. Your best guideline is *never to assume* that you know how the IRS will treat a contribution to a tax-deferred account, a transfer from one tax-deferred account to another or a withdrawal from a tax-deferred account.

Check with your human resources or personnel department and your tax accountant to be sure you understand how the IRS will treat any action you take with your 401(k) money.

26 **Do I pay any taxes at all on the money I contribute to the plan?**

Yes. Your contributions aren't exempt from Social Security taxes. This has a positive aspect: it means your Social Security benefits are unaffected by your participation in the plan.

If you put $1,000 into the 401(k) plan, you'll pay Social Security tax on the entire amount unless you've already paid the maximum Social Security tax for the year. But 401(k) contributions are exempt from federal income tax and state income tax in all states except Pennsylvania. They're also exempt from local taxes in many municipalities. Check with your plan administrator, or human resources or personnel department to see how your municipality treats 401(k) contributions.

27 **After I've made the maximum pre-tax contribution allowed, can I put additional money into the plan if I want to?**

Maybe. Some 401(k) plans permit both pre-tax and after-tax contributions. This arrangement is usually found in plans that existed as savings plans before the 1978 introduction of 401(k)s. Most of the plans adopted since the early 1980s only allow pre-tax employee contributions.

An after-tax contribution doesn't reduce your taxable income. But its earnings in the 401(k) plan are untaxed until you withdraw them. Some employers match your after-tax contributions, but in many plans only your pre-tax contributions qualify for an employer match. (See Questions 17 through 20, page 84 for more information about matching contributions.) PG. 84

28 Are there any other differences between a pre-tax and an after-tax contribution?

The main thing to understand is that eventually, everything is taxable. The big difference between pre-tax and after-tax contributions is *when* the tax falls due. Uncle Sam only gets to take one bite of the apple. You have to pay taxes sooner or later, but not both sooner *and* later.

Pre-tax contributions are taxable when you take them out of the plan because they weren't taxed when they went in. If you take them out before you reach age 59½, you'll also PG. 112 owe a 10% early withdrawal penalty unless you qualify for a special hardship withdrawal. (See Question 69, page 112.)

After-tax contributions are taxed when they go into the 401(k) plan. Because you've already paid taxes on this money, you won't owe additional taxes on it when you take it out of the plan. But when you withdraw after-tax contributions you made after 1986 you must, at the same time, withdraw a proportionate share of the interest they earned. That interest is subject to income taxes and to an early withdrawal penalty if you're under 59½.

29 If I'm saving money that I plan to use before I retire, does it make more sense to do it with after-tax 401(k) contributions, or to save it outside the 401(k) plan?

In general, it's more sensible to do your short-term, after-tax saving outside your 401(k) plan.

It's true that usually you can withdraw your after-tax 401(k) contributions at any time without taxes or penalty, but remember, you'll owe taxes on any interest they earned, as well as a 10% early withdrawal penalty if you're under age 59½. The 10% penalty is an expense you wouldn't have if you saved on an after-tax basis outside your 401(k) plan.

But there are situations where it can make sense to use after-tax contributions for short-term savings: if your employer matches your after-tax contributions and if you're fully vested in the matching contributions by the time you withdraw the money, you may wind up with more money by saving in the 401(k) plan, even after taking the 10% early withdrawal penalty into account.

Eventually, everything is taxable. The big difference between pre-tax and after-tax contributions is when the tax falls due.

401(k) PLANS VERSUS INDIVIDUAL RETIREMENT ACCOUNTS

Many people who participate in 401(k) plans also have IRAs. If you own both types of accounts and can't afford to make contributions to both, you need to know their similarities and differences in order to make an intelligent choice between them. And even if you *can* contribute to both accounts, you should know the differences between them.

 30 **I participate in my company's 401(k) plan but I also want to invest in an Individual Retirement Account. Can I do both?**

Yes. But depending on your salary, your IRA contribution may not be tax-deductible.

Under current law, if you participate in a qualified employer-sponsored pension plan like a 401(k), you can only deduct a $2,000 annual IRA contribution if you are:

a) single and earning less than $25,000, or

b) married filing jointly and together earn less than $40,000.

You qualify for a partial deduction on the IRA contribution if you are:

a) single and earn between $25,000 and $35,000, or

b) married filing jointly and together earn between $40,000 and $50,000.

Of course, even if you make a non-deductible IRA contribution, its earnings won't be taxed until the money is withdrawn.

31 If I decide not to participate in my 401(k) plan, will I be eligible for a fully deductible IRA regardless of my salary?

Yes, provided neither you nor your spouse actively participates in a 401(k) plan or any other qualified pension plan.

You're automatically considered an active participant in a pension plan if you're eligible for a defined benefit plan—the traditional pension that's fully funded by the employer. (See Question 1, page 74.) But in a defined contribution plan like a 401(k), you're not considered an active participant unless you elect to contribute to the plan, or your employer contributes to it on your behalf.

PG. 74

There's a very simple way to determine whether or not you're an active participant in a pension plan: every January or February your employer sends you a W-2 form—the form stating your wages for the year just ended. Take a look at Box 15 on the W-2 form. If there's no X in that box, you don't actively participate in a pension plan and the IRS won't challenge you for taking a deduction for an IRA contribution.

32 If I have to choose between a 401(k) and an IRA, which choice makes more sense?

The 401(k) plan, almost always. This decision is truly a no-brainer if your IRA contributions aren't tax deductible and/or your employer provides a matching contribution to your 401(k) plan. A 401(k) with an employer's match is a much better deal than an IRA that has no matching contribution and won't reduce your current income tax bill.

In fact, unless you're uncomfortable with the 401(k) plan's investment options, it's a better deal even if you don't have an employer match and your IRA contributions are fully tax-deductible. The reason: depending on your salary, a 401(k) plan may let you save up to $9,240 a year. Your maximum annual IRA contribution is limited to $2,000.

It's also easier to save in a 401(k) plan than in an IRA and for a very simple reason: your 401(k) contributions are taken out of your paycheck automatically. Saving in an IRA requires a continuing conscious decision and self-discipline that many of us don't have.

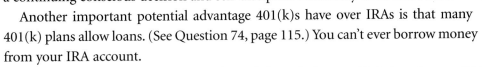

PG. 115

Another important potential advantage 401(k)s have over IRAs is that many 401(k) plans allow loans. (See Question 74, page 115.) You can't ever borrow money from your IRA account.

On the other hand, it is easier to take withdrawals from an IRA than from a 401(k) plan.

PG. 111 You cannot withdraw money from a 401(k) plan before you reach age 59½ unless you qualify for an Internal Revenue Service-approved financial hardship claim. (See Question 66, page 111.)

You don't have to demonstrate a specific, desperate need to make an IRA withdrawal—or even a respectable one. If you want to, you can take money out of your IRA for no better reason than to have a good time at the race track! But an early withdrawal from your IRA is just as expensive as a hardship withdrawal from your 401(k) plan. You'll owe income taxes plus a 10% penalty on what you take out. These taxes could easily add up to 50% of your withdrawal.

33 My spouse and I are both eligible to participate in 401(k) plans at work. We can't afford to put the maximum contribution into both plans. How do we decide how much of our limited retirement money to put into each plan?

You'll have to compare the two plans carefully. Here are the factors you should consider: 1) the amount of each employer's matching contribution; 2) how soon each of you will be fully vested in those matching contributions; 3) how much you like the investment choices available to you in each plan; and 4) which plan allows you to borrow money if you're likely to need a loan.

All things being equal, you should make the maximum contribution to the 401(k) plan with the higher matching contribution. But all things may not be equal. Perhaps one of you is less likely to stay with his or her present employer long enough to become fully vested; it may make more sense to opt for a plan that has a lower matching contribution if you're a lot likelier to become vested in that contribution.

One plan may feature a greater range of investment choices than the other one, or may include investments that have performed better. Be very careful when you compare the investment performance of two 401(k) plan accounts to make sure you're looking at truly comparable investments.

Don't compare a mutual fund that buys bonds with a mutual fund that buys stocks, for example; and when you compare two bond funds, make sure they're the same kind of bond fund. An intermediate-term bond fund buys bonds with an average 5 to 7-year maturity. You shouldn't compare its performance with that of a long-term bond fund, which buys bonds with 15 to 25-year maturities. (For a list of different types of mutual funds, a description of

PG.123 what they invest in and guidelines to use in judging their performances, see pages 123-136.)

You also want to be sure you're looking at how the two funds you're comparing have performed during the same period of time—and that you've subtracted any contributions you made during that time. If you don't do that, you may attribute a rising balance in one fund to better performance when the real reason is simply that you put more money into that account.

Finally, consider whether or not you can borrow from your 401(k) account. Not PG. 115 all 401(k) plans allow you do to this. (See Question 74, page 115.) If you anticipate that you'll need to borrow from your retirement nest egg to cover a major expense—the cost of a college tuition or a down payment on a house—a loan feature could be the determining factor in choosing one 401(k) plan over the other.

Be very careful when you compare the investment performance of two 401(k) plan accounts to make sure you're looking at truly comparable investments.

MOVING YOUR 401(k) ACCOUNT WHEN YOU CHANGE JOBS

The most important single 401(k) tax rule is: *never ever move money out of your 401(k) plan, even into another tax-sheltered account, without first consulting both your human resources or personnel department and your tax accountant about the possible tax consequences.* The money you save will be your own.

Here are answers to some of the most commonly asked 401(k) questions involving taxes.

 34 **Can I roll a 401(k) account from my previous job into the plan I have now?**
Sometimes. Some plans allow you to do this and some plans don't. Assuming your current 401(k) plan does accept rollovers from other plans, the money must be transferred into the plan directly from your previous employer's 401(k) plan or from a rollover Individual Retirement Account. (See Question 37, page 95.) Remember, if this money has passed through any type of account other than a 401(k) plan or a rollover IRA, it's tainted as far as the Internal Revenue Service is concerned. That means it can't be put back into a 401(k) plan.

 35 **If I change jobs, can I leave my money invested in my current employer's 401(k) plan until I retire?**
It depends on the size of your vested account balance. If you have more than $3,500 in the plan and you're under age 65 (or in some cases 62), you have the legal right to leave it where it is. But if your vested balance is less than $3,500, your employer has the right to pay it

PG. 95

to you whether you want it or not. You get to choose how to take that distribution, however.

It can be made directly to you, or to another employer's 401(k) plan, or to a rollover IRA. *Do not* have the money paid directly to you; ask your employer to have it transferred directly to another employer's 401(k) plan or to a rollover IRA. (See Questions 37 and 38, page 95.)

If you've made after-tax 401(k) contributions (see Question 27, page 87), those contribu-
 tions can't be rolled over into an IRA. Ask your employer to return directly to you any after-tax contributions you made to the plan. You won't owe any tax on this money because you've already paid it. But you can and should roll the interest earned by your after-tax contributions into an IRA along with your pre-tax contributions and earnings, and your employer's matching contributions and their earnings.

36 **If I change jobs but I decide to leave my 401(k) account at my former company, can I keep putting money into it?**

No. You can only make pre-tax 401(k) contributions from the salary paid by the plan sponsor. Technically, you participate in the plan by authorizing your employer to take a specific amount out of your compensation and put it into your 401(k) account. In fact, 401(k) plans used to be called salary reduction plans for that very reason.

37 **What if I prefer not to leave my money in this plan—how do I take it out without having to pay taxes on it?**

Have it transferred directly into a rollover Individual Retirement Account and you will preserve its tax-deferred status.

There's a very important difference between a rollover IRA and a regular IRA: *a rollover IRA contains only money that originally came from a 401(k) plan, or other qualified pension plan.*

There are two reasons it's important to keep money from your 401(k) in a separate rollover IRA instead of in a regular IRA. The first is that by using a rollover IRA, you preserve your legal right to transfer this money into another 401(k) plan at a future date. The second is that using the rollover IRA preserves your legal right to favorable tax treatment for this money when you retire. (See page 58.)

Don't make additional contributions to your rollover IRA in the future or you lose those rights. You can always save money in a regular IRA instead.

PG. 95

PG. 87

PG. 58

There's a very important difference between a rollover IRA and a regular IRA: a rollover IRA contains only money that originally came from a 401(k) plan, or other qualified pension plan.

38 **Why is it important to transfer money directly from a 401(k) account to a rollover Individual Retirement Account? Can't I have a check made out to me and then deposit it in a rollover IRA within 60 days?**

You can do that—but if you do, your 401(k) distribution is subject to a mandatory 20% withholding tax.

This means that if your 401(k) account is worth $100,000, you'll get a check for $80,000. The tax is withheld just in case you change your mind about opening that IRA account. If you really do deposit $100,000 in an IRA within sixty days, then the $20,000 that was withheld will be refunded to you by April or May of the following year.

But in the meantime, you face a classic Catch-22 dilemma. How can you deposit $100,000, when all you received from your 401(k) plan is $80,000?

Unless you happen to have a spare $20,000 lying around that you can add to your IRA deposit, you're going to be taxed exactly as if you had taken a $20,000 withdrawal. In other words, if you deposit only the $80,000 you received in the IRA, the government will add $20,000 to your taxable income for the year.

The upshot is that you don't get a $20,000 refund. If you're in the 28% bracket, you get back only $14,400. If you're under age 59½, you'll also owe a 10% early withdrawal penalty, so you get back only $12,400.

If you're leaving your job, don't do anything with the money in your 401(k) plan account until you've opened a rollover IRA. Then have your 401(k) plan administrator do a direct, trustee-to-trustee transfer into your new account. Talk to your human resources or personnel department about this. They're very aware of the 20% withholding rule and will be happy to accommodate your request for a direct transfer to a rollover IRA.

39 **Is there a dollar limit on how much 401(k) money I can transfer to an IRA?**

No. You can roll your entire 401(k) balance into an IRA, provided it contains no after-tax contributions. Any after-tax contributions can't be rolled into an IRA. Take them as a distribution; you've already paid the taxes on that money so it won't cost you anything.

40 **How do I decide whether it makes more sense to leave my money in the company plan or switch it to an IRA when I change jobs?**

It depends on how satisfied you are with your current company plan, and how much investment freedom and responsibility you feel comfortable with.

An IRA gives you unlimited investment choice and the freedom to change investments whenever you want to. That can be attractive or it can be just plain overwhelming, depending on how confident you are about your ability to make those decisions.

In a 401(k) plan, you're limited to the investment choices offered by the plan sponsor and you can only switch your money among those investments as often as the plan rules permit.

If you're leaving your job, don't do anything with the money in your 401(k) plan account until you've opened a rollover IRA. Then have your 401(k) plan administrator do a direct, trustee-to-trustee, transfer into your new account.

RULES ON 401(k) DISTRIBUTIONS

You probably won't think about how you will withdraw your 401(k) account money until you're within a few years of retirement. If you are nearing retirement, you have several key decisions to make about how to take your plan distributions when you do retire. You have a number of financial options. Take time to weigh the pros and cons of each one before you decide what's best for you.

41 What happens to my 401(k) account when I retire?

You get it all. But that still leaves you with several important choices to consider and discuss with your spouse, human resources or personnel department, financial advisor and tax accountant. Rules vary from one plan to another but your choices usually include one or more of the following:

A. You could take all your money in a lump sum. If you do, you'll owe income taxes on all of it. But under current tax law, you may get a special break when this lump sum comes from a 401(k) or a rollover IRA: you can often lower the applicable tax rate by using a calculation called five-year averaging.[1] The government gives you a break on the rate in exchange for collecting tax on the entire amount up front, instead of waiting to collect it little by little as it will if you take IRA distributions.

The advantage of taking your money out in a lump sum is that in some cases you get to pay a substantially lower tax on it than you would normally owe. The disadvantage is that

---

[1] Consult your tax advisor for an explanation of how five-year averaging may be beneficial to you. A common misconception is that the tax on a distribution can be paid over a five-year period; this is incorrect. The tax must be paid in one shot.

after you've taken the lump sum distribution, your money is no longer in a tax-deferred retirement account. That means that the only way to avoid tax on any future earnings is to invest it in tax-exempt instruments.

B. Some plans give you the option of taking a 401(k) payout in the form of a lifetime annuity. An annuity pays a monthly benefit for your lifetime alone or, if you choose a joint-and-survivor annuity, for your lifetime and your spouse's. (For more on joint-and-survivor annuities, see pages 59 and 60.) The advantage of an annuity is that it provides a guaranteed lifetime benefit. The disadvantage is that, because it's a fixed benefit, its purchasing power will be reduced every year by inflation.

C. You could leave some, or all, of the money in your 401(k) plan. You must have at least $3,500 in your account to do this. This choice makes sense if you like the investments available in the plan and the plan rules permit withdrawals that are frequent enough to meet your needs.

D. You could roll your entire balance into an IRA. You can take out money as you need it, paying income taxes only on the amount you withdraw. This gives you more flexibility than any other option. Most of your money will continue to be sheltered in a tax-deferred account. You'll have unlimited choice of investments for that account and you'll be able to change investments at will.

42 **If I roll my 401(k) money into a rollover IRA, when must I start taking money out of that new account?**

Not later than April 1 of the year after you turn 70 ½ years old. In other words, if you turned 70½ in 1994, you'd have to start taking withdrawals by April 1, 1995. This rule applies even if you're still employed.

43 **How much do I have to take out?**

It depends on your life expectancy. (The IRS thoughtfully provides an actuarial table showing how long it expects you to live. See page 61.) You calculate your minimum required distribution by dividing your account balance by the number of years remaining in your life expectancy or by the joint life expectancy of you and your spouse.

Experts say it's worth doing the calculation both ways to see which is better for you. You come up with very different mandatory withdrawal amounts depending on whether you use one life expectancy or two.

PG. 59

You could roll your money into an IRA. This gives you more flexibility than any other option.

You can do this calculation annually because your life expectancy changes every year, or you can choose to lock in a specific number of years over which you will take distributions. (See pages 61 and 62.) You must pay taxes on these mandatory distributions; you can't roll them into an IRA.

 44 **What happens if I don't start taking money out of my account at age 70½?**
You'll regret it. The penalties are severe. The IRS hits you with a 50% excise tax on the difference between what you withdrew from your account and what you should have withdrawn from your account. And you'll owe that excise tax annually until you've made the appropriate withdrawal. In other words, if you should have taken $10,000 from your retirement account and you didn't, you'll owe the IRS $5,000 a year until you take out that $10,000. (When you do take it out, of course, you'll owe income taxes on it.)

This could wipe out your savings in just a few years.

45 **How long after I retire will it take me to get my 401(k) money?**
There's no legal requirement that you must be paid by a specific date. The law just says that your plan must pay you within 60 days after the end of the plan year during which you reach retirement age. Any benefit payment procedures your employer establishes within that guideline are okay, as long as they are uniform and non-discriminatory.

 46 **I am retired and when I got my 401(k) money, the amount was based on the value of my account as of two months earlier. Why didn't I receive any interest for those last two months?**
This is a common complaint, although the time lag you're describing varies from one plan to another. But you aren't being short-changed.

Any 401(k) distribution you receive is based on the most recent valuation of your account. (Valuation is the determination of the exact dollar value of each participant's account on a given date.) Theoretically, your withdrawal and the valuation date match perfectly. But in real life, there's an information lag. If your withdrawal is on December 31, for example, the plan's recordkeeper may not know the exact value of your account on December 31 until several weeks later.

The more frequently a 401(k) plan values accounts, the shorter the time lag. Theoretically, there is no time lag in a plan that is valued daily. In reality, participants don't always receive a distribution check that includes interest up to the date the check was cut.

So what happens to the lost interest? It's credited back to the plan and shared by all the participants. In other words, you have benefitted from this time lag in the past when other people left the plan. In fact, if you've been in the plan for a long time and many other people have left, you may even be ahead of the game.

Your retirement benefit in a 401(k) is exactly equal to the market value of the assets in your account.

HOW SAFE IS MY MONEY?

A 401(k) account can grow very quickly into a substantial sum. The bigger it gets, the more likely you are to ask "Is this money safe?" The answer is yes. Your contributions and their earnings are held in a trust that can't be breached by your employer or (if he goes bankrupt) by his creditors.

But is this safety absolutely guaranteed? No. Unlike a traditional defined benefit pension, your 401(k) plan isn't backed by a federal government promise to make good on investment losses. But there's a reason for that.

Read on.

47 **Does the government guarantee my 401(k) account?**

No. There's no federal agency like the Pension Benefit Guaranty Corporation that guarantees 401(k) benefits. There isn't a need for one.

The PBGC was set up to guarantee pension benefits in case defined benefit plan assets aren't sufficient to pay the promised retirement benefits. Remember, the promised benefits are specific monthly amounts, based on the covered employee's salary and years of service. (See Question 1, page 74.)

PG. 74

That kind of short-fall isn't a risk in a 401(k) plan because your retirement benefit from the plan will never be greater than the assets in your account. In fact, your retirement benefit in a 401(k) is exactly equal to the market value of the assets in your account.

How much or how little your accumulated balance will be worth when you reach retirement is determined by the amount of your contributions and the performance of the investments you choose. You could lose money if your investments perform badly. There is no government guarantee to protect you from investment losses. You may be reassured to learn, however, that a government agency, the Pension and Welfare Benefits Administration, part of the U.S. Department of Labor, is responsible for seeing that employers and 401(k) plan trustees play by all the rules.

48 Do employers guarantee 401(k) accounts?

No. Employers are fiduciaries of 401(k) plans. That means they are legally responsible for supervising your money. They are obligated to protect your financial interests by choosing reputable and competent plan trustees, administrators and investment managers and continuously monitoring their performance of their duties.

If employers choose to follow the voluntary 404(c) regulations established by the Department of Labor, they must give plan participants at least three distinctly different investment choices, each of which has a different level of risk. You must also be given the opportunity to move your money among these investments at least quarterly, and sufficient information to make sensible, informed investment decisions.

But your employer doesn't offer you protection against any investment losses you may suffer.

49 What happens to my account if I'm fired?

That's no different than if you leave your current employment for another job, as far as your 401(k) account is concerned. (See pages 94-97.) If your vested account balance is more than $3,500, you may leave your money invested in the plan.

PG. 94

50 What happens if my employer is acquired by another company?

Several different things can happen, depending on the circumstances. The buyer may own other business units that are covered by a single 401(k) plan. In that case, your company may be required as a new business unit to join the same plan. After the sale is completed, your new 401(k) contributions may have to go into the new company's plan, and the existing account balances in the old plan probably will be transferred to the new one.

On the other hand, the buyer may prefer to have each business unit maintain its own benefit program. In that case, your old 401(k) plan might be retained with little or no change.

The new owner may also decide to terminate the plan if the other business units it owns don't have a 401(k) plan. If your plan is terminated, you can preserve the tax-deferred status of your account by having the current 401(k) plan administrator transfer your money directly into a rollover Individual Retirement Account for you. (See pages 95 and 96.)

PG. 95

51 What happens if my employer goes out of business?

Your money won't be in danger if your employer's business fails.

As plan fiduciaries, employers are legally required to put 401(k) money into a separate trust account or into a contract with an insurance company within a reasonable amount of time after it has been deducted from their employees' salaries. A trust is a separate legal entity from the company and will continue to exist even if the company goes out of business.

The plan trustees are responsible for managing the money in the plan until all benefits have been paid to the participants. The money in the trust is invested in the different investment choices that are offered by the plan as the participants direct; but no matter how many different investments the plan offers, the money is still in a trust. Your employer's creditors have no legal claim to these funds.

52 What happens to my account if I'm disabled?

If you're totally disabled and can't work, you can tap your 401(k) money without being charged a 10% early withdrawal penalty regardless of your age. But you will owe ordinary income taxes on any money you take out.

If you're disabled, you may also be able to take out any matching contributions your employer made even if you haven't completed the years of service normally required for vesting. Most plans provide for full vesting whenever a participant becomes disabled. But each plan has its own definition of what's required to qualify for disability. Ask your human resources or personnel department about your plan's rules.

If your plan does provide full vesting for disabled employees and your employment is terminated as a result of a qualifying disability, you'll receive your vested account balance—your contributions and your employer's contributions and what they earned. If your plan doesn't have a disability feature, or if you don't meet the plan's definition of disability, your distributions from the plan will be processed the same as those of other former employees.

53 **What happens to my 401(k) account when I die?**

When you join your 401(k) plan you must designate a beneficiary who'll receive the money in your account when you die. (If you don't do this, your estate automatically becomes the beneficiary.)

If your beneficiary is your spouse, he or she gets most of the same options with this money that you would have if you were leaving the company: rolling the distribution into an IRA or withdrawing it all and paying income taxes on it. (See Question 41, page 98.) If your survivor elects to withdraw the money and pay taxes on it, the IRS will not impose the 10% early withdrawal penalty, regardless of his or her age.

But unlike a plan participant who is leaving the company, a spouse beneficiary usually doesn't have the option of keeping this money invested in the 401(k) plan. (Different rules apply in the case of divorced spouses, see Question 56, page 106.) A non-spouse beneficiary has fewer options. He or she doesn't have the option of rolling your 401(k) balance into an IRA, for example.

Most plans provide for full vesting when you die, so chances are that any matching contributions made by your employer will be included in the distribution to your beneficiary. If yours doesn't fully vest at death, the amount your beneficiary gets will be determined in the same way as for other former employees.

54 **Can my spouse empty my 401(k) account without my knowledge?**

No. Your spouse can't touch a penny of your retirement account unless you die or get divorced. (See Question 56, page 106.)

Your husband or wife is legally entitled to be the designated beneficiary of your 401(k) account. In fact, the Internal Revenue Code says that on all qualified retirement plans (including IRAs), your spouse must be the named beneficiary unless he or she has signed a consent waiver surrendering the right.

55 **Can I empty my 401(k) account without my spouse knowing about it?**

Maybe not. If your plan follows joint-and-survivor rules, your spouse is legally entitled to the option of receiving a share of your retirement payout in the form of lifetime annuity payments. If that's the case, your plan may require that your spouse approve any loans or hardship withdrawals you take from your account.

56 **If I get divorced, is my spouse entitled to a share of my 401(k) account?**

In all probability, yes. The money that you accumulated in the account during your marriage is considered a marital asset, and marital assets are divided between divorcing spouses. The formula for dividing those assets depends partly on your specific circumstances and partly on the laws of the state in which you live.

In community property states, marital assets in general are split 50/50. This doesn't mean each specific asset is cut in half, but rather that the entire marital estate is divided. The community property states are Arizona, California, Idaho, Louisiana, Nevada, New Mexico, Texas, Washington and Wisconsin.

In equitable distribution states, marital assets are divided equitably—i.e., fairly, which doesn't necessarily mean a 50/50 split. The ultimate decision of what's fair is made by the court. In general, the court determines how much of your pension plan is a marital asset by dividing the number of years you've been married by the number of years you've been a plan participant. For example, if you've been married for two years and a plan participant for three years, two-thirds of your pension would be considered a marital asset. All other things being equal, your spouse would get half of that two-thirds.

After the court has divided your 401(k) account between you and your former husband or wife, it issues a qualified domestic relations order (QDRO). The order requires your 401(k) plan administrator to split your account into two parts. Your former spouse gets all the normal rights of any other plan participant over his or her share, including the right to leave the money invested in the 401(k) plan, unless the court order specifies that it must be paid out immediately.

If your ex-spouse opts not to roll his or her share into an IRA, the money will be subject to income tax; but in a divorce situation, the IRS waives the 10% early withdrawal penalty that would normally be levied on any distribution made to a participant under age 59½.

A divorce court can also order that part of your 401(k) balance go to your children. If that happens, the children can't roll the money into an IRA; taxes will be due on it. The kids don't have to pay the taxes, however. You do.

It's your plan administrator's responsibility to make sure any QDRO fully satisfies all legal requirements before taking any action to divide your account in two.

A divorce court can order that part of your 401(k) balance go to your children. If that happens, the children can't roll the money into an IRA; taxes will be due on it. The kids don't have to pay the taxes, however. You do.

57 **Is my account protected from my creditors if I file for bankruptcy?**

It depends. What you get to keep when you file for bankruptcy depends on state law. Each state has a different list of assets that are exempt. When you file for bankruptcy, some states give you the choice of selecting either the state's list of exempt assets or the list of exempt assets that is included in the federal bankruptcy law.

If you live in a state that gives you that option and you choose the exemptions listed in the federal law, your 401(k) account is protected from creditors if the court finds that considering: 1) your age; 2) the debts you can't avoid even by filing for bankruptcy; 3) your other assets; 4) your dependents; and 5) your future employment prospects, this money is "reasonably necessary" for your support.

But most states only permit you to use the exemptions in their own laws which may or may not exempt 401(k) assets.

Some people assume that 401(k) accounts are protected because of a 1992 ruling by the U.S. Supreme Court (Patterson v. Schumate) which said that retirement assets qualifying under ERISA—most pension plans, including 401(k)s—can't be touched by creditors in a bankruptcy. The Court said a major reason for its ruling is that the debtor has such limited access to those assets.

But unfortunately, it is still unresolved whether the Court's ruling does apply to 401(k)s, which give participants much more access to their money—through loans and hardship withdrawals—than a traditional pension does.

Because there are so many variables, it's a mistake to file for bankruptcy without finding out specifically how it might affect your accumulated retirement assets. Even in the same state, interpretation of bankruptcy law can vary from one court to another. If you contemplate filing for bankruptcy, your best recourse is to consult a lawyer in the district where you live to find out how the local courts treat 401(k) assets.

58 **Can employers use 401(k) money to run their businesses?**

No. Employers are required by law to put your money into the plan trust, to be invested as the law and plan rules direct. The company can't legally use this money for its own benefit.

HOW MUCH CONTROL DO I HAVE OVER MY 401(k) ACCOUNT?

A lot. One of the biggest attractions of a 401(k) plan is its flexibility. The amount of control you have varies from one plan to another because each plan has its own rules. (And of course, all these rules are subject to restrictions imposed by the Internal Revenue Service.) But the trend among plan sponsors today is to give employees increasing freedom in deciding how much to contribute to their accounts and how to invest their money.

 59 What if I decide I can't afford to save this much, or I want to increase the amount I save—can I change my contribution?

Yes. But you may have to wait for a specific date to do it.

Every plan has its own rules about how frequently you can change your contribution. Most plans let you do this on a specific date: at the beginning of every calendar quarter, for example, or at the start of every month. Others permit contribution changes at any time.

 60 Can I stop contributing to my account if my budget is squeezed and I just can't afford to save the money?

Yes. Most plans permit you to stop contributing at any time. But there's no legal requirement to allow this. Some plans lock each participant into a specific percentage contribution for a full plan year. Check your plan's rules with your human resources or personnel department.

 61 **Can I take my money out of the plan if I stop contributing to it?**
No. The fact that you're no longer contributing to the plan doesn't mean you can start taking withdrawals. There are only three ways to take money out of your 401(k) account—distributions, early withdrawals, and loans. You can take distributions after age 59½; you can take early withdrawals only for reasons specifically approved by the Internal Revenue Service. (See Question 66, page 111.) Whether or not you can take a loan depends on your plan's rules.

62 **Can I start contributing again after I've stopped?**
Yes. Most plans let you start contributing again on the specific date when new employees are allowed to enter the plan. But if you stopped making contributions in conjunction with taking a hardship withdrawal from the plan, you may have to stay out for at least one full year depending on your plan's specific provisions. (See pages 111-114 for more on hardship withdrawals.)

63 **Can I switch my money from one investment to another?**
Yes.

 64 **How often can I switch money among investments?**
That depends on your plan's rules. There's no legal requirement your employer has to follow when it comes to frequency of transfers between 401(k) investments.

But employers who have chosen to follow the Department of Labor's voluntary 404(c) regulations must give participants the opportunity to move their money among investment funds at least quarterly, and more frequent transfers must be permitted in instances where the plan offers a very volatile—or high risk—investment. (A very volatile investment is one whose value can change a lot, in either direction, in a very short period of time. For more on the volatility, or risk, of different investments, see pages 15-29.)

One factor that influences a 40l(k) plan's rules on frequency of transfers is the administrative cost of operating the plan. Every time participants switch between investments the administrator must determine the current value of their accounts. Until recently, most plans have valued their participant accounts on a monthly, quarterly or semi-annual basis. So participants were allowed to change their investment choices on these valuation dates.

More recently, many plans have begun to adopt daily valuation systems. Technically, this means they can allow transfers between investments on any trading day because participant account balances are updated every day. But not all plans with daily valuation permit daily transfers.

A major reason for not allowing daily transfers is that many employers worry that they might encourage some plan participants to move their money much too often, jumping into and out of different investment funds based on how they expect those funds to perform in the very short-term.

That kind of investing is called market timing: you try to move in and out of investments in time to catch the market's upward movements and avoid its downward movements. Market timing is a prescription for financial disaster. Its practitioners almost invariably wind up selling an investment that's performing poorly in order to buy one that's per- forming well. In other words, they sell low and buy high—with predictably terrible results. (For more on market timing, see pages 33-36.)

65 **An IRA seems safer than a 401(k) plan. Can I switch my money from my 401(k) into an IRA?**

Not unless you're getting a 401(k) distribution. That doesn't happen unless 1) you're leaving your job; 2) you're older than 59½; or 3) you qualify for a hardship withdrawal. (And if you do qualify for a hardship withdrawal, you'll need every dime of this money for a specific emergency—you won't have anything left to roll into an IRA. See Question 66, page 111.)

But an IRA is no safer than a 401(k) plan. Contrary to what many people assume, IRAs aren't government-guaranteed. And in most cases, an IRA isn't as good a financial deal as a 401(k) plan is. You can contribute a higher annual maximum to a 401(k) than the $2,000 you can put into an IRA, and your 401(k) contribution reduces your current taxes. Depending on what you earn, an IRA contribution might not do that. (For more on IRAs versus 401(k) plans, see pages 90-92.)

HOW CAN I TAKE MONEY OUT OF MY 401(k)?

 66 **What if I need some of this money before I retire? Can I make cash withdrawals from my account while I'm still working?**

Maybe. It depends on what you need the money for. But early withdrawals cost you twice: you'll owe a hefty tax bill on what you take out. And you'll have less when you retire. You'll lose not only the money you withdraw but also all the tax-deferred compound interest it would earn if you left it in the 401(k) plan.

Internal Revenue Service rules permit early withdrawals—withdrawals before you reach age 59½—only in cases of financial hardship and only if you've exhausted all other possible sources of money.

As far as the IRS is concerned, you can claim financial hardship if you need this money to pay for 1) college tuition for yourself or a dependent, provided that it's due within the next 12 months; 2) the down payment on a primary residence; 3) unreimbursed medical expenses for yourself or your dependents; or 4) to prevent a foreclosure or eviction from your home.

Those are the "safe harbor" rules for hardship withdrawals. That means they're not subject to IRS audit and challenge. In general, employers limit permitted withdrawals to the four reasons specifically approved in the Internal Revenue Code. But withdrawal provisions do vary from one plan to another. Some companies allow hardship withdrawals for other emergencies like funeral expenses for a relative or substantial uninsured damage to your primary residence. You'll have to ask your employer what's allowed in your own plan.

NOTE: Plans that permit after-tax contributions usually let you withdraw these contributions for any reason. They won't be subject to taxation since they've already been taxed. But any money those after-tax contributions earned in the 401(k) plan will be subject to the same constraints and taxes as your pre-tax contributions. (See Questions 27 and 28, pages 87 and 88.)

PG. 87

67 How is the 10% penalty on early withdrawals calculated?

The penalty applies to the entire untaxed amount that's distributed to you before you reach age 59½ if you are still employed. (If you are over age 55 and you're retired, you escape the early withdrawal penalty.)

In other words, if you take out $2,000 you'll owe a $200 penalty, in addition to your normal federal, state and local income taxes.

68 Why do I have to pay a penalty for withdrawing my own money?

Because this is a tax-advantaged *retirement* account, not intended to pay for pre-retirement expenses.

The tax breaks you get in a 401(k) plan are the government's carrot to encourage you to save for your retirement and to enable you to save as much as possible. The penalty for early withdrawals is the stick and it's there for the same reason.

69 How do I qualify for a hardship withdrawal?

It depends on the plan. You'll probably have to provide relevant information showing your financial need—an eviction notice, a contract to buy a primary residence, unreimbursed medical bills or a college tuition bill.

Some plans require that you sign a form stating that you have no other source of money to deal with this emergency. Other companies instead consider that you've exhausted all other resources if 1) you've have taken all permissible loans from the plan; 2) you make no plan contributions for the next 12 months; 3) you make only limited contributions in the year after that; and 4) you withdraw only as much as you need to cover the immediate emergency.

70 **Is there a dollar limit on the amount I can take in a hardship withdrawal?**

In general, you'll be limited to the amount of your own pre-tax contributions. Within that limit, you can take out whatever is necessary to satisfy your financial emergency, plus the amount that's needed to cover the taxes you'll have to pay. Be sure you don't spend what you need to cover the taxes.

 71 **What taxes will I owe on a hardship withdrawal?**

You'll owe ordinary income taxes on everything except amounts that you originally contributed to the plan on an after-tax basis. (See Question 28, page 88). You'll also owe a 10% early withdrawal tax penalty. Many people assume that if they meet the IRS definition of financial hardship they won't owe the 10% penalty. They're wrong. To avoid the penalty, you have to be in truly dire straits. (See Question 73 page 114.)

Let's say you're under age 59½ and you withdraw $20,000 from your account for a qualifying hardship situation—to make the down payment on a house, for example. If your combined federal, state and local tax rate is 40%, then $8,000 of your withdrawal will go to pay income taxes. Plus, you'll pay an additional $2,000 in early withdrawal penalty tax. So you'll wind up with only $10,000 of your $20,000 withdrawal. That's why you should consider an early withdrawal from your 401(k) plan only as a last resort. It's terribly expensive money.

 NOTE: If you are taking a hardship withdrawal, remember that your employer will only withhold 20% of your distribution for taxes. When you file your next income tax return, you'll owe the rest of the taxes due on that distribution. If you've spent it all, you'll be in a jam. To make sure you have enough to cover the taxes and penalty you'll owe the following April, either set the money aside immediately or ask your employer to withhold more than the customary 20%.

72 **Are my employer's contributions available to me if I make a hardship withdrawal, or can I only take out my own contributions?**

For plan years starting after December 31, 1988, a hardship distribution is limited to your own contributions. Your employer's contributions are usually subject to other rules for hardship withdrawals. Check to find out what rules apply in your plan.

73 **Are there any circumstances in which I can withdraw my money before I retire without paying a penalty?**

Yes. But you won't like them.

The IRS waives the penalty if 1) you're totally disabled; 2) you're dead, and your beneficiary is getting the money; 3) you're in debt for medical expenses that exceed 7.5% of your adjusted gross income; 4) the money is going to your divorced spouse by court decree; 5) you've taken early retirement and you're at least 55 years old; or 6) you set up a payment schedule for withdrawing the money in substantially equal chunks over the course of your life expectancy.

Don't forget, even if you meet these conditions and the IRS waives the 10% penalty, your withdrawals will still be subject to ordinary income taxes.

The silver lining is Option 6. That choice has more flexibility than it seems to because the payments don't really have to continue for the rest of your life. Here's how it works:

You set up a schedule for withdrawing the money in substantially equal, periodic payments over the rest of your life expectancy, or over the joint life expectancies of you and your spouse, or another beneficiary. (The IRS provides an actuarial table to help you calculate your life expectancy. See page 61.) If your life expectancy is 20 years, for example, and you have $100,000 in your account, you could take out $5,000 a year.

 Once you begin taking withdrawals, you have to stick to the payment schedule for at least five years, *and* until you reach age 59½. Then if you want to, you can stop taking withdrawals and let your money continue to grow untaxed until you reach age 70½. (See Question 42, page 99.)

This gives a lot more flexibility to older people than younger ones. If you're 30 years old for example, you have to keep taking money out until you reach age 59½. But if you're 57 years old, you only have to keep taking money out for five years. Then if you wish, you can leave the balance in your 401(k) or rollover IRA account to continue earning tax deferred interest until you reach age 70½.

BORROWING FROM MY 401(k)

74 **Can I borrow from my 401(k) account instead of making withdrawals?**

Maybe. It depends on your plan's rules. Most employers do allow plan participants to take loans, but they don't have to.

Legally, loans can be allowed for any reason. But most plans permit them only in specific, approved situations, such as if you're using the money to buy a house or pay for college tuition. Employers have two good reasons for restricting plan loans. One is that loans add to the cost of administering the plan. The other is that allowing loans for any reason can defeat a 401(k) plan's main purpose, to ensure that you retire with a substantial nest egg.

When a loan is allowed, it's definitely preferable to a withdrawal. Instead of costing you money, a 401(k) loan earns you money because you'll pay yourself interest on the amount you borrow. And borrowing from a 401(k) is easier than borrowing from a bank because there are no credit standards to meet. As a plan participant, you automatically qualify for a loan if the plan permits them.

75 **How much of my total account can I borrow?**

It depends on the plan. But the most you can borrow is half of your account balance up to $50,000. (That's the legal limit; some plans impose a lower ceiling on the total amount you can borrow.)

76 Must my spouse agree to the loan?

Maybe. Some plans follow joint-and-survivor rules, which means that you and your spouse must have the option of receiving your retirement payout in the form of lifetime annuity payments. If your plan follows these rules, your spouse may have to sign off on loans you take from the plan. Ask your human resources or personnel department what applies in your company's plan.

77 What will a loan cost me?

The IRS doesn't let your plan give you a sweetheart deal. It must charge a market rate—in other words, what a bank would charge you on the same loan. That means you'll probably pay one or two percentage points above the prime rate, which is the interest rate that banks charge their best corporate customers. Many plans also charge loan processing and administrative fees.

But you're much better off than you would be if you borrowed from a bank—even if you qualified for its prime rate—because you're paying the interest to yourself. Your loan becomes a fixed-rate investment for your 401(k) account.

78 If my money is divided among several different funds within the plan, which one should I borrow from?

Some plans tell you which fund you must borrow from. Some plans automatically take a proportionate amount from each investment in your account. Others let you make the choice.

From your 401(k) account's perspective, your loan is a fixed-rate investment. To maintain your current mix of investments, you should borrow the money from a fixed-rate fund.

Let's say that you have $45,000 in your account and it's currently divided equally between three funds: $15,000 in a diversified stock fund, $15,000 in a corporate bond fund and $15,000 in a Guaranteed Income Contract (GIC) fund. Of those three investments, only the GIC fund pays a fixed rate of return. So if you want to stay with that investment mix, you'll borrow from the GIC fund. (For more information about different types of investment funds offered in 401(k) plans and how to select an investment mix that is right for you, see pages 14-50 and 122-136.)

79 **Is the interest I pay on a 401(k) loan tax-deductible if I use the money to buy a house?**

No. Interest on home loans is only tax-deductible when the house is the collateral for the loan. A bank will take a house as collateral for a loan but a 401(k) plan will not. When you borrow from your 401(k) account, it's your remaining balance that serves as collateral for the loan.

As far as the IRS is concerned, your loan is a tax-deferred investment, like everything else your 401(k) account puts money into. Giving you a tax deduction on the interest you're paying yourself would amount to giving you a tax-break on top of a tax break. The IRS isn't that generous.

 **NOTE:** Before borrowing to buy a house, ask the local mortgage lenders if they accept 401(k) loans as down payments. Most banks don't like your borrowing down payment money because if you default on your mortgage, they don't want any other creditor coming forward with a claim on the house. But many banks make an exception for 401(k) loans because the loan comes from your own savings.

80 **How soon do I have to repay the loan?**

The loan must be repaid through a series of regular payments which are usually deducted from your paycheck automatically. The entire amount you borrowed must be repaid within five years with one exception: if you took a loan to buy a principal residence, the law says that it must be repaid in a "reasonable" period of time. Most plans give you up to 25 years to pay it back, but the term of the loan can't extend beyond your normal retirement date, as defined by the plan.

81 **Is there any drawback to taking a loan from my account that I should be aware of?**

Yes, and it can be a significant drawback, depending on your circumstances.

Very few plans allow a former employee to continue repaying a 401(k) plan loan. If you leave your job, voluntarily or involuntarily, you'll almost certainly have to repay the outstanding balance within 60 days—into the 401(k) plan or into a rollover IRA—or the IRS will treat it as an early withdrawal on which you owe income taxes and an early withdrawal penalty. If you've spent all the money, that puts you in a very tough spot.

The entire amount you borrow from your 401(k) account must be repaid within five years with one exception: you may get up to 25 years to repay a loan to buy a house.

82 **Can I use my 401(k) account as collateral for a bank loan?**

Probably not, because your 401(k) account is protected from your creditors under federal bankruptcy law. (See Question 57, page 107 for information on bankruptcy protection.)

Your 401(k) balance may improve the impression you make as a would-be borrower because it shows the lender what a hard-working, thrifty, fiscally responsible person you are. But most banks are unlikely to accept collateral that they might be legally barred from collecting if you filed for bankruptcy. (For more on how your 401(k) may be treated in a bankruptcy filing, see Question 57, page 107.)

PG. 107

MORE IMPORTANT INFORMATION ON MY 401(k)

83 **What recourse do I have if my employer and I disagree about my 401(k) account?**

Your employer is required by law to include a claims review process in which you can file a written claim with the plan administrator. That's the person or committee responsible for handling the day-to-day administration of the plan.

The plan administrator must respond to participant questions and give an explanation for any denial of benefits. If you don't find the explanation acceptable, you can request a review of the matter. If you're still not satisfied, you should seek outside support from an attorney and/or the Department of Labor.

84 **Who picks the investment manager for my company's 401(k) plan?**

The plan trustee—your employer, or an institution selected by your employer to act as trustee—is legally responsible for choosing the organization or organizations that invest the money contributed into the 401(k) plan. The choice must be based solely on the "best interest" of the plan participants. The trustee is also responsible for monitoring the investment managers' ongoing performance.

85 **Who picks the 401(k) plan investments?**

The employer, as plan sponsor, decides which investments it will offer participants.

86 **Do I get to decide how to invest all the money in my 401(k) account?**

Not necessarily. Some plans let you decide how your own contributions will be invested, but not how your employer's matching contribution to your account will be invested. In some plans, for example, the employer's matching contribution is always in company stock. (See Questions 17 and 18, page 84.)

PG. 84

87 What can I do if I don't like my plan's investment options?

Talk to your human resources or personnel department. Your employer really wants the 401(k) plan to meet your needs. (See Question 16, page 83.) Most companies are quite receptive to employee suggestions about how the 401(k) plan could be improved; in fact, many employers periodically survey their plan participants to find out how the plan can be made even more responsive to their needs.

PG. 83

On the other hand, don't expect the plan to be tailored to your preferences if they aren't shared by most other plan participants. Your employer may well consider adding an international fund to the 401(k) plan menu if many employees express interest in it, for example, but that doesn't mean you'll succeed in talking him into offering a little fund that specializes in Mongolian oil stock futures.

88 How many investment options must be offered in a 401(k) plan?

The Department of Labor has issued regulatory guidelines to help employers choose the investment menu they offer. But there's no legal requirement that a 401(k) plan has to offer a specific number of investments.

The Department of Labor guidelines, commonly called 404(c) regulations, recommend that employers offer at least three distinct investment choices—investments with notably different risk and reward characteristics. One example of three distinct investments is a money market fund, a stock fund, and a bond fund. (For an explanation of how these three types of funds differ, see pages 15-23.)

PG. 15

The 404(c) guidelines are voluntary; employers aren't penalized if they don't follow them. But even employers who haven't adopted the guidelines usually offer at least three 401(k) plan investment options. Many plans offer eight or nine. Most employers are reluctant to offer more than eight or nine investment choices; they believe that participants confronted with too many investment options will wind up feeling confused and overwhelmed, rather than well-served.

PART FIVE

WHAT ARE YOUR INVESTMENT CHOICES?

Understanding your plan's investment options

As a mutual fund shareholder, you get a proportionate slice of the fund's profits and losses, as well as a proportionate share of any dividends it earns on its investments.

UNDERSTANDING YOUR PLAN'S INVESTMENT OPTIONS

Typically, you get a choice of either mutual funds, insurance company separate accounts, or bank commingled trust accounts. There are technical differences between these three investment vehicles, but from a plan participant's viewpoint, commingled accounts and separate accounts are almost indistinguishable from a mutual fund. You may notice one or two differences: unlike mutual funds, commingled accounts and separate accounts aren't available to retail investors. Therefore, they usually don't have prospectuses and aren't listed in the daily newspapers. They're also less likely than mutual funds to be valued daily and often charge lower investment management fees.

The most commonly offered 401(k) investments are mutual funds. Mutual funds are run by investment management companies which pool the money of thousands of investors to buy specific types of investments. Some mutual funds offer broadly diversified stock and/or bond portfolios, while others specialize in the stocks of specific industries—technology or health care companies, for example. Through mutual funds, you can invest in every variety of U.S. and foreign stocks and bonds, as well as in real estate, gold and other precious metals and commodities like forest products and natural gas.

HOW DOES A MUTUAL FUND WORK?

When you put money into a mutual fund, you're buying fund shares whose value rises and falls depending on how the mutual fund's investments perform. The price of a mutual fund share is called its Net Asset Value, or NAV.

As a shareholder, you get a proportionate slice of the fund's profits and losses, as well as a proportionate share of any dividends it earns on its investments. If you invest in a mutual fund outside a 401(k), you might opt to take your dividends in cash. You can't do that in a 401(k) plan because withdrawals from the plan are very strictly limited by law. (See Question 66, page 111.) Any dividends you earn in a mutual fund in your 401(k) are automatically reinvested in more fund shares.

By pooling their money, a mutual fund gives people who have only a few hundred dollars to invest the same advantages as corporate investors and very wealthy individuals: a professional portfolio manager, a research staff and the ability to diversify. As a fund shareholder, you're investing in hundreds of different stocks or bonds instead of only a handful. That makes you much less vulnerable to the poor performance of any one stock or bond.

Your expenses are also lower as a fund shareholder than as an individual investor. A mutual fund commands lower fees because it buys and sells stocks and bonds in such huge volume. This matters—because assuming equal investment performance, the lower your expenses, the bigger the return on your investments.

89 What investments does my plan offer?

Most 401(k) plans offer a limited selection of investment choices. These typically include at least one from each of the three main asset categories (see pages 15-23). The most commonly offered choices include:

Cash Equivalents/Stable Value
➢ Money market fund
➢ Guaranteed Investment
   Contract (GIC) fund

Fixed-Income
➢ Government bond fund
➢ Corporate bond or income fund

Asset category blends
➢ Balanced fund
➢ Lifestyle or asset allocation fund

Growth
➢ Growth and income fund
➢ Growth fund
➢ Aggressive growth fund
➢ Index fund
➢ International fund
➢ Emerging markets fund

WHAT ARE THE MAIN ADVANTAGES AND DISADVANTAGES OF EACH OF THESE INVESTMENTS?

90 What is a stable value or GIC fund?

A GIC, or guaranteed investment contract, is a short-term loan that you and your fellow 401(k) plan participants make to an insurance company. The insurance company guarantees you a fixed interest rate for the term of the loan, usually from one to five years. The insurer guarantees to pay the interest on time and return your principal at the end of the contract term.

A GIC fund is a pool of GICs from different insurers. A certain percentage of the fund's assets will mature and be reinvested every year. The fund may pay a fixed rate for a year at a time, or it may change its rate on a much more frequent basis as it buys new contracts.

If GICs sound familiar, it may be because they're very much like Certificates of Deposit. But there's an important difference: GICs are guaranteed only by the insurance company that issues them, not by the federal government or by your employer. Your assurance of timely interest payments and return of principal depends on the issuer's ability to honor its guarantee. If the insurer fails, GIC investors may be forced to accept a lower interest rate than they were promised and may have to wait longer than expected to get their principal back—and they may never get it all back.

This doesn't happen often, but it does happen: since 1991, three reputable insurers[1] that sold GICs have faltered or failed financially and have been taken over by regulatory authorities.

An insurer's ability to honor its obligations is reflected in credit ratings from organizations like Standard & Poor's, Moody's Corp., and Duff & Phelps. If your 401(k) plan offers a GIC fund, your human resources department can tell you how the issuing insurer or insurers are rated by these agencies. (For more on credit ratings, see page 17.)

PG.17

91 What are GIC funds' main advantages and disadvantages?

The main advantage of a GIC fund is stability of principal. This is a fancy way of saying that the value of your original investment doesn't fluctuate as it would in a stock or bond fund. (In fact, a GIC fund is sometimes called a stable value fund.) If you invest

---

[1] In 1991, Executive Life Insurance Company and Mutual Benefit Life Insurance Company; and in 1994, Confederation Life Insurance Company.

$1,000 for example, your investment's value won't ever fall below $1,000. (For more on stability of principal in GICs and other investments, see pages 15-23.)

Your risk of losing your original investment in a GIC fund is low because the term of the loan you're making to the insurer is so short.

The big disadvantage is that your principal doesn't grow enough in a GIC fund to withstand the ravages of inflation. Many plan participants like the fact that with a GIC fund, they know in advance exactly what rate of interest they'll earn. But although this may be a peace-of-mind advantage, it isn't really a financial advantage: typically, a 401(k) investment must meet a goal that is many years away, and a GIC's pre-determined interest rate is guaranteed only for a short term.

History shows that for a goal that's ten years or more into the future, you're likely to earn a better return in a mixture of stock and bond investments than in cash equivalent investments or GICs. (See chart, page 33.)

92 What is a money market fund?

A fund that invests in very short-term, high quality loans. It's a way for you to buy Treasury Bills, bank Certificates of Deposit, and commercial paper (the very short-term IOUs of corporations with excellent credit ratings). You earn a fluctuating interest rate in a money market fund because the fund is constantly buying and selling these loans. This can be an advantage or a disadvantage, depending on which way interest rates move.

Your original investment, or principal, remains stable. It's converted into shares with a fixed value of $1 each. This is different from a stock or a bond mutual fund, in which your share price fluctuates depending on how well or how poorly the fund's investments perform.

The main advantage of a money market fund is this stability of principal. Another plus is that your investment is more diversified than it is in a GIC fund because you're lending to a wide range of corporate borrowers and to the federal government. In a GIC fund, you are lending to borrowers only within one industry: the insurance industry.

The main disadvantage of a money market fund is that your principal doesn't grow. It's very vulnerable to inflation, just as it is in a GIC fund. History shows that after inflation and taxes, a money market fund investment like Treasury Bills barely grows at all over periods of ten years or more. (See chart on page 29.)

History shows that for an investment goal ten years or more into the future, you're likely to earn a better return in a mixture of stock and bond investments than in cash equivalent investments or GICs.

93 Why doesn't my 401(k) plan allow me to transfer money from a GIC fund to a money market fund?

Many plans restrict direct transfers from a GIC fund to a money market fund.

The fixed rate you earn on a GIC is conditional on leaving your money invested for the term of the contract. Insurers that sell GICs to 401(k) plans often don't allow you to switch out to take advantage of a higher money market rate before the contract expires.

The reason: GICs are backed by long-term investments whose predictable income lets the insurer offer a relatively high fixed rate on its short-term GICs. If GIC investors cash out early because interest rates have gone up, the insurer might have to sell long-term investments at a loss to give them their money.

94 What is a government bond fund?

A mutual fund that buys IOUs issued by the U.S. government and/or its agencies. The federal government issues three basic IOUs: 1) Treasury Bills, which mature in one year or less; 2) Treasury Notes, which mature in one to ten years; and 3) Treasury Bonds, which mature in ten years or longer.

The interest on these government loans is lower than the interest on corporate bonds of similar maturities because there's virtually no risk that the federal government and its agencies will default on their loans. (Unlike corporations, the government can always raise money by increasing taxes or imposing new ones.) *But just because there's no default risk doesn't mean that government bonds or government bond funds are risk-free.*

If you buy an 8% government bond and hold it to maturity, you get a fixed 8% yield for the life of the bond. But if you buy shares in a government bond fund, your interest isn't fixed because a mutual fund doesn't hold bonds to maturity. The fund is constantly buying and selling bonds. The interest earned by fund shareholders fluctuates.

The value of your principal in a government bond fund doesn't remain fixed, either. It rises and falls as interest rates change. If the prevailing interest rate goes up, the value of your principal—and the Net Asset Value (NAV) of your fund shares—will go down. Rising interest rates always reduce the value of existing bonds. Why? Because no one will pay full price for a $1,000 bond that pays 7% if newly issued $1,000 bonds are paying 8%.

If you think that all of this means that the term "fixed-income fund" is somewhat misleading, you are perfectly right. Neither interest nor principal value is fixed in a fixed-income fund.

The risk that your principal will shrink because of rising interest rates is called **interest rate risk.** All bonds carry interest rate risk, including government bonds.

Don't judge a bond fund's performance by yield alone. Always look at total return: the yield plus or minus any changes in the value of your principal as reflected in the price of your shares. As junk bond fund investors discovered when interest rates rose in 1989 and 1990, a bond fund can pay a very high yield but have a terrible total return. The result: investors earn high interest while their principal dwindles away.

Some government bond funds also have **pre-payment risk.** These are funds that buy mortgage-backed bonds from government agencies like the Government National Mortgage Association, commonly known as Ginnie Mae. Some mutual funds specialize in Ginnie Mae bonds. Other government agency bonds are Freddie Macs (issued by the Federal Home Loan Mortgage Corporation) and Fannie Maes (issued by the Federal National Mortgage Association).

The stream of income paid by Ginnie Maes, Fannie Maes and Freddie Macs comes from homeowners' mortgage payments. The mortgages in question are guaranteed by federal agencies, so there's no default risk.

But there are other risks. Most mortgage-backed bonds have 30-year maturities, but in reality they mature much faster. The reason: homeowners prepay their mortgages when they move or when they refinance because interest rates have gone down. In reality, a 30-year mortgage typically is repaid in seven years when the average house is sold or the mortgage is refinanced.

This makes mortgage-backed bonds particularly vulnerable to interest rate changes. Like all bonds, they lose value when interest rates rise. But they also lose value when interest rates fall significantly because millions of homeowners refinance. They pay off the mortgages backing Ginnie Maes and other mortgage-backed bonds and take out new mortgages at the prevailing lower rate. When that happens, investors in Ginnie Mae bonds get their principal back much sooner than they expected and must reinvest it at a lower interest rate.

Ginnie Maes and other mortgage-backed bonds typically yield somewhat more than other government bonds to compensate investors for this pre-payment risk.

95   What is a corporate bond fund?

A mutual fund that buys the IOUs of corporations.

Short-term bond funds usually buy bonds with a maturity of less than three years.

Intermediate-term bond funds invest in bonds that mature in three to ten years. Long-term bond funds usually have a maturity of ten years or longer.

You usually earn higher interest on corporate bond funds than on government bond funds of similar maturities because even a top-rated corporation isn't as sure to repay its loans as the federal government.

Although bond funds are also called fixed-income funds, the interest you receive in a bond mutual fund isn't fixed at all; it fluctuates constantly as the fund buys and sells bonds. The value of your principal investment also fluctuates: your shares increase in value when interest rates fall, making old bonds that pay a higher rate more valuable. Your shares lose value when interest rates rise because newly issued bonds now pay a higher rate than old ones. (For more on how interest rates affect principal in a bond investment, see page 18.)

The longer the maturity of a bond, the more value it gains if interest rates fall, and the more value it loses if interest rates rise. Long-term bond funds are much more volatile than short or intermediate bond funds, because they react more dramatically to changes in interest rates.

Your total return from any bond fund is the interest you earn, plus or minus any changes in the value of your principal, as reflected in the market price of your fund shares.

96 What are the advantages and disadvantages of bond funds?

The advantage of short to intermediate-term bond funds is that they provide a steady stream of income, while keeping your principal fairly safe. Short to intermediate-term bond funds also tend to be less volatile than stock funds, so keeping part of your 401(k) account in a bond fund can help lower the overall volatility of your portfolio.

A long-term bond fund involves more risk. It provides a relatively high stream of income and has a potentially higher total return than shorter-term bond funds. If interest rates fall, the value of long-term bonds can grow quite dramatically. The risk is the flip side: if interest rates rise, the value of your shares could plummet. (See chart, page 18.)

The main disadvantage of bond funds is **interest rate risk.** (See page 28.) All too often, bond fund investors don't realize that their principal will shrink if interest rates rise. They mistakenly assume that their principal will be stable in a bond fund the way it is in a money market fund or a GIC fund.

Bond funds also have a major disadvantage as a long-term investment: historically, they haven't stood up well to inflation. (See chart, page 29.) But this doesn't mean that bonds have no place in a portfolio invested for a long-term goal. It's always a good idea to diversify your long-term investments—there have been decades (from 1928 to 1937, for example) when the bond market outperformed the stock market.

97   What is a balanced fund?

A fund that invests in both stocks and bonds. The portfolio manager's freedom to decide what percentage of fund assets to invest in bonds and what percentage to invest in stocks depends on the individual fund. You can find out what kind of leeway the manager has by reading the fund prospectus, a legal document that describes the fund's investment objectives and strategy. (See Question 114, page 135.)

98   What are the advantages and disadvantages of balanced funds?

A balanced fund is designed to provide you with both income and growth. It's a compromise: in a rising stock market, a balanced fund won't earn as high a total return as a pure stock fund. But in a falling stock market, it won't lose as much as a pure stock fund, because its income from interest and dividends will cushion the fall. When interest rates fall, balanced funds do very well because falling interest rates are good for both bond and stock prices. But when interest rates rise, the value of both stocks and bonds is likely to fall.

When you buy shares in a balanced fund, you're paying a portfolio manager to decide how to divide your money between stock and bond investments. Alternatively, you could make that decision yourself by investing in a combination of stock and bond funds.

99   What is a growth and income fund?

Growth and income funds invest in blue-chip stocks: the stocks of established companies with a long history of steadily growing earnings and reliable dividends.

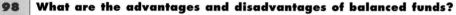

In a falling stock market, a balanced fund won't lose as much as a pure stock fund.

100 **What are the advantages and disadvantages of growth and income funds?**
Growth and income funds are a good investment for relatively conservative investors who want long-term growth. In a rising stock market, they won't grow as rapidly as pure growth funds; but in a falling stock market, they don't lose as much, partly because blue chips' dividends offset some of the decline in the stock prices.

101 **What is a growth fund?**
A fund that invests in the stocks of companies whose earnings the portfolio manager thinks will grow faster than average. The main goal of a growth fund isn't to earn current income for its investors, but to grow the value of their principal by investing it in growing companies.

102 **What are the advantages and disadvantages of growth funds?**
The main advantage of a growth fund is that over the long term, the companies it invests in are likely to grow at a faster rate than inflation. If that happens, the real buying power of your principal will grow faster than inflation, too.

The main disadvantage of a growth fund is that your investment is very vulnerable to short-term market fluctuations. Over periods of ten years or longer, the stock market has historically increased in value. But in any two or three-year period, the price of stocks 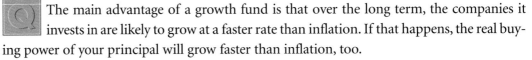 can seesaw up and down for a wide variety of reasons. (See page 22 for a discussion of stock market performance over time.)

A growth fund isn't a good investment for anyone who'll need his or her money back in one or two years and might have to cash out at a time when the fund shares have lost value.

103 **What is an aggressive growth fund?**
Aggressive growth funds are sometimes called capital appreciation funds. They're like growth funds, only more so. Their goal is to achieve the highest possible growth of your principal—and they assume high risk to get high return. An aggressive growth fund invests in the stocks of smaller, less established companies than a growth fund does.

In a rising stock market aggressive growth funds may outperform the average stock fund. But in a falling stock market, they lose more value than the average stock fund.

104 What is an index fund?

An index fund is a fund that can be managed by a computer instead of a human being.

No portfolio manager or research staff decides what an index fund will buy or sell; it simply invests in all the stocks or bonds that make up a particular market index. The Standard & Poor's 500 Index, for example, consists of the stocks of 500 companies: 400 industrial companies, 40 utilities, 40 finance companies, and 20 transportation companies. Together, these companies have the greatest market value of stock outstanding in the United States. The performance of these 500 stocks is a handy way to measure the stock market's overall performance. An S&P 500 Index fund buys the 500 stocks that make up the index.

Other major indexes include the Russell 2000 which tracks the performance of the stocks of 2,000 medium to small companies; the Shearson Lehman Brothers Government/Corporate Bond Index, which tracks the performance of investment grade bonds (the IOUs of borrowers with good credit ratings); and the Dow Jones Industrial Average, which tracks the performance of 30 blue-chip stocks. (Blue-chips are the stocks of large, very stable companies with long track records of reliable earnings and dividends.)

When you invest in an index fund, you earn the average return and you suffer the average losses of the particular market that index represents.

105 What are the advantages and disadvantages of index funds?

When you buy shares in an actively managed fund, you're hiring a portfolio manager who tries to pick investments that perform better than average: better than the market as a whole.

But historically, only about 33% of actively managed funds have achieved this goal—and even fewer have done so consistently. Most actively managed funds *underperform* the market as a whole. In other words, an index fund that performs as well as the market will have a better return than most actively managed funds.

What's more, an index fund has lower operating expenses than an actively managed fund. These funds don't pay a star portfolio manager or a big research staff and they don't have a lot of trading expenses since they simply buy and hold one group of stocks or bonds. These lower costs mean a higher return for their shareholders.

The disadvantage? *Some* actively managed funds do outperform the market, sometimes by a substantial margin. An index fund will never outperform the market, in good times or bad. In a falling stock market, the index fund falls too. A talented or lucky investment manager can minimize an actively managed fund's losses in a down market by changing its portfolio mix, and selling and buying the right assets at the right time.

106 What is an international fund?

International funds invest only in non-U.S. stocks or bonds. Don't confuse them with global funds, which can invest in any country, including the United States.

When you invest in an international stock fund, you're buying shares in foreign companies doing business outside the United States. When you own shares in an international bond fund, you're lending money to foreign companies and/or governments, which often pay a higher interest than you could obtain in a domestic bond fund.

107 What are the advantages and disadvantages of international funds?

As the politicians keep reminding us, we now live in an international economy. Today the U.S. stock market represents only about one-third of the world's publicly traded stocks—down from two-thirds of the world's total stock market a mere 20 years ago. So if you limit yourself only to U.S. stocks, you're ignoring two-thirds of the investment opportunities in the world. Some of those investment opportunities are in economies that are growing more rapidly than ours.

Another reason to own international stocks is that it diversifies your total portfolio. Foreign stock markets don't move up and down in tandem with the U.S. stock market; a good performance by international investments can help cushion your total portfolio at a time when the U.S. market is falling.

One disadvantage of international investments is that they expose you to currency risk. Before the fund can buy shares on a foreign stock exchange, its dollars must be converted into local currency, and when the fund sells shares, its investment is converted back into dollars.

Like all risks, this currency risk works both ways: if the U.S. dollar falls in value compared to other currencies, your shares in an international fund can increase in value; but if the dollar rises in value relative to other currencies, the price of your fund shares can drop. When the Mexican peso plummeted in early 1995, for example, investors in American mutual funds that owned Mexican stocks lost money.

108 | **What is an emerging markets fund?**

An emerging markets fund is an international fund that invests in developing countries, such as Indonesia, Malaysia, the Philippines, Singapore, South Korea, Thailand and the former Iron Curtain countries of Eastern Europe. Some of these economies are growing at 15% or more a year—much faster than the mature U.S. economy which grows at about 3% a year. The companies in these emerging markets are likely to grow much more rapidly than American companies.

109 | **What are the advantages and disadvantages of emerging markets funds?**

The economies of emerging markets countries have the potential to grow rapidly. Your investment in an emerging markets fund gives you a chance to profit from that growth.

The enormous potential demand for goods and services in developing nations is going to make many companies (and their shareholders) very rich. Just think of all those millions of people in the former Iron Curtain countries who have yet to buy disposable razors, breakfast cereal, life insurance, automobiles and countless other products an American consumer takes for granted.

But the road from communism or dictatorship to a free market economy is far from smooth, as anyone reading headlines or watching the evening news can testify. Emerging markets countries are very vulnerable to economic and political crises and you should expect any emerging markets investment to be much more volatile than an investment in a domestic fund or an international fund that invests primarily in the world's developed nations.

110 | **What is a lifestyle or asset allocation fund?**

These funds are relatively new—only about five years old. A lifestyle or asset allocation fund invests in several different types of assets—U.S. stocks and foreign stocks, bonds, real estate stocks, money market instruments—that you'd normally buy in separate funds. The goal is to give you the diversification to weather virtually any market or economic environment.

Often, a 401(k) plan will offer several asset allocation funds, each with a different investment mix ranging from very conservative to very aggressive.

Some asset allocation funds keep a fixed percentage of their total assets in each different

You should expect any emerging markets investment to be much more volatile than an investment in a domestic fund or an international fund that invests primarily in the world's developed nations.

type of investment. Others give portfolio managers the freedom to change the mix,  emphasizing the investments they believe will perform best in the current environment. (See pages 32-36 for a discussion of market timing.) With a lifestyle fund, you've hired a portfolio manager to make your asset allocation decisions for you. Alternatively, you might prefer to retain control of those decisions by investing in several different types of fund.

PG. 32

111 What is company stock?

Many 401(k) plans offer you the chance to purchase stock in the company you work for. Also, some employers give their matching contribution in company stock rather than in cash. (See Question 18, page 84.)

PG. 84

112 What are the advantages and disadvantages of owning company stock in my 401(k) account?

You probably know more about the company you work for—its strengths, weaknesses and future prospects for growth—than any other. This is an advantage; you're an informed investor.

But it's risky to have both your current income and your retirement nest egg riding on the success of a single company, no matter how wonderful. If the company experiences difficulties, your paycheck and your retirement savings could be impacted simultaneously. Even a great company whose stock is world-renowned for dependable growth isn't immune to bad times. Consider IBM: between mid-1992 and mid-1993, Big Blue downsized by 65,000 employees, while its stock price fell from $100 a share to just over $41. By early 1995, the stock had climbed up to $84 a share.

If you already receive company stock through your employer's matching contribution, that's great. But you should carefully evaluate the risk before you increase your investment in the stock by purchasing additional shares for your account.

113 What happens to the company stock in my account if I leave the company?

Some companies automatically distribute the shares of stock you own. (That means they'll be transferred into a rollover Individual Retirement Account at your direction.) Other companies give you the option of taking the stock or its cash value. Some companies automatically sell the stock for you, and distribute cash to your IRA.

114 **What should I look for in a mutual fund prospectus?**

A prospectus is a long legal document that reveals everything the Securities and Exchange Commission believes you should know about a mutual fund before investing in it. Unfortunately, a prospectus is written by and for lawyers, which makes for extremely dull and often unintelligible reading. Fortunately, the most valuable information is in the first few pages.

Look for the **investment objectives**. This tells you the fund's goal and its basic strategy: how the manager intends to reach the goal. In a growth and income fund, for example, the primary objective might be capital appreciation (growth of your principal) and current income might be a secondary objective. In a government bond fund, on the other hand, the primary objectives might be current income and safety of principal.

The description of a stock fund's **investment strategy** should tell you whether the portfolio manager is a value investor who looks for stocks selling at cheap prices relative to their true value, or a growth investor who buys stock of companies expected to enjoy rapid earnings growth.

Other things to look for under **investment objectives**: Will the fund try to time the market? If the portfolio manager believes the stock market is going into a decline, for example, will he or she switch out of stocks and into money market instruments in an attempt to minimize losses? Or does the manager intend to stay fully invested in stocks at all times, riding out the market's ups and downs? (For more on the pros and cons of market timing, see pages 32-36.)

Obviously, you want a fund with investment objectives and strategies that fit your own.

Under investment objectives you'll also learn something about out what the fund intends to invest in. Here's an excerpt from the prospectus of a small cap fund, for example:

> *The fund normally invests at least 65% of its assets in common stocks of small and medium size companies in the early stages of their life cycle. It may invest up to 20% of its assets in foreign securities.*

And here's the prospectus description of a conservative, short-term bond fund:

> *The fund seeks income, consistent with low risk to principal and liquidity; total return is a secondary objective. The fund invests in U.S. government obligations and related repurchase agreements, mortgage and asset-backed securities, investment-grade corporate debt securities, and foreign debt securities. Average weighted maturity may not exceed five years.*

A mutual fund prospectus tells you the fund's investment goal and its strategy: how the manager intends to reach the goal.

Look for the **fees and operating expenses**. The most important number is the **expense ratio**, which shows you the fund's annual operating expenses as a percentage of its total assets. The lower this ratio, the lower the fund's expenses. This matters, because expenses reduce your return. In 1993 for example, actively managed stock funds had an average expense ratio of 1.43%; the lowest-cost index fund, by contrast, had an expense ratio of just 0.19%. This has a real impact on your bottom line. When two mutual funds have the same performance, the fund with the lower expense ratio will have the higher return.

The prospectus section on **fees and expenses** will also have an illustration showing how much the expenses would reduce your return on a hypothetical $1,000 investment that earned a hypothetical 5% a year over a one, five and ten-year period.

Finally, look at **performance history.** This tells you how the fund has performed over different periods of time in the past. Be sure you compare the fund's past performance only with the performance of funds with similar objectives. Often, a prospectus will suggest an appropriate benchmark to use in judging a fund's performance. A growth fund or a growth and income fund might use the Standard & Poor's 500 Index as a benchmark, for example. A small cap stock fund might use the Russell 2000 Index.

 115 How can I get more information about the funds I've invested in?
If your 401(k) offers widely available mutual funds, you can learn more about them at the public library. Check the reference shelves for *Morningstar Mutual Funds* or Value Line's *Mutual Fund Survey*. Both publications analyze and report regularly on more than 1,000 different mutual funds, ranking their performances on both the returns they achieve and the risks they take.

116 If I decide to invest in a stock fund, how can I tell when the market is likely to move up or down so I know when it's a good time to buy and when it's a good time to sell?
You can't tell which way the market is going to move—and that's no reflection on your financial expertise. Nobody else can tell, either. Don't waste your time and energy worrying about it. (For more on market timing, see pages 32-36.)

PART SIX

FOR YOUR
QUICK REFERENCE

An easy way to find the

information you need

6

A

Asset: Any property that has monetary value. Your personal assets include your house, car, clothes, jewelry and, of course, your savings and investments.

Asset allocation: The process of dividing your money between different types of assets—such as stocks, bonds, cash, and real estate—in a combination intended to generate the overall return you need, while at the same time minimizing your overall risk.

The underlying idea is that if you own assets that behave differently, you'll always have one or two investments that are doing okay. There's plenty of evidence to show that asset allocation works. The history of financial markets shows, for example, that owning both stocks and bonds is less risky than owning only stocks or only bonds. (see chart, page 33.)

Average maturity: A bond matures when it stops paying interest and repays investors' principal. The average maturity of a mutual fund's bond portfolio is the average length of time it takes those bonds to mature.

A fund's average maturity tells you a lot about how you can expect it to behave. A fund with a longer average maturity pays a higher yield, for example. But if the prevailing interest rate rises, your principal will lose more value than it would in a fund with a shorter average maturity. (See Interest rate risk.)

B

Basis point: A unit of measurement that makes it easy to measure dollar amounts smaller than one percent. One percentage point equals 100 basis points. In other words, an investment that yields 3.5% pays 500 basis points more than one yielding only 3%.

Bear market: Bad news. A bear market is one that loses value for an extended period of time, typically a year or more. If you're bearish about something, you're pessimistic about its prospects. (A bear market shouldn't be confused with a market correction, which is a short-lived drop in prices.)

Big cap stocks: The stocks of companies whose market value—the total number of shares outstanding multiplied by their price—is more than $10 billion. Big cap companies are well-established corporations with a long track record of steady earnings growth and reliable dividend payments.

Blue-chip stocks: In a poker game, blue-chips traditionally are the most valuable. In Wall Street slang, blue-chip stocks are shares in the nation's biggest and most consistently profitable companies. Needless to say, there's no official list of blue-chip companies because they keep changing.

Bond: An IOU issued by a corporation or by a government. The bond issuer is borrowing money from you and other members of the public. (The U.S. government is the nation's biggest borrower.) Most bonds pay interest at regular intervals until they mature, at which point investors get their principal back. Alternatively, some bonds are sold at a discount to their face value—$800 for a $1,000 bond, for example. The investor gets $1,000 when the bond matures, receiving interest and principal repayment in a lump sum.

Bond rating: A way of measuring the bond issuer's ability to make good on its IOUs. The major bond rating agencies are Standard & Poor's Corp. and Moody's Inc. (For more on bond rates, see page 17.)

PG. 17

Buy-and-hold: A long-term investing strategy. Buy-and-hold investors maintain their holdings, ignoring short-term market fluctuations. The opposite of buy-and-hold is market timing: trying to anticipate market trends in order to sell investments before prices fall, and buy again before prices rise.

NOTE: Following a buy-and-hold strategy doesn't mean sticking with a poor investment—one that consistently underperforms comparable investments in its category. Long-term investors should periodically compare their investments' performance with appropriate benchmarks. If you own a growth stock mutual fund, for example, you should compare its performance with the average performance of all growth stock mutual funds, or with an appropriate market index, over the same period of time. (See Index.)

Average mutual fund performance numbers are published quarterly in *Barron's*, available at most newsstands, and can also be found in newsletters by Morningstar and Value Line which should be available in the reference section of your public library.

Bull market: Good news. A bull market is one that gains value for an extended period, often several years. Even in a bull market, however, prices fluctuate from day to day.

Capital appreciation: The growth of your principal. If you invest $100 in a stock mutual fund and its value increases to $120, that $20 increase is called capital appreciation.

Capital gain: When you sell an investment for more than you paid, your profit is called a capital gain. If you sell for less than you paid, you have a capital loss.

Cash investment: A very short-term loan to a borrower with a very high credit rating. Examples of cash investments are bank certificates of deposit (CDs), Treasury Bills (T-Bills) and money market funds. A cash investment typically offers investors great principal stability, but little long-term growth.

C

Commercial paper: Very short-term IOUs of highly rated corporate borrowers. The maturity of these loans ranges from overnight to 90 days. Money market funds are a big buyer of commercial paper.

Commodities: Raw materials like wheat, gold, silver, oil, pork bellies, oranges, cocoa. Commodities are an extremely volatile investment—their value can soar or plummet overnight.

Common stock: An ownership share in a corporation.

Compounding: Compounding happens when you earn interest not just on your original investment, but also on the interest it has already earned. If you earn 10% a year on an investment for four years, and let your interest compound, for example, instead of earning 40% over these four years, you actually earn 46.4%. The longer you stay invested and automatically reinvest your earnings, the more dramatically compounding can increase the value of your investment.

Correction: A relatively short-lived drop in market prices. (It's called a correction because professionals consider it a return to appropriate values.)

Credit rating: See Bond rating.

Debt: On Wall Street, "debt" is a synonym for investments in which you lend your money for a specific term and rate of interest—i.e., bonds.

Default: The bond issuer's failure to pay the interest or principal that has come due on his bonds.

Distribution: A mutual fund's payment to shareholders of the profits, interest, or dividends it has earned on its investments. Outside a 401(k) account, distributions would be taxable income unless they represented interest the mutual fund earned on tax-exempt investments. But inside a 401(k) account, your distributions are tax-deferred and automatically reinvested, giving you the great benefit of compounding. (See Compounding.)

Diversification: A fancy way of saying don't put all your eggs in one basket. You diversify by spreading your money among several different investments; that way, you won't be too badly hurt if any one of them performs poorly.

Dividends: Income paid by your investments. Both stocks and bonds can pay dividends. Mutual funds pass the dividends they earn on their investments to their shareholders. In a 401(k) account, these dividends aren't paid to you in cash, but are automatically reinvested to buy more shares for you.

D

Dollar cost averaging: An investment technique in which you invest a fixed amount at regular intervals—$100 at the beginning of every month, for example. With dollar cost averaging, you automatically buy more shares when the price is low and fewer shares when the price is high. As a result, your average cost is less than the average share price.

Dow Jones Industrial Average: The stock price average of 30 blue-chip (see above) stocks that represent about 15% to 20% of the market value of the stocks traded on the New York Stock Exchange. The daily performance of the Dow Jones Industrial Average is used on nightly television news broadcasts as an indicator of the New York Stock Exchange performance—but it may not be any indication of how your mutual funds performed.

Equity: Equity is an ownership interest. Your equity in your house, for example, is the percentage of its value that you own outright. (The balance of its value is your mortgage.) On Wall Street, "equity" is often used as a synonym for stock—i.e., an equity investor is a stockholder. By contrast, a debt investment is one in which you lend money. You invest in a debt instrument when you buy a bond.

E

Expense ratio: The percentage of a mutual fund's net assets that is used to pay its expenses. The higher a fund's expense ratio, the bigger the bite being taken out of your return to pay those expenses.

Fixed-income: A synonym for bonds, which promise a fixed rate of interest until they mature. Bond mutual funds are called fixed-income funds, but the name is misleading because in a bond mutual fund your income fluctuates. Your principal value also fluctuates (both in individual bonds and in bond funds) as the prevailing interest rate changes. When the interest rate rises, existing bonds lose value because they now pay a lower-than-prevailing rate. When the interest rate drops, the value of existing bonds goes up because they now pay a higher-than-prevailing rate.

F

Ginnie Mae: See Government National Mortgage Association

Global fund: A mutual fund that invests in stocks and bonds all over the world, including the United States. By contrast, an international fund invests all over the world except in the United States.

G

Government National Mortgage Association (GNMA): A federal agency of the Department of Housing and Urban Development more commonly known by its nickname, Ginnie Mae. The GNMA guarantees the full and timely payment of all interest and principal on mortgage-backed bonds sold to mutual funds and other investors. Ginnie Mae bonds are backed by residential mortgage loans which in turn are insured or guaranteed by the Federal Housing Administration, the Farmer's Home Administration or the Veteran's Administration.

NOTE: Ginnie Mae bonds are not risk free. Like all bonds, they carry interest rate risk — their principal value falls when the prevailing interest rate rises. Like all mortgage-backed bonds, they also carry pre-payment risk, which is the danger that interest rates will fall, causing homeowners to pay off their existing mortgages. When that happens, investors in Ginnie Mae bonds get their principal back much sooner than they expected, and must reinvest it at the lower prevailing interest rate.

Growth investment: An investment whose main objective is to grow your principal rather than to generate income. A house, a gold coin, and a stock mutual fund are all growth investments. You hope to make money in a growth investment by eventually selling it for a lot more than you paid for it.

Guaranteed Investment Contract (GIC): A contract between an insurance company and an investor like your 401(k) plan. The contract promises to pay a fixed rate of interest and to return the investor's principal after a specified term, usually one to five years.

NOTE: "Guaranteed" doesn't mean you can't lose money. A GIC is guaranteed only by the issuing insurer, not by the government or by your 401(k) plan.

Income investment: An investment whose main objective is to generate income in the form of interest or dividend payments, rather than to grow your principal. A bond fund, for example, is an income investment.

Individual Retirement Account (IRA): A personal tax-deferred retirement account. An IRA itself is not an investment—it's an account that can hold any type of investment. You can own IRAs at many different financial services companies, but your total annual IRA contribution cannot exceed $2,000. Whether or not your IRA contribution is tax-deductible depends on your income and on whether you participate in a pension plan or 401(k) plan at work. (See page 90 for IRA deductibility rules.)

PG.90

Index: A statistical model that serves as a handy reference for judging how well an investment is performing. The benchmark most often used for stock market performance is the Standard & Poor's 500 Index, which measures the average performance of 500 widely held common stocks. Over periods of 15 years or longer, the stock market, as measured by the S&P 500 Index, historically has earned an average 10% annual return.

Other frequently used indexes are the Dow Jones Industrial Average; the Russell 2000, which is used as a benchmark for smaller company stocks; the Wilshire 5000, which is used as a benchmark for the entire U.S. stock market—including both the big company stocks that make up the S&P 500 Index and the smaller stocks represented in the Russell 2000; the Morgan Stanley Capital International Europe, Australia, Far East Index (EAFE), which is used as a benchmark for foreign company stocks; and the Shearson Lehman Brothers Government/Corporate Bond Index, which is used as a benchmark for investment-grade (good quality) bonds.

Index fund: A mutual fund that buys the stocks or bonds that make up a widely used market index. The goal of an index fund is to mirror market performance.

Inflation: An increase in the cost of goods and services, most often measured by the Consumer Price Index. When too much money chases too few goods, inflation is the result. Economic growth often causes moderate inflation by increasing consumer spending at a faster rate than the production of goods.

International fund: See Global fund.

Liquidity: The measure of how quickly an investment can be turned into cash. A mutual fund typically is a very liquid investment, because you can redeem your shares at any time. A house, by contrast, is a very illiquid investment.

L

Lump sum distribution: A single payment representing the entire amount due to you from your 401(k) plan.

Management fee: The fee a mutual fund pays to its investment advisers. This fee is expressed as a percentage of fund assets, and is paid by the mutual fund's shareholders.

M

Market timing: An investment strategy based on predicting market trends. A market timer may buy or sell investments based on a conviction that interest rates will rise or fall, for example. The goal of market timing is to anticipate trends, buying before the market goes up and selling before the market goes down. In practice, this is impossible to do with any consistency.

The opposite strategy, called buy-and-hold, is used by investors who realize they can't predict when the market will rise and when it will fall, and don't want to waste their time, energy, and money by guessing. Buy-and-hold investors expect to ride out the market's ups and downs and make money in the long-run.

Maturity: A bond's maturity is the length of time it takes to repay investors' principal. (See Average maturity.)

Money market fund: A mutual fund that invests in the very short-term IOUs of the government and highly rated corporations. Money market funds pay a fluctuating interest rate, but maintain a fixed $1 per share value. (See Net Asset Value.)

Mutual fund: An investment company that pools the money of many individual investors and uses it to buy stocks, bonds, money market instruments and other assets.

Net Asset Value per share (NAV): The value of a single share in a mutual fund, which is determined daily by dividing the total assets of the fund, minus its liabilities, by the total number of shares outstanding.

Principal: The amount you originally invested.

Portfolio: Portfolio is the collective noun for investments—a portfolio of investments is like a flock of swans, a gaggle of geese, or a pride of lions. Your portfolio is all your investment holdings.

Pre-payment risk: A risk assumed by anyone who invests in mortgage-backed bonds. The risk is that the prevailing interest rate will fall, causing homeowners to pay off their existing mortgages. When that happens, investors in mortgage-backed bonds get their principal back much sooner than they expected, and must reinvest it at the lower prevailing interest rate.

Prospectus: A legal document that contains all the information the Securities and Exchange Commission says an investor must have in order to make an informed decision about whether or not to buy a stock or shares in a mutual fund. Among other things, a mutual fund prospectus tells you a fund's investment goals and strategy, performance record and fees.

Rollover: Moving money from a 401(k) plan into another tax-deferred retirement account, like an Individual Retirement Account, so that you avoid any tax liability.

Share: A unit of ownership in a corporation or a mutual fund.

Small cap stock: The stock of companies whose market value—total number of shares outstanding multiplied by their price—is less than $500 million. Small cap companies grow faster than big cap companies and typically use any profits for expansion rather than for paying dividends. But they're also more volatile than big cap companies and fail more often.

Standard & Poor's 500 Index: See Index.

Total return: The total that you're earning on an investment. Total return is the dividends and interest you get, plus any change in the value of your principal, or original investment. If your mutual fund share price increased from $23 to $25, and you also received a 20 cent per share

N

P

R

S

T

dividend, your total return was $2.20—a little over 9%.

Trade: To trade shares of stock (or mutual fund shares) is to buy or sell them.

Treasuries: The IOUs of the U.S. government. The federal government borrows money by selling Treasury Bills, which range in maturity from 90 days to one year; Treasury Notes, whose maturity ranges from one to ten years; and Treasury Bonds, whose maturity ranges from ten years to 30 years.

Treasuries are considered to have no risk of default. But like all bonds, they are vulnerable to **interest rate risk.**

Turnover ratio: The percentage of a mutual fund's holdings that was replaced during a one-year period. A fund's turnover ratio tells you how aggressively the portfolio manager buys and sells investments. You can find this information in the prospectus.

V

Value: In Wall Street slang, a value investor is an investor who looks for stocks selling for less than they're really worth. By contrast, a growth investor looks for stocks of companies whose earnings are growing rapidly.

Vesting: Your ownership rights in your 401(k) plan account. You are fully vested in your own contributions at all times. But you aren't vested in your employer's matching contributions until you have worked at a company for a specific length of time. Vesting rules vary from one plan to another, but by law you must be fully vested in your employer's contributions at the end of seven years of service.

Volatility: The measure of an investment's tendency to rise or drop in value. A very volatile investment is one whose value can change dramatically in a short period of time.

Yield: The annualized rate at which your investment earns income.

Y

NOTE: Yield is not the same as total return. It's possible to earn a good yield on an investment, but lose money anyway because of a drop in principal value. A $1,000 bond that pays 10% will continue paying 10% after the prevailing interest rate rises to 11%—but the bond will be worth less than $1,000. (See chart, page 18.)

After-tax contributions 88, 89, 95, 96, 112
Aggressive growth fund 123, 130
Asset allocation fund: see Lifestyle fund
Asset categories or asset classes 14, 20, 30, 31, 32, 39, 40, 47, 123
Balanced fund 123, 128, 129
Bankruptcy: see 401(k) plan; filing for bankruptcy
Bond fund 18, 19, 25, 28, 29, 30, 32, 34, 46, 53, 81, 92, 116, 120, 126-129, 142, 152
    total return 18, 25, 127, 128
    yield 18, 25, 127
Bonds vs. bond mutual funds 19, 141
Borrowing: see 401(k) plan; loans from
Capital appreciation 130, 135, 139
Capital appreciation fund: see Aggressive growth fund
Certificate of deposit 15, 31, 63, 124, 125, 139
College cost 9, 16, 35, 45, 47, 55, 93, 111, 112, 115
Commercial paper 15, 125, 140
Company stock 84, 120, 134
Compounding 4, 13, 21 37, 39, 58, 140
Credit rating 15, 17, 28, 29, 72, 124, 131, 139, 140
Defined benefit plan 74, 75, 91, 102, 156
Defined contribution plan: see 401(k) plan
Disability: see 401(k) plan; disability
Diversification 4, 25, 30, 31, 32, 39, 133, 140
Divorce 35, 45, 105, 106, 114, 155
Dollar cost averaging 4, 35, 36, 38, 39, 141
Early withdrawal penalty 88, 89, 96, 104, 105, 106, 112, 113, 117
Emergency account 16, 23
Emerging markets fund 123, 133, 152
Equity income fund 64
Fiduciary 83, 103
Fixed-income 14, 17, 18, 19, 20, 21, 23, 25, 27, 30, 40, 44, 46, 47, 65, 122, 126, 128, 140, 141
Foreign stocks and bonds 24, 31, 32, 34, 143
  (see International fund)
401(k) plan:
    being fired 103
    changing jobs 8, 58, 94, 95, 97, 103, 149
    death and 62, 105
    disability and 71, 104
    disputes with employer 119
    distributions from when you retire 52, 58, 59, 60, 61, 62, 64, 65, 98, 100, 104, 109, 140, 150
    divorce and 105, 106, 114
    early withdrawals from 88, 89, 92, 96, 104, 105, 106, 109, 111, 112, 113, 117
    eligibility to participate in 86, 90, 91
    employer being acquired by other company 103
    employer going out of business 103
    employer's matching contributions 75, 84, 88, 89, 91, 92, 95, 104, 105, 113, 120, 134, 145,
    expenses of 79, 81, 86, 109

    filing for bankruptcy and 106, 107, 118
    financial statement 81
    hardship withdrawals from 88, 92, 105, 107, 109, 110, 111, 112, 113
    income taxes and 9, 62, 74, 75, 76, 88, 92, 98, 99, 100, 104, 105, 112, 113, 114, 117
    investment goal 27, 29, 63, 125, 135
    investment manager 81, 83, 103, 119, 132
    investment menu 39, 120, 121, 123
    loans from 45, 46, 91, 92, 93, 105, 107, 109, 112, 115, 116, 117, 118
    moving money from one investment to another 109, 110
    safety of money in 102-110
    vesting in matching contributions 84, 85, 92, 94, 103, 145
    your contributions to 9, 46, 53, 74, 75, 76, 78, 79, 80, 81, 83, 85, 87, 88, 90, 91, 93, 95, 96, 102, 103, 105, 109, 113
404(c) rules 103, 108, 120
Ginnie Mae fund, 122, 126, 127, 141, 142
Global fund; see International fund
Government bond fund 14, 19, 23, 64, 122, 126, 127, 128, 135
Growth and income fund 64, 122, 123, 129, 130, 135, 136
Growth fund, 123, 130, 136
Guaranteed investment contract (GIC) 14, 15, 16, 17, 25, 26, 35, 38, 53, 80, 116, 123, 124, 125, 126, 128, 142
High-yield bond: see junk bond
House: buying or selling; see Life events
Index 20, 22, 23, 131, 139, 142, 143
Index fund 131, 132, 136, 142, 143
Individual Retirement Account 31, 58, 82, 90, 94, 95, 96, 104, 134, 142, 144
    rollover 60, 64, 94, 95, 96, 98, 99, 104, 114, 117, 134, 144
Inflation 9, 12, 13, 17, 20, 23, 25, 26, 27, 29, 31, 33, 42, 43, 44, 48, 59, 63, 64, 65, 66, 67, 76, 79, 99, 125, 129, 130, 142, 143, 156, 157, 158
International fund 32, 120, 123, 132, 133, 141
  (See Foreign stocks and bonds)
Investment choices: see 401(k) plan; investment menu
Investment goals: see 401(k) plan; investment goal
Investment return 26, 32, 40, 66
Investment volatility 22, 109, 128, 144
Investments 122-136
    cash equivalent 14, 15, 16, 17, 19, 23, 25, 27, 122, 125
    fixed-income 14, 17, 18, 19, 20, 21, 23, 25, 27, 30, 40, 44, 46, 47, 65, 122, 126, 128, 140, 141
    growth 14, 19, 20, 22, 25, 27, 43, 44, 48, 64, 142
    long-term 17, 20, 23, 32, 40, 126, 129
    short-term 16, 23
Investments outside your 401(k) plan 16, 31, 40, 45, 46, 81, 88, 89, 123, 140
Junk bond 17, 29, 127
Life events 35, 45
    birth of child 35
    buying a house 16, 35, 45, 56, 93, 113, 115, 117, 118

death of spouse 45
divorce 35, 45, 105, 106, 114, 155
inheriting money 35
marriage 35
selling a house 55, 56, 65
Life expectancy 44, 48, 50, 53, 54, 60, 61, 62, 63, 65, 77, 99, 100, 114
Lifestyle or asset allocation fund 34, 123, 133
Loans: see 401(k) plan; loans from
Market timing 32, 33, 34, 36, 110, 134, 135, 136, 139, 142, 143
Medicare 73, 74, 155
Medigap 71, 74
Money market fund 15, 16, 18, 26, 30, 31, 33, 46, 53, 58, 80, 120, 123, 125, 126, 128, 139, 140, 144
Mortgage-backed bond 127, 141, 142, 144
Mutual fund 14, 15, 17, 18, 19, 20, 22, 23, 25, 27, 28, 31, 39, 56, 64, 80, 81, 85, 92, 122, 123, 125, 126, 127, 128, 132, 135, 136, 138, 139, 140, 141, 142, 143, 144, 145
  fees and expenses 81, 135, 136
  investment objectives 135, 136
  performance history 136
  prospectus 85, 134, 135
  turnover rate 145
Pension Benefit Guaranty Corp. 75
Pension plan: see Defined benefit plan
Profit-sharing plan 75
Real estate 9, 20, 22, 33, 38, 56, 122, 133, 138
Rebalancing a portfolio 34, 40
Retirement account: see Individual Retirement Account
  mandatory minimum distributions 60, 61, 62
  naming a beneficiary 60, 61, 105, 114
  payment method 52, 60, 61, 62
Retirement 52-72
  applying for Social Security 69, 70
  drawing on capital in 64, 65, 66
  expenses in 47, 52, 55, 56, 57
  financial moves to make within five years of 53
  investing in 62, 63, 64, 65, 66
  meaning of 54, 55
  selling your house in 55, 56, 57
  where to live 57
  working in 54
Risk 26-40
  business risk 27
  credit risk 28
  inflation risk 26, 27
  interest rate risk 28
  market risk 27, 28
  personal tolerance for 48, 49
Rollover: see Individual Retirement Account
Social Security 54, 64, 66, 67, 69, 71, 72, 73, 76, 77, 87, 155, 156
  estimate of your retirement benefit 69

forfeit for working after retirement 71
spousal benefit 69, 70
survivor's benefit 69, 70
taxes on retirement benefit 67
when to start collecting 70
S&P 500 Index 22, 23, 37, 43, 131, 142, 143
Stock dividends 20, 21, 64, 123, 129, 130, 131, 140, 144
Stock market 20, 21, 23, 24, 27, 30, 32, 33, 34, 36, 38, 43, 48, 64, 66, 129, 130, 131, 132, 135, 142, 143
  chance of loss in 23, 27, 43, 48
  historic return 20, 36, 66
  long term performance of 20, 30, 32, 36
  short term performance of 23, 30, 32, 43
Stocks: see Stock market
  big cap 20, 21, 22, 138, 144
  foreign 24, 31, 32, 34, 143
  growth 22, 31, 64, 123, 130, 136, 139
  mid cap 21, 22
  small cap 21, 22, 135, 136, 144
  value 22, 30
Time horizon 13, 16, 19, 22, 25, 26, 29, 42, 43, 44, 45, 48, 50
Treasuries 28, 33, 36, 56, 125, 136, 139, 144 , 145
Vesting 84, 85, 92, 94, 103, 145
Years of service: see Vesting

LIST OF ILLUSTRATIONS

INVESTMENT TIME HORIZON AND GOAL 13
TIME IS MONEY 15
BOND PRICES VS. INTEREST RATES. 17
A BOND'S VALUE FLUCTUATES 18
THE GROWTH OF $1 INVESTED FROM 1926-1994:
  PERFORMANCE OF DIFFERENT INVESTMENTS OVER TIME 19
HOW INFLATION SHRINKS THE VALUE OF A DOLLAR 21
HOW DIFFERENT INVESTMENTS HAVE PERFORMED OVER TIME . . 29
COMPARING ASSET ALLOCATION STRATEGIES. 33
DOLLAR COST AVERAGING 35
THE MAGIC OF COMPOUNDING. 37
HOW TIME HELPS MANAGE RISK 43
YOUR ASSET MIX DEPENDS ON YOUR TIME HORIZON 44
DEFINING RISK OVER THE SHORT-TERM (1-3 YEARS) 49
DEFINING RISK OVER THE LONG-TERM (10-20 YEARS) 49
IRS LIFE EXPECTANCY TABLES 61
TAPPING YOUR NEST EGG IN RETIREMENT 64
HOW MUCH OF YOUR INCOME WILL SOCIAL SECURITY REPLACE . 67
TAX-DEFERRED VS TAXABLE SAVINGS 71
A 401K CONTRIBUTION LOWERS YOUR INCOME TAXES 76
SIX-PACK SAVINGS ADD UP 79

CHAPTER ONE: HOW DOES A 401(k) PLAN WORK?

1. How is a 401(k) different from a regular pension?............................ 74
2. How is a 401(k) different from a profit-sharing plan?......................... 75
3. How do I contribute to the 401(k) plan?.................................... 75
4. How do my contributions lower my income taxes?......................... 76
5. Why is the government giving me this tax break?.......................... 76
6. Won't Social Security be there for future retirees?........................ 76

CHAPTER TWO: 401(k) CONTRIBUTIONS

7. How much can I put into the 401(k) plan?................................. 79
8. How little can I put in?... 79
9. Are my 401(k) contributions deducted from all the pay I receive, including bonuses and overtime?.. 79
10. I've heard that if I earn over a certain amount, my 401(k) contributions are capped. Is that true, and if so, why?...................... 80
11. What happens to the money I put into the 401(k) plan?..................... 80
12. How do I know how well my investments are doing?....................... 81
13. What does the 401(k) plan cost — and who's paying for it?................. 81
14. If I leave this job, is the money I put into the plan mine to take with me?........ 82

CHAPTER THREE: EMPLOYERS' OBLIGATIONS FOR 401(k)s

15. Does my employer contribute to my 401(k) account?........................ 83
16. Why do employers contribute to 401(k) plans if they don't have to?.............. 83
17. What is a matching contribution?... 84
18. Is there any other way my employer can contribute?....................... 84
19. Do my employer's contributions go into the plan at the same time as mine?...... 84
20. At what point do I own my employer's contributions to my account?........... 84
21. How are my years of service determined?................................. 85
22. What if my company has many different business units, and some units have 401(k) plans and some don't? How are my years of service determined if I'm transferred from a unit without a 401(k) plan to a unit that has one?....... 85
23. What information about my 401(k) plan am I legally entitled to have?.......... 85

24. Does participating in a 401(k) affect any of my other benefits? 86

25. How long do I have to wait after being hired to join the 401(k) plan? 86

CHAPTER FOUR: TAX RULES

26. Do I pay any taxes at all on the money I contribute to the plan? 87

27. After I've made the maximum pre-tax contribution allowed,
    can I put additional money into the plan if I want to?. 87

28. Are there any other differences between a pre-tax and an after-tax contribution?. . . 88

29. If I'm saving money that I plan to use before I retire, does it make more sense
    to do it with after-tax 401(k) contributions, or to save it outside the 401(k) plan? . . 88

CHAPTER FIVE: WHICH IS BETTER FOR ME: 401(k) OR IRA?

30. I participate in my company's 401(k) plan, but I also want to invest
    in an Individual Retirement Account. Can I do both?. 90

31. If I decide not to participate in my 401(k) plan, will I be eligible for
    a fully deductible IRA, regardless of my salary? 91

32. If I have to choose between a 401(k) and an IRA, which choice makes more sense?. 91

33. My spouse and I are both eligible to participate in 401(k) plans at work.
    We can't afford to put the maximum contribution into both plans. How do
    we decide how much of our limited retirement money to put into each plan? 92

CHAPTER SIX: TAKING MY 401(k) MONEY WHEN I CHANGE JOBS

34. Can I roll a 401(k) account from my previous job into the plan I have now? 94

35. If I change jobs, can I leave my money invested in my current employer's
    401(k) plan until I retire?. 94

36. If I change jobs, but I decide to leave my 401(k) account at my former
    company, can I keep putting money into it?. 95

37. What if I prefer not to leave my money in this plan — how do I take it out
    without having to pay taxes on it?. 95

38. Why is it important to transfer money directly from a 401(k) account to
    a rollover Individual Retirement Account? Can't I have a check made out
    to me and then deposit it in a rollover IRA within 60 days? 96

39. Is there a dollar limit on how much 401(k) money I can transfer to an IRA? 96

40. How do I decide whether it makes more sense to leave my money in the

company plan or switch it to an IRA when I change jobs? 97

CHAPTER SEVEN: RULES ON 401(K) DISTRIBUTIONS

41.   What happens to my 401(k) account when I retire? 98

42.   If I roll my 401(k) money into a rollover IRA, when must I start
      taking money out of that new account? 99

43.   How much do I have to take out? 99

44.   What happens if I don't start taking money out of my account at age 70½? 100

45.   How long after I retire will it take me to get my 401(k) money? 100

46.   I am retired and when I got my 401(k) money, the amount was based on the
      value of my account as of two months earlier. Why didn't I receive any
      interest for those last two months? 100

CHAPTER EIGHT: HOW SAFE IS MY MONEY?

47.   Does the government guarantee my 401(k) account? 102

48.   Do employers guarantee 401(k) accounts? 103

49.   What happens to my account if I'm fired? 103

50.   What happens if my employer is acquired by another company? 103

51.   What happens if my employer goes out of business? 104

52.   What happens to my account if I'm disabled? 104

53.   What happens to my account when I die? 105

54.   Can my spouse empty my 401(k) account without my knowledge? 105

55.   Can I empty my 401(k) account without my spouse knowing about it? 105

56.   If I get divorced, is my spouse entitled to a share of my 401(k) account? 106

57.   Is my account protected from my creditors if I file for bankruptcy? 107

58.   Can employers use 401(k) money to run their businesses? 107

CHAPTER NINE: DO I CONTROL MY 401(K) ACCOUNT?

59.   What if I decide I can't afford to save this much, or I want to increase
      the amount I save—can I change my contribution? 108

60.   Can I stop contributing to my account if my budget is squeezed and
      I just can't afford to save the money? 108

61.   Can I take my money out of the plan if I stop contributing to it? 109

62. Can I start contributing again after I've stopped?. 109

63. Can I switch my money from one investment to another? 109

64. How often can I switch money among investments? 109

65. An IRA seems safer than a 401(k) plan. Can I switch my money
    from my 401(k) into an IRA?. 110

CHAPTER TEN: HOW CAN I TAKE MONEY OUT OF MY 401(k)?

66. What if I need some of this money before I retire? Can I make cash
    withdrawals from my account while I'm still working? 111

67. How is the 10% penalty on early withdrawals calculated?. 112

68. Why do I have to pay a penalty for withdrawing my own money? 112

69. How do I qualify for a hardship withdrawal? 112

70. Is there a dollar limit on the amount I can take in a hardship withdrawal? 113

71. What taxes will I owe on a hardship withdrawal?. 113

72. Are my employer's contributions available to me if I make a
    hardship withdrawal, or can I only take out my own contributions? 113

73. Are there any circumstances in which I can withdraw my
    money before I retire without paying a penalty? 114

CHAPTER ELEVEN: BORROWING FROM MY 401(k)

74. Can I borrow from my 401(k) account instead of making withdrawals? 115

75. How much of my total account can I borrow?. 115

76. Must my spouse agree to the loan? 116

77. What will a loan cost me? 116

78. If my money is divided among several different funds within the
    plan, which one should I borrow from? 116

79. Is the interest I pay on a 401(k) loan tax-deductible if I use the money
    to buy a house?. 117

80. How soon do I have to repay the loan?. 117

81. Is there any drawback to taking a loan from my account that I should be aware of? 117

82. Can I use my 401(k) account as collateral for a bank loan?. 118

CHAPTER TWELVE: MORE IMPORTANT INFORMATION ON MY 401(k)

83. What recourse do I have if my employer and I disagree about my 401(k) account? 119

84. Who picks the investment manager for my company's 401(k) plan? 119

85. Who picks the 401(k) plan investments?. 119

86. Do I get to decide how to invest all the money in my 401(k) account?. 119

87. What can I do if I don't like my plan's investment options? 120

88. How many investment options must be offered in a 401(k) plan? 120

PART FIVE: WHAT ARE YOUR INVESTMENT CHOICES?

89. What investments does my plan offer? 123

90. What is a stable value or GIC fund? 124

91. What are GIC funds' main advantages and disadvantages? 124

92. What is a money market fund? 125

93. Why doesn't my 401(k) plan allow me to transfer money from
a GIC fund to a money market fund? 126

94. What is a government bond fund? 126

95. What is a corporate bond fund? 127

96. What are the advantages and disadvantages of bond funds? 128

97. What is a balanced fund? 129

98. What are the advantages and disadvantages of balanced funds? 129

99. What is a growth and income fund? 129

100. What are the advantages and disadvantages of growth and income funds? 130

101. What is a growth fund? 130

102. What are the advantages and disadvantages of growth funds? 130

103. What is an aggressive growth fund?. 130

104. What is an index fund?. 131

105. What are the advantages and disadvantages of index funds?. 131

106. What is an international fund? 132

107. What are the advantages and disadvantages of international funds?. 132

108. What is an emerging markets fund? 133

109. What are the advantages and disadvantages of emerging markets funds? 133

110. What is a lifestyle or asset allocation fund?. 133

111. What is company stock?. 134

112. What are the advantages and disadvantages of owning company
stock in my 401(k) account? 134

113. What happens to the company stock in my account if I leave the company?. 134

114. What should I look for in a mutual fund prospectus? 135

115. How can I get more information about the funds I've invested in? 136

116. If I decide to invest in a stock fund, how can I tell when the market is likely
to move up or down so I know when it's a good time to buy and when it's
a good time to sell? 136

YOUR NEST EGG MATTERS...TO US!

Investors Press invites you to send us any question about your 401(k) that you would like included in future editions of **Building Your Nest Egg.** Send to: Investors Press, Questions Editor, PO Box 329, Washington Depot, CT 06794

1. GENERAL INFORMATION ON FINANCE AND INVESTING

BOOKS

The following is a list of easy-to-understand books that explain all the basics of financial planning and give reliable, objective advice on how to invest to achieve your goals, including planning for a comfortable retirement:

Making the Most of Your Money by Jane Bryant Quinn, Simon & Schuster, 1991 ($27.50)

The New Century Family Money Book by Jonathan Pond, Dell, 1994 ($29.95)

The Consumer Reports Money Book by Janet Blamford, Jeff Blyskal, Emily Card, Aileen Jacobson, Greg Daugherty, and the editors of Consumer Reports Books, Consumers Union, 1994 ($29.95)

The Lifetime Book of Money Management by Grace W. Weinstein, Visible Ink, 1993 ($15.95)

Personal Finance for Dummies by Eric Tyson, IDG Books, 1994 ($16.95)

PUBLICATIONS

In addition to general news magazines available on the newsstand and at the public library like *Time, Newsweek, U.S. News & World Report* and *Business Week,* which regularly cover personal finance and investing, there are magazines that specialize in personal finance. Among them: *Money, Kiplinger's Personal Finance Magazine, Worth,* and *Smart Money.* Your local newspaper probably reports regularly on personal finance issues, as well.

Smart Pill: *The Wall Street Journal's* personal finance column, "Your Money Matters," runs almost every day on page C1. If you don't already read *The Wall Street Journal,* you may feel intimidated by the fact that it's the nation's premier business newspaper. You'll get over your shyness very fast if you read a few of these columns—they're very informative and easy to understand.

2. INFORMATION ON FINANCIAL ISSUES IN RETIREMENT

Look Before You Leap: A Guide to Early Retirement Incentive Programs
Published by the American Association of Retired Persons, free of charge even to non-members. For a copy, write to AARP Fulfillment, 601 E Street NW, Washington DC 20049.

Finances After 50 For a copy, send your order and $14.50 to the United Seniors Health Cooperative at 1331 H Street NW, Suite 500, Washington, DC 20005.

Retirement Ready or Not: How to Get Financially Prepared—In a Hurry
By Lee Rosenberg. For a copy, send your order and $18.45 to Career Press, PO Box 34, Hawthorne, NJ 07507.

You've Earned It, Don't Lose It: Mistakes You Can't Afford to Make When You Retire
By Suze Orman, Newmarket Press; available at bookstores for $22.00.

Investment Swindles: How They Work and How to Avoid Them
How to protect yourself against illegal, yet legitimate-sounding telemarketing and direct mail offers. Free from the Commodity Futures Trading Commission. Mail your order and $1 service charge to S. James, Consumer Information Center - 5A, P.O. Box 100, Pueblo, CO 81002.

3. INFORMATION ABOUT FEDERAL PROGRAMS

Understanding Social Security
Explains retirement, disability, survivor's benefits, Medicare coverage, Supplemental Security Income and more. Social Security Administration, 41 pages.

A Woman's Guide to Social Security
Explains benefits upon retirement, disability, widowhood and divorce. Social Security Administration, 20 pages. Mail your order and $1 service charge to S. James, Consumer Information Center-5A, P.O. Box 100, Pueblo, CO 81002.

The Medicare Handbook
Explains who is eligible, how to apply, fill out claims, what is and isn't covered and your right to appeal. 64 pages. Mail your order and $4.00 to R. Woods, Consumer Information Center-5A, P.O. Box 100, Pueblo, CO 81002

Smart Pill: The National Council on Aging conducts one-day, 8-hour workshops on how to prepare for retirement, financially and emotionally. The cost is $95 and the program has been highly praised. Corporations sometimes pay the cost for workers who face lay-offs. Workshops are scheduled periodically across the country. For more information on workshops in your area, call the National Council on Aging at 202-479-6971.

HOW MUCH DO YOU NEED TO SAVE FOR YOUR RETIREMENT?

This worksheet* states all dollar amounts in terms of today's dollar equivalent and assumes a 4% annual inflation rate. It also assumes you'll be in the same tax bracket after retirement as before retirement.

Use the Conservative Return Estimates Chart on page 158 to estimate the annual return you expect your nest egg to earn, before and after you retire.

1
$

The annual income you think you'll need in retirement................................

(Many retirement professionals suggest that you use 60% to 80% of your current gross salary as an estimate for what you'll need in retirement.)

The annual amount you expect from sources other than your 401(k) plan—like Social Security, a defined benefit pension plan if you have one, and income from work you may choose to do after you retire................

2
$

(For an estimate of your Social Security benefit in retirement, call the Social Security Administration at 800-772-1213. Ask for a Request for Earnings and Benefit Estimate Statement. Four to six weeks after you complete and mail back this form, you'll get an estimate of your future benefit. If you have a defined benefit plan, ask your personnel department for an estimate of your retirement income from the plan.)

3
$

Subtract Line 2 from Line 1 and put the result on Line 3................................

This is the amount of annual income you want in retirement that won't be covered by Social Security, your defined benefit pension, and your estimated earnings in retirement.

Multiply Line 3 by your annuity factor to find out how big your nest egg will have to be when you retire in order to generate the amount on Line 3.

(To find your annuity factor, look at Table 1, page 159. Find the number of years you expect to live in retirement; then go across until you find the rate of return you expect to earn on your nest egg during retirement. The corresponding figure is your annuity factor.

4
$

Line 3 x Annuity Factor................................

* This worksheet is adapted from a model prepared by Maria Crawford Scott, American Association of Individual Investors, Chicago, Illinois.

The amount on Line 4 is the value—in today's dollars—of the amount you will need to have saved by the time you retire in order to have your desired annual income for as many years as you expect to live in retirement. (This is always an enormous number. Take a deep breath and keep going.)

5
$

Your current savings..

This is the total amount in your 401(k) plan and any other retirement accounts you may have.

To find out how much your current savings will have grown by the time you're ready to retire, multiply Line 5 by your savings growth factor.

(To find the savings growth factor, look at Table 2, and find the number of years until you will retire; then go across until you find the rate of return you expect to earn on your nest egg during this period. The corresponding figure is your savings growth factor.)

6
$

Line 5 x Savings Growth Factor..

This is what your current savings will be worth when you retire, if you don't add to them and you earn the return you expect.

7
$

Subtract Line 6 from Line 4 to find your savings shortfall..............

Now calculate how much you should save every year to make up this shortfall. Start by finding your annual payment factor. Look at the first column in Table 3 and find the number of years until you retire; then go across until you find the rate of return you expect on your savings during this period. The corresponding figure is your annual payment factor.

8

Annual payment factor..

Multiply your annual payment factor by the amount on Line 7 (your savings shortfall). The result is the value in today's dollars of the amount you need to save annually until you retire to make up the shortfall..............................

9
$

If you can afford to save this much every year, congratulations—you're in a tiny minority.

The amount on Line 9 will have to increase every year to keep up with inflation. If you think your salary will keep pace with inflation, you can calculate the necessary annual contribution as a percentage of your salary. Simply divide the amount on Line 9 by your current salary. The result is the percentage of your salary you need to save every year to reach your stated goal..........................

10 ____ %

If you're not sure your salary will keep up with inflation, you can calculate the annual 401(k) contribution needed to make up the shortfall by using a fixed dollar amount that factors in inflation. To find your fixed dollar payment factor, look at the first column in Table 4 and find the number of years until you retire; then go across until you find the rate of return you expect to earn on your savings during this period. The corresponding figure is your fixed dollar payment factor..

11 ____

Multiply the amount on Line 7 (your savings shortfall) by the fixed dollar payment factor. The result is the fixed dollar amount you need to save each year......

12 $ ____

If you're like almost everyone else, this number is absurdly high. There's no way—absolutely none—that you can save that much every year!

So go back and do the calculation again, but with different assumptions. What if you earn a higher return on your investments, before and after you retire? What if you retire a few years later? What if you reduce your stated goal and live more modestly? Remember, you may move to a less expensive part of the country.

The objective here isn't to suggest that you should deprive yourself of the basic necessities and comforts of life to save for retirement—that would be absurd. Rather, it's to give you a way to experiment on paper, to find out what difference it would make to change your investment mix to shoot for a higher return, or to postpone your projected retirement date.

Living comfortably in retirement is important—but it's not more important than living comfortably before you reach retirement. This worksheet is a tool to help you figure out a way to compromise between these conflicting demands on your money.

CONSERVATIVE RETURN ESTIMATES
BASED ON THE PAST 50 YEARS

ANNUAL RETURN	
Small Company Stocks	12.0%
Large Company Stocks	10.0%
Bonds	5.5%
Cash	3.5%

TABLE 1 - ANNUITY FACTOR

NO. OF YEARS IN RETIREMENT	EXPECTED RETURN ON SAVINGS IN RETIREMENT				
	4%	6%	8%	10%	12%
20	20.00	16.79	14.31	12.36	10.82
25	25.00	20.08	16.49	13.82	11.80
30	30.00	23.07	18.30	14.93	12.48
35	35.00	25.79	19.79	15.76	12.95
40	40.00	28.26	21.03	16.39	13.28

TABLE 2 - SAVINGS GROWTH FACTOR

NO. OF YEARS UNTIL RETIREMENT	EXPECTED RETURN ON SAVINGS UNTIL RETIREMENT				
	4%	6%	8%	10%	12%
5	1.00	1.10	1.21	1.32	1.45
10	1.00	1.21	1.46	1.75	2.10
15	1.00	1.33	1.76	2.32	3.04
20	1.00	1.46	2.13	3.07	4.40
25	1.00	1.61	2.57	4.06	6.38
30	1.00	1.77	3.10	5.38	9.24
35	1.00	1.95	3.75	7.12	13.38
40	1.00	2.14	4.52	9.43	19.38

TABLE 3 - ANNUAL PAYMENT FACTOR

NO. OF YEARS UNTIL RETIREMENT	EXPECTED RETURN ON SAVINGS UNTIL RETIREMENT				
	4%	6%	8%	10%	12%
5	0.200	0.189	0.178	0.168	0.159
10	0.100	0.090	0.081	0.073	0.065
15	0.067	0.057	0.049	0.041	0.035
20	0.050	0.041	0.033	0.026	0.021
25	0.040	0.031	0.024	0.018	0.013
30	0.033	0.024	0.018	0.012	0.009
35	0.029	0.020	0.013	0.009	0.006
40	0.025	0.017	0.011	0.006	0.004

TABLE 4 - FIXED DOLLAR ANNUAL PAYMENT FACTOR

NO. OF YEARS UNTIL RETIREMENT	EXPECTED RETURN ON SAVINGS UNTIL RETIREMENT				
	4%	6%	8%	10%	12%
5	0.225	0.216	0.207	0.199	0.192
10	0.123	0.112	0.102	0.093	0.084
15	0.090	0.077	0.066	0.057	0.048
20	0.074	0.060	0.048	0.038	0.030
25	0.064	0.049	0.036	0.027	0.020
30	0.058	0.041	0.029	0.020	0.013
35	0.054	0.035	0.023	0.015	0.009
40	0.051	0.031	0.019	0.011	0.006

ORDER FORM

ADDITIONAL COPIES .... $14.95 plus $3.05 for shipping and handling
(25 OR LESS)   Please mail your $18.00 payment to:

Investors Press, Inc.
P.O. Box 329 - BYNE
Washington Depot, CT 06794
Or call 1-800-773-401(k)

BULK PURCHASES .... Please contact Publisher: Investors Press, Inc.

Voice Mail: 203-868-6148 Ext. 95
Telephone: 203-868-9411
Fax: 203-868-9733

INVESTORS
PRESS